WHAT EVERY LIBRARIAN SHOULD KNOW ABOUT ELECTRONIC PRIVACY

WHAT EVERY LIBRARIAN SHOULD KNOW ABOUT ELECTRONIC PRIVACY

Jeannette Woodward

U N L I M I T E D

A Member of the Greenwood Publishing Group

Westport, Connecticut • London

Library of Congress Cataloging-in-Publication Data

Woodward, Jeannette A.
  What every librarian should know about electronic privacy / Jeannette Woodward.
    p. cm.
  Includes bibliographical references and index.
  ISBN-13: 978-1-59158-489-6 (alk. paper)
    1. Public access computers in libraries—United States. 2. Internet access for library users—
United States. 3. Confidential communications—Library records—United States. 4. Computer
security—Law and legislation—United States. 5. Data protection—Law and legislation—United
States. 6. Privacy, Right of—United States. I. Title.
  Z678.93.P83W66 2007
  025.50285—dc22   2007013566

British Library Cataloguing in Publication Data is available.

Library of Congress Catalog Card Number: 2007013566
ISBN-13: 978-1-59158-489-6

First published in 2007

Libraries Unlimited, 88 Post Road West, Westport, CT 06881
A Member of the Greenwood Publishing Group, Inc.
www.lu.com

Printed in the United States of America

The paper used in this book complies with the
Permanent Paper Standard issued by the National
Information Standards Organization (Z39.48–1984).

10   9   8   7   6   5   4   3   2   1

To Lowell, Laura, Chris, and John with all my love.

Contents

Introduction

Few professionals are as concerned about the privacy of their customers as librarians. We want our libraries to be places where they can explore ideas of all persuasions and need never worry that big brother is looking over their shoulders. Just consider, for example, our spirited opposition to the Patriot Act. While the librarians collectively known as "John Doe" made national news when they refused to surrender library records without a warrant, the American Library Association challenged the constitutionality of the law (Cowan 2000). Again and again, librarians have defended the right of citizens to read and inform themselves, free from intrusion and free from censorship.

Because librarians believe that citizens in a democracy need unrestricted access to information, we have also been leaders in providing public access computers. Our commitment to an information literate society has led libraries to make computers available to those who lack either the financial resources or the technical sophistication to purchase and maintain their own machines. In fact, computers have totally transformed libraries in recent years. They are now used to perform a wide variety of clerical and administrative tasks. In addition, they have replaced the old card catalogs with much more efficient online public access catalogs, and provide access to thousands of digitized journals. Computers are ideally suited to the library environment, and we have embraced them enthusiastically. We may, however, be allowing our computers to inadvertently jeopardize the privacy of our users.

THE LIBRARY'S RESPONSIBILITY

The ALA Council's, "An Interpretation of the Library Bill of Rights" adopted June 19, 2002 makes clear the position of the library community regarding individual privacy. "Privacy is essential to the exercise of free speech, free thought, and free association ... In a library (physical or virtual), the right to privacy is the right to open inquiry without having the subject of one's interest examined or scrutinized by others ... When users recognize or fear that their privacy or confidentiality is compromised, true freedom of inquiry no longer exists" (American Library Association 2002).

The fear of Islamic terrorism pervades much of contemporary American life. As has occurred repeatedly throughout our history, fear sometimes causes people to temporarily devalue their freedoms and those of their fellow citizens. Readers of the well-written and informative book *Jihad: the Rise of Militant Islam in Central Asia* by Ahmed Rashid have experienced some of the overreaction that inevitably occurs when people are frightened. The book jacket displays the single word Jihad in very large letters, large enough that they are visible from a considerable distance. Commuters on subway trains have reported their fellow passengers to the police, simply for carrying or reading the book (Robinson 2006).

In such an environment, protecting the freedom to read and to seek out information becomes much more difficult. The role of librarians does not end with simply making information available to users. It must extend to protecting those users from overzealous or paranoid elements of our society who equate ignorance with patriotism. In his article "Librarians at the Gates," Joseph Huff-Hannon summed up this responsibility: "Be it in the capacity of archivist, reference librarian, or information technology professional, a common thread is the profession's dogged commitment to safeguarding books, research, and information to make knowledge more widespread, not less" (Huff-Hannon 2006).

LIBRARY COMPUTER USERS ARE AT RISK

Although it may not be immediately obvious, our determination to protect our users' privacy can sometimes conflict with our commitment to provide the public with access to online resources. The public library probably provides more opportunities for free Internet access than any other organization. We encourage our patrons to use our computers to satisfy their information needs, and most libraries allow them to take advantage of e-mail and/or other recreational resources. The access we provide, however, is necessarily limited. Because they have fewer opportunities, our users tend to be less informed and more at risk than computer owners.

For example, most of the millions of people who use the library's public computers have signed up for e-mail accounts like Hotmail and Yahoo. Their e-mail messages are stored on the computer servers of those service providers, and their accounts are accessed in much the same way that computer owners access the e-mail programs on their personal computers. However, those messages and other documents that comprise "Web mail" receive only weak privacy protection. Government agencies do not need search warrants to access personal Web mail as they would to search privately-owned computers.

Library computer users are often novices and may not be aware that even seemingly innocuous information supplied to Web sites can be mined by both government agencies and unscrupulous businesses. The recent discovery that online service providers have been supplying vast quantities of data to government agencies without the public's knowledge has highlighted the threat.

Comparing Libraries of Yesterday and Today

This era in which libraries and their users are now struggling, is different in one way from any other period in human history. Never before was it possible to gather vast quantities of personal information, and bring it all together to create a detailed profile of each and every individual. It was common knowledge that our Social Security numbers and driver's license information were available to various government agencies. In fact, quite a lot of personal information was filed away somewhere, but it was difficult to locate and gain access to it. There was no way that one careless individual could take home the Social Security numbers of the 26 million veterans and make them available to thieves, as happened in a 2006 laptop theft (Lemos 2006).

Privacy threats posed by overzealous marketers are also relatively new. We have known that businesses collect information about us for some time. Some kept our names and addresses in their records, sending us sales promotions. Today, however, marketers have created vast databases full of highly confidential information about our personal habits. For example, the mammoth data broker ChoicePoint inadvertently gave an identity thief access to the personal information, including Social Security numbers, of 145,000 people (Zeller 2005). Their goals are essentially the same as they always were: to sell us more of their merchandise and services. However, the techniques they employ are just as invasive as those used by government agencies, and they cannot be justified by threats to national security.

Laws Must Catch-Up with Technology

Technology has progressed much more rapidly than state and federal privacy legislation. Both marketers and overly enthusiastic government officials are unconstrained by the usual laws, regulations, and ethical guidelines that would normally prevent the misuse of personal information. Additionally, there has been a dangerous confluence of disaffected, highly skilled computer specialists and cyber-thieves. Both legislators and law enforcement agencies are slow to respond, leaving millions of individuals open to attack. Only recently have we fully realized how dangerous personal information can become in the wrong hands. Not only do thieves steal billions of dollars, obtaining loans and charging merchandise against the credit cards of innocent people, but they have also committed violent crimes in their names, literally stealing their homes and abducting their children.

Privacy is not a Political Issue

In our private lives, we librarians bridge the full political spectrum from right to left. It is important that we not view privacy as a political ping pong ball, bounced back and forth between parties when it suits their purposes. Privacy is much more than political rhetoric; it is a cornerstone of our professional ethics. It does not matter which party is in power; we have an obligation to protect the privacy of our users as a matter of principle. It is essential that our enthusiasm for our cause not wax and wane, depending on the occupant of the White House or the composition of Congress.

Perhaps Justice Louis Brandeis put it best when he called privacy "the right to be left alone." Without well-considered legislation, there is nothing to stop marketers and government agencies from keeping track of the books people buy, the illnesses they suffer, the checks they bounce, the places they visit, or the personal problems they endure.

Searching for Terrorists

It has recently become clear that the National Security Agency (NSA) is monitoring millions of telephone calls, theoretically intended to help fight the war on terror. Concurrently, NSA and other government agencies have developed vast databases of personal information to be used for data mining (the trolling of billions of bits of personal information) searching for patterns that match government profiles of the typical terrorist.

The problems with such a strategy are numerous. First, there really is little scientifically reliable evidence that such profiling can effectively identify terrorists. Sadly, government workers have repeatedly identified innocent people who happen to share names, personal habits, travel destinations, and financial activities with the few known terrorists whose biographies are available. Too many intelligence agency projects appear to be the product of overly imaginative government functionaries who were influenced by fictional exploits like those portrayed in the movie "Mission Impossible."

Furthermore, as was made clear in the incident of the 26 million Veteran's records, the people who staff those government agencies are fallible human beings. People often take shortcuts, become careless, or put their personal needs above the demands of their jobs. In the case of the veterans' records, the practice of copying personal data to agency laptops and home computers had been widespread for years. It was considered more convenient to do so. In other government agencies, access to personal records has been so widely available, and supervision so lax, that staff members actions have led to numerous felony charges.

Collecting Data Just in Case

As we in libraries know, there is a natural urge to collect data just in case we need it someday. Our patron information records contain fields that no library should ever use, but blame cannot be placed entirely at the door of our vendors. As we work with them in developing more functional library systems, the thought keeps recurring: "That would be interesting to know." We are charmed by all the reports that can be produced with the click of a mouse and we imagine that we could do our jobs better if we knew more about our patrons. That's true, but at what price do we collect this unneeded data? Almost every library has discovered, especially when faced with a search warrant or other request for information by a law enforcement agency, that it has inadvertently collected far too much data from its users.

Keeping Up with Breaking News

As this book goes to press, news concerning the Patriot Act, data mining, and other privacy matters is breaking daily. With the recent changes in Congress have come numerous investigations into the way the Justice Department and other federal agencies have used or misused their authority. It is inevitable that the investigations will result in new policies and even new laws. Similarly, upcoming court decisions will profoundly affect privacy issues. Since these developments will be of great interest to readers, Libraries Unlimited will add a new section to its Web site to update you on breaking news, legislation, court decisions, and new information regarding upcoming investigations. You will find more information about these updates at the end of the book.

Computers in the Library

This book is intended for librarians and library supporters representing most types of libraries. Public, school, and academic libraries routinely provide public computers to meet the needs of their users. Libraries of every type including medical, law, and corporate libraries, use computers to maintain records of both their patrons and their materials. This means that the information stored in library staff computers could compromise the privacy of many individuals by revealing personal information about their lives and their reading habits. Although librarians are committed to protecting the privacy of their users, they may not be aware of the broad range of privacy issues that surround electronic data. Patrons may be subjected to unnecessary and unwanted threats to their personal privacy.

This book is intended to be a practical guide on the issue of electronic privacy in the library. It focuses on real library users rather than on abstract concepts. It is not intended to be a comprehensive or technically sophisticated overview of the issues. When technical strategies are mentioned, they are never described in detail, leaving it to you, the librarian, to bring such matters to the attention of technical staff.

Although we may find it difficult and demanding to protect our users, we have no choice but to do so. Jonathan Turley, law professor at George Washington University, sums up our responsibility succinctly when he writes, "It is only in the assurance of privacy that free thoughts and free exercise of rights can be truly exercised. Such privacy evaporates with doubt; it is why the Constitution seeks to avoid the chilling effect of uncertainty in government searches and seizures."

REFERENCES

American Library Association. 2002. Privacy: An Interpretation of the Library Bill of Rights. Adopted June 19, 2002, by the ALA Council. http://www.ala.org/ala/oif/statementspols/statementsif/interpretations/privacy.htm.

Cowan, Alison Leigh. 2006. U.S. ends a yearlong effort to obtain library records amid secrecy in Connecticut. *New York Times*, June 27. http://select.nytimes.com/search/restricted/article?res=FA0C1EFD3C540C748ED DAF0894DE404482.

Godwin, Jennifer. 2000. Librarians at the gate. *Forbes*, July 24, p. 184.

Huff-Hannon, J. 2006. Librarians at the gates. *Nation Magazine*, August 22. http://www.thenation.com/doc/20060828/librarians/.

Lemos, R. 2006. Veterans Affairs warns of massive privacy breach. *Security Focus*, May 22. http://www.securityfocus.com/news/11393.

Robinson, Eugene. 2006. Fear is driving U.S. public opinion. *LJ World*, May 18. p. B6. http://www2.ljworld.com/news/2006/may/18/fear_driving_us_public_opinion/.

Turley, Jonathan. 2006. "Big brother" Bush and connecting the data dots: the total information awareness program was killed in 2003, but its spawn present bigger threats to privacy. *Los Angeles Times*, June 24. http://www.commondreams.org/views06/0624-29.htm.

Zeller, Tom. 2005. Breach points up flaws in privacy laws. *New York Times*, February 24, p. C1. http://www.nytimes.com/2005/02/24/business/24datas.html?ei=5088&en=1a34f1accdb516d9&ex=1267160400&partner=rssnyt&pagewanted=print&position=

For the latest updates on Electronic Privacy in the Library, please visit this book's companion Web site at the Libraries Unlimited Web site, www.lu.com/e-privacy.

CHAPTER 1
Portrait of a Library Computer User

If you were to walk into any public library at almost any hour of the day, you would probably find many library users clustered around a group of public computers. In academic and school libraries, many areas of the library might be sparsely occupied while every computer workstation is in use. Library users have become accustomed to conducting a significant part of their business, academic, and personal lives on the library's computers. They have come to depend on them for recreation, social interaction, and to satisfy their information needs.

PROTECTING LIBRARY COMPUTER USERS

Our customers use library computers to check the news and weather, e-mail or instant message friends and relatives, meet new people at social networking sites, file their taxes, and search for information about their medical conditions. They may shop and make purchases, find their soul mates, submit copies of medical records to doctors, check their bank accounts, and apply for automobile loans online. A few library users even operate small home businesses like the older woman who supplements her Social Security check by making dolls and selling them on EBay. Unemployed patrons job hunt online by submitting resumes and completing employment applications.

Librarians have come to accept the presence of large numbers of computer users as a matter of course. We treasure them for the healthy gate counts they produce, but begrudge taking staff members off other important tasks to attend to public computer duties. Too often we fail to look closely at our computer users or see them as individuals. We don't make it our business to consider whether they are putting themselves at risk. Most libraries, often inspired by the dire warnings delivered at Gates Foundation training sessions, have taken some precautions to secure and protect their computers. They may not, however, have given much thought to protecting their computer users. The majority of Americans now own a computer or have access to one at home. This is not usually true of library computer users, many of whom depend almost entirely on the library for computer access. Children and teenagers may use library computers to escape parental supervision or because they aren't permitted to use the computer at home.

WHO USES LIBRARY COMPUTERS?

It is difficult to talk about library computer users in the abstract. Who are they? Why do they use library computers instead of purchasing their own? Let's take a closer look at some typical customers staring intently at those glowing computer monitors.

Low-Income Adults

While other library customers are generally drawn from the middle class, this is not always true of our computer users. They may be adults who are either unemployed or whose low wages make it impossible for them to purchase costly electronic equipment. This is a group we have long wanted to serve and have been largely unsuccessful in attracting. Although public computers provide an excellent opportunity to get to know these people and learn more about their needs, we are still getting acquainted.

In general, this group lacks computer proficiency because they don't have opportunities to practice their skills. Public libraries usually limit computer sessions to thirty minutes. A few libraries have express e-mail stations with fifteen minute limits, and still others may permit users to remain at a computer for a full hour. Most computer owners spend several hours a day at their personal computers and at their workplace computers. People learn by doing. They encounter a problem, solve it, and gradually develop more sophisticated computer skills. The skills of occasional computer users tend to remain at the same level.

Poverty has always limited access to information. A single mother working two jobs to put food on the table has little time for surfing the web. Such a patron may see the library computer as a brief respite or focus on the ways in which library computers can save time and reduce expenses. A free e-mail account is a godsend to someone whose telephone has been turned off. Web sites promise free services and gifts for consumers who complete surveys. Every online advertisement seems to promise "You can win a luxury automobile!" Just as the poor are more vulnerable to scams in the non-virtual world, they are more likely to be victimized by cyber criminals online.

Seniors

Older adults are also attracted to our public computers. Although they may have limited incomes like the group above, they also use our computers because they know that staff are available to help them if they run into problems. Some of our more affluent seniors may have purchased computers that sit in their dens gathering dust. They discovered computers late in life and didn't grow up playing computer games or zapping aliens. The eye-hand coordination that comes so easily to young people becomes a huge hurdle as we grow older. Seniors' initial experiences with computer technology may be frustrating ones, and they may lack the incentive to work through problems unaided. Older adults may also be suffering from failing short-term memory and may be continually frustrated by the computer's insistence on exact repetition.

Technically-Challenged Adults

Not everyone feels comfortable with computers. No matter what their age or budget constraints, some of our customers have almost literally been brought into the computer age "kicking and screaming." These are the people who ask us the same questions, day after day, insisting that they did exactly what they were supposed to do. It's not their fault that the computer hates them.

Although computers have become much more user friendly, this group continues to experience frequent difficulties. Poor cognitive skills account for some of their problems but many of these people handle life's other demands very successfully. We all have a friend or acquaintance who just doesn't get it, and even the simplest explanations are misinterpreted. To them, the computer will always be a magic box and there will always be a capricious imp inside who is bent on frustrating their efforts.

People with Time on their Hands

This catch-all category includes the mentally ill, the physically and developmentally disabled, and the very lonely. They have always come to the library to be with other people, to read our magazines, and to attend our programs. The library is an important part of their lives and library computers can provide an even richer experience. Computers offer lonely people the opportunity to reach out to others who share their disability or their sense of isolation. Unfortunately, this group is among the most vulnerable. Their need for sympathy and companionship can cause them to let down the protective barriers we all place between ourselves and strangers.

High School Students

Teenagers are going through the most vulnerable period of their lives. They desperately seek acceptance and agonize over their looks, personality, and status. Although they use school and public library computers for homework, they are far more interested in the social networking opportunities they provide. To whatever extent libraries permit, teens are avid users of chat rooms, Internet messaging programs, e-mail, and bulletin boards. While parents worry about online predators and librarians wonder if these activities are a waste of precious computer resources, teens find relief from their problems in talking endlessly about themselves.

College Students

Academic libraries also experience heavy public computer use. College students may have computers at home or in their dorms, but they use the library's computers when it is more convenient. In fact, college students seem to be tethered to computers, using them for many of their personal and academic needs. Like high school students, they are avid users of social networking sites and spend hours sharing personal information on sites like MySpace and Friendster.

Criminals, Terrorists, and Others Seeking Anonymity

Most of us would rather not talk about this group but, since these library users are well-known to law enforcement agencies, we must face facts. If we were criminals who needed to communicate with our fellow miscreants, library computers would offer a near perfect opportunity. A few years ago, we would have been forced to write a letter, but it would have to be sent to a real-world address. The envelope would also bear a postmark so post office employees, nosy landladies, and criminal investigators might discover the plot. We might instead have chosen to meet at a bar or inconspicuous place. However, we could be followed and any number of people might eavesdrop on our conversation.

Imagine how much safer it would be to send a message using an anonymous e-mail account accessed on an anonymous library computer. Foul deeds could be planned with very little possibility of discovery. It is now clear that this is exactly what some of the terrorists from the September 11th attacks did. They were identified by both library patrons and library staff as frequent computer users (Regan 2004). Identity thieves have used library computers to purchase expensive merchandise and apply for auto loans (I describe my own personal experience with juvenile identity thieves purchasing high-end athletic shoes in the next chapter). Some criminals even gave the library as their home address and audaciously collected their mail from the library staff.

Of the millions of people who use library computers, this group constitutes only a very tiny part. However, it is their omnipresence in the public imagination (and in the media) that is largely responsible for Congress's refusal to exclude library records from the Patriot Act.

Children

The Children's Internet Protection Act has drastically changed the way that children use computers in both school and public libraries. Whether or not you have decided to install the mandated filters, you have undoubtedly spent hours mentally weighing the children's ardent appeals for Internet access against fears for their safety. For every child the library serves, there are parents or guardians who must be considered. What do they know about computers? Are they aware of what their children are doing at the library? Are they providing the kind of guidance their children need or do they themselves need guidance from the library?

Tourists

Depending on whether your area attracts large numbers of visitors, you may have found that tourists and other travelers are among your library's most frequent computer users. Americans are becoming so computer dependent that they find it painful to be separated from their e-mail correspondence while they are on vacation. Many travelers are aware that public libraries provide Internet access and often make a point of heading for the library when they first arrive in a new city or town.

Because they are separated from the resources of their home communities, travelers may be prone to taking unacceptable risks to obtain information. They may check their bank accounts and online brokers for current information about their finances. Many libraries are installing Wi-Fi networks that make it possible for visitors to connect to the Internet with their own laptop computers. Unfortunately, many libraries take pains to secure their wired desktop computers while they leave their wireless networks unprotected.

Immigrants

In some respects, immigrants are not really so different from the groups described above. They may be young or old, underemployed, or technically unsophisticated. However, in one respect they are different: they are outsiders. They depend on library computers to communicate with friends and family in their homeland, find jobs, and help them assimilate into American culture. However, immigrants may not speak or read English well enough to really understand the new world they have entered. They may find it necessary to use library computers to transfer money, communicate with immigration authorities, and complete online forms that require divulging very personal information.

PEW STUDY

The Pew Internet and American Life Project is a non-profit research organization funded by the Pew Charitable Trusts. It was created to study the social impact of the Internet on contemporary life, and has produced a number of well-researched reports that can tell you a lot about the people who use the Internet. One report of interest to librarians is entitled "People Who Use the Internet Away from Home and Work" (Harwood 2004). The study found that 23% of adult U.S. Internet users have gone online from someplace other than their homes or workplaces. Of this group, 26% accessed the Internet from libraries. However, students who used the Internet in their school libraries were classed under schools, so the number of library computer users is actually substantially higher.

Most of the statistical information gathered in the report concerns the entire group of Internet users who go online from a third place; but nevertheless it is extremely informative. In general, the study confirms our own experiences with library computer users. For example, students make up a substantial portion of this group. In fact, age is the most important factor that determines who uses the Internet away from home or work. Nearly half of Internet users between the age of 18 and 24 say they have used the Internet in a third location. About 45% of full-time students have accessed the Internet at a library, while 27% of part-time students have done so.

Income is a big factor in determining use. The same study showed that 28% of Internet users with annual household incomes of less than $30,000 have accessed the World Wide Web from someplace other than their home or work. Of this lower income group, 30% used library computers. Although high income Internet users logon from other places as well, it is often because they are traveling. They may use their own laptops or hotel computers and are attracted to libraries that offer wireless access. African Americans and Hispanics are also more likely to use the Internet away from home or work than whites. An especially interesting finding is that while males are more likely to access the Internet away from their home or workplace, women are more likely to use the library when online outside of home or work. Young men will often go to a friend's house to surf the Web. Perhaps men are also more inclined to use it while traveling on business. One finding that does not seem to reflect our own experience in the library is that older Americans are the least likely to use the Internet away from home or work. Only 10% of Internet users age 65 and over have gone online away from their home or their workplace.

The Digital Divide

Susannah Fox, an Associate Director at the Pew Internet and American Life Project, testified at Federal Trade Commission (FTC) public hearings on the subject "Protecting Consumers in the Next Tech-ade" (Fox 2004). Her research confirms our own views on the information gap that separates rich and poor. In recent years, the Internet has become an integral part of the daily lives of many Americans. "We found that the Internet helped people get through some of what we called 'major life moments' like buying a car, changing jobs, dealing with a serious illness, or finding a new place to live" (Fox 2004). However, a disproportionate number of whites had access to these resources compared to African Americans and Hispanics. While Fox's findings were reported in 2004, they are still relevant today. 73% of white Americans reported that they went online as compared to 61% of African Americans. Only a third of Spanish-speaking Latinos ever accessed the Internet. While every age, ethnic and economic group depends on access to the Internet to satisfy their information needs, such statistics make it clear that many of our library computer users have few choices. Although senior centers may offer computer access to some older Americans, and some school computer labs allow students to use computers for activities unrelated to school, many of our users are different from the larger population because they have almost no other options.

LIBRARY COMPUTER USERS ARE MORE VULNERABLE

What the library computer users described above have in common (with the probable exception of the criminal group) is their increased vulnerability. Immigrants are at increased risk because of the personal information they are likely to share. Their limited language skills further endanger them, and their lack of familiarity with American culture makes them more vulnerable to phishing scams and other opportunities for identity theft. Immigrants, however, are not the only group who may be ignorant of the dangers that await library computer users.

Children and teenagers, though they may be technically skilled, do not fully understand why they must protect their privacy, and their personal needs often drive them to talk about themselves to strangers. Inexperienced adult users do not really understand the nuts and bolts of the Internet and have no intuitive sense for what constitutes safe use, and what activities are potentially dangerous. People of all ages feel a need to reach out to those they imagine are like themselves. When a cyber acquaintance shows an interest, users are often flattered and curious.

Inexperienced Computer Users

Of course, these are not the only people who use our computers, and many don't fit into any convenient categories. Working people some-times spend their lunch hours in the library catching up on their e-mail and others just happen to be passing by the library. Mothers may wile away the time while their preschoolers are enjoying story hour. Nevertheless, it is true that most library computer users are not comfortable with the computer age in the same way as computer owners. They are acquainted primarily with the software loaded by the library, usually limited to Web browsers, word processors, and other easy-to-use programs. Any library patron who uses only library computers for a half hour here and fifteen minutes there is unlikely to be tuned in to the technology grapevine, the computer articles in the local newspaper, or the personal computing Web sites like PC World.

THE UNIVERSAL NEED FOR PRIVACY

In another sense, however, library computer users are just like computer owners. In fact, they share a characteristic with every other group on the globe: to grow and thrive, they need a private world. To be fully themselves, they need both a physical and a virtual door to shut out prying eyes. In other words, they need to be assured that their per-sonal lives—their thoughts and their life experiences—are private. They are theirs alone, to be shared only when they choose to share.

In this era when the right to privacy is frequently ignored by both the business and government sectors, we often hear the same excuse: anyone who objects to giving out personal information must have something to hide. The individuals brandishing this excuse are being unfaithful not only to their fellow human beings, but to themselves as well. Only the shallowest people (and some immature teenagers) would be comfortable sharing the most personal parts of their lives. There are big secrets, of course, like the gay college student who chooses to remain in the closet or the HIV-positive woman who should not be at the mercy of gossipy neighbors. But there are small secrets too, and every adult has dozens of them. Disturbing things have happened to all of us. We may feel guilty, we may feel hurt, but there is usually no reason why anyone needs to know about these experiences.

Library Materials and Privacy

The books and other library materials that patrons borrow are often associated with those secrets. People turn to books to help them deal with their problems. Why else would we librarians purchase so many books on depression, grief, phobias and fears, alcoholism, and family dysfunction? We know from long experience that people turn to us for help in coping with life's problems. No one has ever asked me for a book on building bombs, but many have approached the checkout desk trying nervously to obscure the cover of a book on divorce or mental illness.

When Privacy is Lost

In our present post-9/11 world, we may think of all secrets as being suspect. If people want to hide information about themselves, perhaps their secrets are dangerous and should be brought out into the open. We have become accustomed to probing the personal lives of public figures as if we were entitled to their innermost thoughts and we have extended this sense of entitlement to anyone who awakens our curiosity. After all, we rationalize, there may be a terrorist in our midst.

The subject of secrets brings to mind the ordeal of a friend who was accused of sexually abusing a child. It occurred during the 1980s when a wave of hysteria created by the McMartin Preschool case gripped the country. A neighbor child, angry at not getting a promised treat, made up a tale of abuse. Her story probably had its basis in an overheard adult conversation or possibly the evening news. During the trial that followed, the child's story fell apart and it became very clear that she was not the victim of abuse but rather of an overactive imagination. Over a year passed, from the date of the initial accusation to the final exoneration in the court room. During that time, my friend saw his own face on the front page of the local newspaper and endured the hatred of much of his community. Every aspect of his private life was exposed. Most of us can't even imagine the kind of agony he went through. He later disclosed that it was only the support of his close friends and family that kept him from suicide.

Aftermath

When the jury's not guilty decision was announced, the newspaper article wasn't nearly as long as the one that announced his arrest.

Most readers soon lost interest and turned their attention to more exciting stories. Unfortunately, the verdict did not lift the entire burden from the accused. He would always carry with him the memories—the hateful comments, the embarrassment, and the anxiety at meeting new people. In fact, he will probably never be able to escape the pain, even though he has been able to move on with his life. Although the circumstances of this case are unusual, most people have lived through traumatic experiences and at such times, they frequently turn to their libraries for information and consolation.

Earlier in this chapter, I spoke of business owners and government officials who invade the private lives of their fellow citizens, and then insist that only the guilty have anything to fear. It seems to me it would be just punishment to force those selfish and sanctimonious souls to walk in the shoes of this innocent man. They too could feel discomfort when a conversation ends abruptly as they approach, sense the unspoken belief that maybe he was guilty after all. They too could cringe when yet another tactless acquaintance blurts out a bit of gossip.

Because of its official nature, nothing could have kept my friend's agonizing experience from public view. Most of us, fortunately, have not had to endure such public humiliation, but that doesn't make it any easier when our lives are pried open for public view. Before the arrival of computers, the part of our lives that was known to the public was quite limited. If we got into trouble with the law, our neighbors knew about it. Gossip traveled rapidly, but it was generally based on observable behavior. However, in general, what went on within the walls of our homes was our own business. Thoughts, plans, and interests were unknown to others until we turned them into actions.

WHEN LIBRARY USERS GO ONLINE

Now let's look at one of our library computer users typing a search into a search engine like Google. In this case, it's a senior looking up information on Alzheimer's disease. Another user is completing an online application for welfare assistance, and a lonely patron is writing a personal ad on the Yahoo! Web site. None of these activities is in any way criminal, but they are private. These library computer users would not want the world at large to look over their shoulders. Nevertheless, Google keeps a record of all our searches in its vast computer servers. When library computer users sign up for services like Yahoo! or Google's Web mail, they are asked personal questions. Their answers are stored permanently in large databases and this information can be associated with their searches. Google or Yahoo! can then sell personal data to companies marketing rest homes, Alzheimer cures, or supplemental insurance policies. In other words, collecting and keeping such data has proven highly lucrative to dot coms. You may recall that in 2006, Google pleased privacy advocates by refusing to surrender search data to the National Security Agency (NSA). Eventually, the company negotiated the surrender of a smaller quantity of data, and it was revealed that Yahoo! and other services provided data that they said excluded personally identifiable information.

Pressure to Share Confidential Information Online

A woman applying for public assistance is in a vulnerable position. Increasingly, government agencies are exerting pressure on applicants to complete online applications. This allows a computer program to screen applications, checking data against that already stored in their databases. Programs can also check public records databases and flag applications where fraud is suspected. It is easier and faster to apply for Social Security or a student loan online than by mail. However, surrendering personal information to public computers is a dangerous practice. An elderly man searching for Alzheimer's information risks only a mailbox full of junk mail or inclusion in one of the federal government's data-mining projects. The library user who must use a public computer for personal business risks victimization by identity thieves, stalkers, and other criminals.

SUMMING IT UP

It's easy to see that library patrons are not your average computer users. Without libraries, many of them would be completely left out of the computer revolution. In many ways, their lives would be less enjoyable and less satisfying. However, public computer use must be seen as an integral part of the library's mission. Our role is different from that of the local coffee shop that offers Wi-Fi access. Unlike the coffee shop, we can't simply say "Here's your latte and your computer access. Go to it." Our services must result in better informed citizens who are able to satisfy their information needs.

REFERENCES

Fox, Susannah. 2004. Internet usage trends: through the demographics lens. Protecting Consumers in the Next Tech-ade, Public Hearings on Protecting Consumers in the Next Tech-ade. http://www.pewinternet.org/ppt/Fox_FTC_Nov_6_%202006.pdf

Harwood, Paul, and Lee Rainie. 2004. People who use the Internet away from home and work. Internet and American Life Project, Pew Charitable Trusts. http://www.pewinternet.org/pdfs/PIP_other_places.pdf/

Regan, Tom. 2004. New skirmishes in the Patriot Act battle. *Christian Science Monitor*, July 14. http://www.csmonitor.com/2004/0714/dailyUpdate.html.

CHAPTER 2
Protecting Library Users from Identity Theft

The Better Business Bureau defines identity theft as occurring "... when someone uses your name, Social Security number, credit card number or some other piece of your personal information to apply for a credit card, make unauthorized purchases, gain access to your bank accounts or obtain loans under your name." There is ample evidence that library computer users are often the victims of identity theft and are occasionally perpetrators.

OBSERVING TYPICAL LIBRARY COMPUTER USERS

A good way to approach the subject of identity theft might be to make yourself invisible, perhaps borrow young wizard Harry Potter's invisibility cloak, and peer over the shoulders of several library computer users. In the last chapter we grouped our computer users into some broad categories that made it possible to generalize about their needs. We saw that most are using the library's computers because, for some reason, they are unable to join the majority of Americans who own their own computer equipment. Let's take a closer look.

The Student

Brendan is a high school student planning to enter college next year. He is going to need a student loan and has been told that it is best to apply for financial aid online. At the Free Application for Federal Student Aid (FAFSA) Web site, students are encouraged to submit electronic applications. Here is a quote from the homepage. "It is recommended that you use the FAFSA on the Web because:

- It's Quick: You'll get your results as much as three weeks faster than using the paper FAFSA.
- It's Easy: FAFSA on the Web has detailed help screens for every question.
- It's Accurate: FAFSA on the Web points out inconsistent answers and gives you the chance to correct mistakes before submitting the application.
- It's Safe: FAFSA on the Web uses encryption when transferring data so that anyone attempting to access your information will not be able to read it."

But is it safe if you do not have a computer of your own and must use school or public library computers? The answer is usually no. Brendan, however, is in a hurry and it's important for him to get his results early. Because he is not a computer owner, his computer knowledge is limited to Web browsers and word processing programs, or in other words the low-end software available on public computers. Because he is a novice, he believes what he is told about computers, and the student loan Web site assures users that it is safe to complete his application online.

Beware the Key-logger

What Brendan doesn't know is that another student, Joe, sat in the same seat a short while ago. He popped his own CD into the computer drive, and, before he gave up his seat to another user, he left behind a small piece of software. This keylogging program was nothing very complicated. Almost any novice programmer can write one in a day or two and there are hundreds of keylogging programs floating around the Internet. Primitive as they are, keyloggers can record every keystroke made by every computer user.

As Brendan answers the questions on the FAFSA student loan application, he types his name, address, phone number, date of birth, high school, Mother's maiden name, and Social Security number, as well as his own and his parents' financial information, all of which is being recorded as he types. He also chooses a user name and a password so he can log in from time to time and check on the status of his application.

When Joe Keylogger returns, he discovers that he has hit the jackpot. He has most of the information he needs to become Brendan. Because the application goes into detail about all Brendan's income sources, he may also be able to assume the identity of Brendan's mother, father, or other family members. By the way, Joe needn't return to the library to claim the personal information waiting on the computer. The keylogging program can simply send it to Joe's e-mail address, probably a free one like Yahoo! or Hotmail that requires no personal information about Joe himself.

Sharing Your Identity with a Criminal

What can Joe Keylogger do with the information? How can he use it for financial gain and bring incalculable harm to Brendan? To begin with, Joe probably has enough information to apply for a raft of credit cards and perhaps a car loan or two as well. It is easy to get credit, and by the time Brendan becomes aware that there's a problem, he could find that thousands and thousands of dollars worth of merchandise have been charged on cards he never applied for. Joe might also apply for credit cards in the names of Brendan's mother and father. In similar situations, keyloggers have applied for driver's licenses under their assumed names, hired rental cars using this license and one of their many credit cards, and then stolen the car. If it is too difficult to obtain official identification cards like driver's licenses, computers make it relatively easy to produce fake ones.

Brendan is just starting out in life. Unlike his parents whose retirement savings are at risk and who could even end up declaring bankruptcy, Brendan has almost no savings or possessions. However, what he stands to lose is his reputation, and this cannot be measured in dollars and cents. Many employers perform background checks on job applicants, and for the foreseeable future, Joe Keylogger's presence will be felt whenever Brendan's credit history is viewed or when public records are checked. Since Joe is a criminal, we can reasonably assume that he will continue to commit crimes. Brendan's name may, therefore, be included in court records as one of Joe's aliases. Since court records are included in background checks, Brendan may be refused credit or turned down for jobs because he appears to have a criminal record.

Identity Theft and Public Records

In a New York Times article, Tom Zeller Jr. described an identity theft victim he calls Anthony (Zeller 2005). Anthony's name and birth date were acquired by repeat offender Josh Morris (his real name), who was arrested in Sacramento, California. Because Morris had used Anthony's name, it was listed in court records as one of Morris's aliases. Court records are available to the public and because there is such a huge Internet business in public records, databases are copied, sold, and resold. That meant that the court case came up whenever any employer, credit card company, or law enforcement agency did a background check. The structure of the database was designed for the Sacramento court and perfectly intelligible to its staff. However, when its contents were merged with thousands of other small, local databases, it appeared as if Anthony had committed a crime.

While Anthony's name has been purged from the court's database, the mix-up remains in many of the massive public records databases. Public records vendors are none too careful about where they get their records or how often they update them. In some cases, databases have been copied from one another, not from the original source. Josh Morris was arrested in 2000, and later tried and convicted, but Anthony was still battling the consequences of identity theft in September 2006. Although he has made repeated efforts to correct the record, Anthony's name is still linked with Morris's crimes when background checks are performed. "If errors are found, it is generally futile to complain to a data broker because the companies are not the original source of the data," explains Tena Friery, Research Director for the Privacy Rights Clearinghouse of San Diego. "It's really an uphill battle" (Zeller 2006).

The photocopy chain, Kinko's, also provides public computers to its customers. Juju Jiang is the unusual name of a very proficient key-logger who managed to install a keylogging program in fourteen Kinko stores. An enterprising Boston College student was able to install his keylogging program on over one hundred publicly accessible campus computers. "I am very concerned about [keylogging software] given the enormous number of public access computers at schools, copy shops, and libraries," says John Grossman, Chief of the Massachusetts Attorney General's Corruption, Fraud, and Computer Crimes Division. "Those people have a responsibility to make sure their boxes are locked down. I think consumers need to be careful about where they use their credit card numbers and various other private information" (Poulsen 2003).

The Traveler

Brendan submitted his application from either a school or public library. If he were a college student, he might use a computer in his college or university library. Let's imagine that he was using his neighborhood public library and that he left the library happily unaware that he will be spend the next few years trying to reestablish his identity, his credit rating, and his innocence. Perhaps he notices Donna, looking somewhat lost and unfamiliar with her surroundings, as she signs up for a library computer. Donna and her husband are on vacation and the library is Donna's first stop after checking into a local hotel. She's worried that the vacation is turning out to be more expensive than she expected and she just wants to take a quick look at their bank balance to be sure they are not overdrawn.

Accessing Financial Information

Of course, there is an ATM machine just down the street, but Donna would have to pay a two dollar fee since it is not her own bank. Besides, the library is more comfortable than standing outside pressing buttons. Donna sits down in front of a computer (not the one Brendan used), and loads the library's Web browser. Then she types her bank's web address or URL into the box at the top of the page. The familiar page appears, and she is asked for her user name and password. After she enters it, she sees another familiar screen, this time informing her that the service is temporarily unavailable. She is asked to try again later. Although this all sounds perfectly normal, Donna has been victimized by spyware.

Spyware

Joe Keylogger may have other talents, or another library computer user may be the culprit. This time a program has been loaded onto the library computer that redirects users from established Web sites to scam sites. This spyware program diverts browsers from the URLs of large commercial Web sites including banks, airlines, online brokers, and travel services like Travelocity and Priceline. It then sends the Web browser to a page that looks almost identical to the one being requested. That is because the real page has been copied. The web address at the top of the page also looks similar to the real thing but it is faked as well.

The Long Distance Cyber-Thief

To add a little variety to our scenario, we'll invent Ted. Ted is seated somewhere across town or even in a foreign country watching as Donna types her user name and password into what she thinks is her bank's Web site. In reality, of course, it is Ted's site and the information Donna is typing is for Ted to do with as he likes. If Ted is really talented, Donna may next see a screen that tells her the bank's server cannot find her account. She is then asked for more information like her bank account number or her Social Security number. It would be handy for Ted to know her e-mail address as well. When Donna gets home from vacation, she will might find that her bank account has been completely cleaned out and she may even be overdrawn by thousands of dollars.

Like Brendan, she is the victim of identity theft. Somewhere out in cyberspace, there is someone who is pretending to be Donna. It might be Ted or someone to whom Ted has sold Donna's identity. In fact, Ted may have sold Donna's identity to dozens of his Internet customers. Those someones have enough confidential information that they can continue to cash checks and make purchases. Even though Donna's accounts are closed or frozen, Ted and his friends have plenty of time to run the many new accounts they opened into the ground. Donna and her husband may not realize the real dimensions of their problem until they begin receiving calls from collection agencies.

Don't Remember Me

Even if no evildoer has loaded spyware on a library computer, it is still unwise for library computer users to access financial or other personal information. Remember that each time you are prompted for a username or password, no matter what the site, a small window appears that asks whether you want the computer to "remember me." Inexperienced patrons may not really understand what this question means. Of course, they want their bank or broker to remember them. Otherwise, there's no reason to answer "Yes." Obviously, the correct answer is "yes." As most of us are aware, however, it isn't the bank but the computer that remembers that user name and password. It stores the information in a small file, usually a cookie on its hard drive. This is convenient for people who own their own computers and use them in the privacy of their homes. It is extremely dangerous to leave such information on a public computer, awaiting the experienced user who searches the hard drive looking for just such information.

The Unemployed Computer User

But Donna has left the library, so we'll turn our attention to a new arrival. Henry has been out of work for several months. A man in his

50's, he is becoming desperate. He needs to get out of the house during the day and so he spends many hours in the library. Henry is the one who always asks why the local paper hasn't been put out or when he can expect the next issue of a weekly news magazine. One reason why Henry has not been successful finding a job is that he has weak computer skills. The library staff members know Henry as the patron who asks the same questions nearly every time he uses a computer.

Job Hunting on the Internet

A big part of Henry's reading consists of job-hunting books and articles. He was particularly interested to learn that over half the people who find jobs do so on the Internet. They learn of job openings online and often apply by completing online forms. Many job hunters post their resumes on large Web services like Monster.com, Career Builder, Craig's List, and Yahoo!. Since he found many tips encouraging him to do so, Henry posted his resume on half a dozen of the larger Web sites. Unfortunately, it did not occur to Henry that he should not include his Social Security number on the resume.

Believe it or not, this mistake is much more common than you might think. Latanya Sweeney, an associate professor of computer science at Carnegie Mellon University, wrote a software program that scans Google search results for files containing names with Social Security numbers. She found hundreds of numbers that were included in online resumes (Bray 2005). In a sense, the Social Security number is considered the ultimate prize for identity thieves. Armed with this number and some publicly available information (like that found in the phonebook or at online Web sites like Switchboard), criminals have many options. However, when one adds all the information contained in a multi-page resume like Henry's, the possibilities are almost limitless.

Identity-Theft and Medical Records

Since Henry is unemployed, his financial condition is perilous. He cannot afford the kind of havoc that identity theft might wreck on his finances. Henry is also at an age when his health necessitates fairly frequent visits to the doctor and occasional hospital stays. Although most people don't realize it, becoming a victim of identity theft can be life-threatening. Cyber-thieves are like the rest of us in that they too have medical conditions that require attention

Let's invent still another imaginary character, Daryl, who has taken Henry's identity. Daryl is a drug user and his unhealthy lifestyle has meant frequent visits to the hospital emergency room and persistent medical problems. Since Daryl long ago compromised his own credit standing, he will use Henry's name and Social Security number for these encounters with the medical profession. The hospital where he has received treatment keeps track of his conditions in its patient database. Patient medical histories are not part of any public records so one would think that this information would not affect Henry. However, hospitals are frequently owned by large corporations and may store patient information in a single shared database. If Henry should be admitted to the same hospital where Daryl was treated or one of the hospitals owned by the corporate group, Henry will inherit Daryl's medical history, and he may be treated for those same conditions.

PREVENTING CYBER-THEFT

In each of these situations, the library computer user submitted highly confidential information not knowing that it was being shared with others. It is obvious to most of us that typing a Social Security number or bank password into a public computer is dangerous. We may not be aware, however, that much less sensitive information can also be risky. Each time a cyber-criminal obtains one bit of information, even if just a name and address, it becomes easier to obtain the next piece of the puzzle. Online services like Intelius will provide an extraordinary amount of personal information for a fee. This information is usually obtained for such reasons as employee screening, background checks, phone number verification, and other activities performed routinely by business and industry. However, anyone can sign up for their services. When a library computer user completes an online survey or signs up for a free e-mail account, he or she may be providing just the kind of information that serves as a starting point for the cyber-thief.

Criminals in the Library

When we allow library users to inadvertently reveal personal information to strangers, we put them at risk of being misrepresented, misjudged, and harassed. Even more dangerous, we put them at risk of sharing their very identities with criminals. We may also be providing the means by which identity thieves collect on their crimes.

Joe Keylogger and Ted will soon be spending a lot of ill-gotten money, and most of these transactions require a computer. With their stolen identities, they will be applying for credit cards and will use those cards to make expensive online purchases. They will also be applying for loans to purchase automobiles, boats or other big-ticket items.

Recognizing Cyber-Thieves

Although it is possible to submit applications and make purchases anonymously from their home computers, cyber-thieves may prefer to use the library's public computers. After all, it doesn't matter what traces they leave behind. They're leaving other people's personal information, not their own. If you have already created a mental picture of Ted and Joe, you may be in for a surprise, Rather than hardened criminals with sophisticated tech skills, they may be kids from your local junior high school.

That was the case when my own library was victimized by a group of juvenile delinquents. None was over fourteen and all looked to be typical kids who giggle a lot, and beg to play games on the library's public computers. Although their technical skills were minimal, they had managed to amass a collection of credit card numbers, most of which were traded across the Internet. Their tastes ran more to $200.00 running shoes and expensive athletic equipment than to boats or cars. They might never have been caught if they had not gotten so excited about their purchases. Like children discussing their letters to Santa Claus, they argued the merits of different wish list additions. At first, the library staff and other computer users thought that's all it was. Then it became clear that they were calling out long numbers to one another. No criminal was ever more obvious and yet it was quite some time before we began putting two and two together. Most cyber-criminals are much more circumspect.

Staff Awareness

In future chapters, you'll learn some good ways to secure library computers. It is possible to prevent users from loading keylogging software or spyware. It is also possible to eliminate cookies that can contain usernames and passwords. However, it is much more difficult to prevent criminals from purchasing merchandise and completing loan applications on library computers. It requires a level of awareness among library staff members that we are often uncomfortable with. It means occasionally taking a good look at public computer monitors and making note of regular customers and their habits.

This means that to protect the privacy of our users, we must occasionally invade it. It may be easier to do this with children and teenagers, but we nearly always feel guilty peering over an adult's shoulder. It may be easier, if staff make it a point to look for certain signs. For example, if users are obviously purchasing merchandise, we're fully justified in stopping them. Explain that personal financial information should never be entered into public computers. In most cases, users will be grateful for the tip. If you have surprised someone in an illegal activity, then it has been effectively interrupted, and he or she will think twice completing the transaction or continuing to use the library for such purposes.

THE TALE OF A PHISHING EXPEDITION

There are some identity thieves who never come near the library. In fact, they may be pursuing their illicit activities from another country. These people are phishers who specialize in e-mail-based fraud. When library computer users sign up for free e-mail accounts, they quickly find their mailboxes full of spam. Spam is usually defined unsolicited bulk e-mail and is usually not illegal. As long as they do not cross the line, spammers can usually stuff mailboxes with unlimited junk mail. Phishers, however, go several steps further. Their spam is very illegal and very dangerous to your users.

Since we've gotten pretty good at imagining library users, let's imagine yet another customer. This time we'll call her Louise. A library staff member helped her set up her free e-mail account and she has been delighted with it. The account has helped her to stay in close touch with her children and grandchildren. She has rediscovered old friends through her high school alumni Web site and she spends quite a lot of time in the library taking care of her voluminous correspondence.

A while back, Louise found a message from the Red Cross in her inbox. She was not surprised because she frequently receives advertisements and solicitations. This one, however, touched her heart. It went into detail about the plight of the victims of Hurricane Katrina. Graphics showed a flooded New Orleans and people who were obviously suffering. After making an impassioned plea for help, the message provided a link to a Web page where Louise could make a donation to the Red Cross for Katrina relief. That's exactly what Louise did. When the Web browser loaded the page, it looked exactly like the legitimate Red Cross site although it was actually a Phishing scam maintained on a server in Korea.

Ploys that Rely on Fear

Another library user received a message from the Internal Revenue Service (IRS) requesting information about a tax return. Again the message sent the reader to a Web site, and again the Web site looked exactly as it should. At this point, the scam is almost identical to the one that Donna encountered when she attempted to access her bank account. However, these con games are much safer and more productive for cyberthieves who may be on the other side of the globe and not even subject to American law. They can send out thousands or even millions of spam messages with impunity. In fact, they will obtain so much information that they cannot possibly use all of it themselves. Instead, they will sell it on the Internet black market to other cyber-criminals. Gartner Inc., a research and consulting firm, reported in June 2005 that 73 million Americans received an average of 50 phishing e-mails in the previous year. Of these victims, 1.2 million reported losing money totaling nearly $929 million (Gowan 2005).

Educating Users

Protecting computers from spyware and other illicit software will not protect library patrons from phishing expeditions, and peeking over their shoulders is equally ineffective. Educating our users is really the only way that we can effectively reduce the dangers they face. When your library decides to provide public computers, it must accept some responsibility for their welfare. Of course, we can't prevent all our users from making foolish mistakes, but we can make sure that they understand what they are getting into.

In the last chapter of this book, we will be discussing effective programs for educating library computer users. It should, however, be a library policy that every single library computer user is cautioned against entering personal information or conducting financial transactions online. Since e-mail-based phishing scams are the ones that the library staff is least likely to be aware of, they should be a focus of whatever educational programs are devised for library computer users. Users must understand that neither the IRS nor their bank would ever contact them using a free e-mail account, especially when the address was never given to them.

Why Users Yield to Temptation

It is convenient to transact business using the library's public computers. It would be considerably less convenient for Brendan to obtain a printed FAFTA application form and wait three or four additional weeks to learn whether he will receive a student loan. If Donna's own bank does not have a local branch equipped with an ATM machine, then she will just have to blow the $2.00 and use the one that is available. Henry's problem is a little more difficult. Not only is he a novice, but he will always remain a novice. Although Henry is not stupid, there's just something about computers that doesn't really make sense to him. He probably needs to be cautioned again and again in a variety of ways since one warning or one sign is unlikely to make a permanent impression.

Recognizing a Phishing Scam

The TechSoup Web site provides some excellent advice on how to avoid phishing expeditions. There are almost always clues that a message is spurious. Here are the most common tip-offs.

- The message has a sense of urgency. Something must be done immediately. Your bank account is going to be closed or someone is trying to clean out your account. In the case of the Katrina e-mail, something terrible was going to happen to the victims unless the Red Cross acted immediately.
- Although the message was sent to you by your bank or the IRS, it includes no information that is uniquely about you. In reality, of course, the message was sent to thousands of people. Although it may have been able to get your name from your e-mail program, it can't include specific information that is not equally applicable to all the other recipients.
- The message requests a lot of information about you, especially highly confidential information like your Social Security number.

- The subject line doesn't really seem to go with the message or it is crafted to get your immediate attention (e.g., "Important notice about your account"). The reason that the subject and the content may not seem to go together is that the phisher must evade the filters used by your e-mail provider to detect spam and fraudulent messages. If a word is misspelled, it may be deliberate.
- The sender's address is faked but it may be such a good fake that it is impossible for the average person to detect it. Computer users who have their own computers, often have e-mail programs that include an option to display raw message header information. This can reveal the fact that a message was sent from a different server than the address indicates. However, library computer users do not have this option. A few Web mail providers, however, are becoming more alert to fraudulent practices and may soon offer such a feature.
- There may be no effective way to tell a message from a reliable source from a fraudulent one on the basis of message content. The cooked-up one may include a genuine logo, graphics, privacy policy and other verbiage copied from the real organization's Web site. Occasionally, phishers' grammar or spelling may give them away, especially if they are not native English language speakers.
- The e-mail message contains a link to a Web site that appears to be legitimate. However, phishing messages are nearly always written in HTML rather than in simple text. This makes it possible to hide the real address of the destination server behind a bogus link that appears to be going to a legitimate business. In other words, the link you see is not the one to which you are sent. It may not, however, be difficult to discover this subterfuge. Most e-mail programs and Web browsers have a menu option, "show source," that can reveal the hidden text.
- Once you arrive at the Web site, the URL address may continue to look legitimate. Remember, however, that the domain name (the server on which the Web site's files are stored) appears at the top of the page just before the dot com. In other words, the final period and the three letters that indicate the kind of site you have reached (com, net, edu, gov, etc). Often, the actual domain name is something very neutral that you may fail to notice because the name of your bank, etc. is prominently displayed in the space to the left. The URL may read "www.usbank.info.com"

or "www.citibank.admin.com" (if these were legitimate domains, "usbank" would come after "info" and "Citibank" would come after "admin"). Occasionally, the scammer is so skilled that he has gotten into one of the domain name servers (DNS) that route messages across the Internet. In this case, the address may actually appear to be correct but its numerical equivalent, in other words the address that the computer itself understands, is bogus.

- Some people imagine that if they see a logo like Verisign, they can be assured that they are on a secure, legitimate site. Remember that it is easy to simply copy and paste the Verisign graphic from another site.
- Most people don't look too closely at the address bar at the top of the page. In fact, they probably won't notice if there are two address bars. Pfishers may go one step further in making their web pages look legitimate by adding a fake address bar of their own, complete with a very official looking URL.
- Occasionally, the scammer is able to hack his way into a respected site without the Web master being aware of his presence. Once he has access to the site, he can insert a popup window that asks visitors to click on a link. Of course, the link takes them to the scammer's site.

MONEY MULES: THE OTHER LIBRARY VICTIMS OF PHISHING SCAMS

This odd name refers to a particularly nasty scam that actually implicates the unwary Internet user in a crime. It does not directly result in identity theft but aids and abets cyber-thieves who perpetrate this crime. Because library computer users may trust strangers with confidential information about themselves and may assume that e-mail correspondents are who they say they are, they are at high risk of falling for this type of scam.

Novice Internet users are often delighted when they open their inboxes and find messages waiting for them, even if they are from strangers. They may be much more trusting of strangers who approach them in this way than they would of a stranger greeting them on the street. There is ample evidence that inexperienced Internet users simply do no not exert the same caution that they would in face-to-face situations because so many of the usual cues are missing. This makes it possible to get themselves into compromising situations before they really know what is happening. The Money Mule scam is a good example of how this can happen.

Choosing a Victim

To better understand this somewhat technical activity, let's go back and revisit Henry, our older, out-of-work computer user. Some time ago, Henry opened a free e-mail account, which he checks daily. Like Louise above, Henry receives plenty of junk mail, but he still enjoys finding messages waiting for him. One day, however, the message in his inbox seemed like a gift from heaven. It was a job offer sent by an international company and inviting him to become their American agent or representative. In his excitement, Henry didn't read the message very carefully but there was some vague mention of his past experience and his suitability for the job. Of course, Henry had posted many copies of his resume online, so he assumed the message was a response. As the company's American agent, Henry would be receiving payments for the company and transferring funds overseas, always keeping a healthy commission for himself.

The company made it clear that no risk would be involved. Henry need not spend any money of his own. This was not an investment scheme but a real job with real money. The company assured Henry that he was the right man for the job because he had a good reputation and could be trusted with their money (actually, they did not mention Henry by name but made it clear that he was known for his sterling character.

Offshore Schemes

The message explained that an agent was needed because U.S. law places tight restrictions on the bank accounts of foreign companies, and a U.S. citizen is not subject to these strict laws. All Henry would need to do was to initiate wire fund transfers whenever he received payments for the company. Henry was invited to look them up on the Web to confirm that they were a legitimate company. When Henry clicked on the link provided in the e-mail message, he did, indeed, find a Web site that looked very legitimate and professionally produced.

In reality, this was not really a company but an individual who needed a patsy to receive funds obtained through fraudulent phishing scams similar to the ones previously described. The cyberthief who recruited Henry also sent out thousands of e-mails purporting to be from a large bank like Wells Fargo or CitiBank. He tricked some recipients into sharing their bank passwords and then emptied their accounts. The stolen funds were sent to Henry or transferred directly into Henry's bank account. Eventually, of course, law enforcement agencies were able to follow the trail that led directly to Henry. He became liable for all the funds that went through his hands (or his bank account) and an attempt was even made to press criminal charges against him.

Lest you think that "money mule" scams are infrequent, let me tell you about an e-mail message that was downloaded to my computer only minutes ago. As I was making changes to this chapter, my e-mail program alerted me to a new message. Here it is in its entirety:

Good day
Accept my apology for writing you in this mode, I got your contact from the International directory and will be glad to do business with you. I came across your contact in my search for a reliable person who will assist me in transferring a large amount of money lying dormant in a bank into a safe and secure account.

If interested get back with your position, private telephone and fax numbers for easy and effective communication. I hope i can count on your confidentiality and honesty. On receipt of your mail i will give you more details on this transaction.

Regards
Dr Emmanuel Silver

As a librarian, you would immediately question the supposed International Directory in which the writer discovered your name, but the message sounds somewhat plausible. Most of the grammar and spelling are acceptable, although one immediately wonders why the writer can't simply transfer funds to his own bank account if they belong to him. Presumably, you would receive a somewhat plausible explanation if you responded. If this were the message that Henry received, his gullibility was perfectly understandable. He needed money and someone called Dr. Emmanuel Silver (a nice professional sounding name) was offering him an opportunity to earn some.

Protecting Library Users

Henry should have been cautioned to ignore e-mails from strangers. He should have been warned that in most cases, real business contacts who wish to reach him will not know about his e-mail account. There is really no such thing as an Internet telephone book despite the claims of some Web sites. The unsolicited messages he finds in his inbox are almost inevitably spam. Senders do not know Henry, even though they may pretend to have information about him. Vague compliments should be an immediate tip off that senders are up to no good.

Checking Out Credentials

The supposed international company sent Henry to a Web site to verify that they were who they said they were. If Henry had more sophisticated Web skills, he could have gone to the Web site at http://www.betterwhois.com to check up on the company. Scammers usually register their fake sites just days before they send out their bulk e-mail messages. They can't afford to leave their Web sites up too long since authorities might be able to trace them. Henry would probably have found that the supposedly well-established international company had applied for its domain name and uploaded its files less than a week earlier, an obvious indication that there was something rotten in Denmark. If Henry were more sophisticated about the Net, he would also discover that the Web site was registered in a country with very lax laws. Con artists deliberately operate out of certain countries in Africa and the Caribbean because they do not enforce the conventions of international law.

WHEN THE WORST HAPPENS

Despite your best efforts, one or more of your library computer users may become the victim of identity theft. Spyware and scams like those described earlier are only some of the means by which unscrupulous thieves obtain personal information. For example, college students continue to leave their purses and backpacks behind when they visit the restroom. Whether information is obtained by high-tech or low-tech means, the results are the same. Since this is such a common crime (various surveys put the number of victims in the U.S. between 700,000 and 9 million depending on how identity theft is defined), information to assist victims should be readily available in your library.

Many organizations offer free or inexpensive leaflets with step-by-step instructions for getting one's finances back together. However, it's also easy for the library to produce a short list of things to do immediately if one suspects identity theft. The sooner the crime is discovered and the victim takes action, the less damage will result. The following information can be made available in a flyer, brochure, or even on a bookmark:

Contact the Local Police Department

Although it is essential to contact the police immediately if one suspects identity theft, most library users have no idea that they are about to become victims. What they really need is to be informed about cyber scams before they first sit down at a library computer. Inexperienced computer users will be unaware that they have been crime victims unless they can spot the clues. Even then, however, they may only have vague suspicions, so it is the responsibility of the library staff to encourage them to contact the police. The sooner a possible crime is reported, the less devastating the consequences. The call to the police department should be made by the victim, not the library staff. There's a thin line between carrying out the library's responsibility to protect patrons and becoming entangled in their lives.

Obtain a Copy of the Police Report

Any time law enforcement officers respond to a call, they write up a report of the incident. This report is stored in their computer system and is available to crime victims. Your patron will need to send copies of this report to a variety of different businesses and government agencies including credit reporting services, collection agencies, banks, and other creditors. Be sure the library patron asks where and when the report can be obtained.

Contact One of the Three Major Credit Reporting Agencies

Anyone can find contact information for credit agencies online, but the library should also have the information readily available. Encourage the possible victim to request a credit report and then to review it for signs of possible fraudulent activity. Patrons should look for accounts they can't recall opening, applications for credit, and incorrect information. Then they should report any inaccuracies in writing to the credit reporting agency and follow their instructions carefully. You might

---

want to suggest, either in a brochure or when you're talking with worried patrons, that they talk with a real human being at the credit reporting agency. There are various steps that can be taken to protect their credit, but they can be quite inconvenient if there is only a small chance that they have been victimized

Notify Credit Card Companies

Let them know that fraudulent activity is suspected. Companies will usually want to cancel your cards and issue new ones. This is a good time, however, to decide whether the credit card is really needed. It may be possible (though less likely) for a cyber-thief to find out about the new card.

Complete an ID Theft Affidavit

This is a single, standard document to report identity theft to multiple organizations. This document can be obtained from the Federal Trade Commission (FTC) Web site (http://ftc.gov) as an Adobe PDF file. This same government Web site has a very complete summary of the types of problems victims may encounter. Suggestions are provided for dealing with each type of incident.

Consider Submitting a Fraud Alert

This involves calling the toll-free number of any one of the three reporting agencies and asking the customer service representative to place a fraud alert on your file. This alerts potential creditors that a problem exists and that they should take special precautions. However, this may make it difficult for the theft victim to obtain credit.

Consider Submitting a Victim Statement

This statement tells creditors to contact you before granting credit or other services. The advisability of doing this depends on how likely it is that your credit is in danger. It will impede your own legitimate access to credit more than necessary if there is only a vague suspicion of fraud.

Continue to Monitor Credit Status

Identity theft victims often believe that once they have taken the appropriate steps, their problems are over. Unfortunately, it sometimes takes a year or more for all the problems to surface. Nothing may happen until the victim's information is sold to a third party. As we saw above, identity problems can continue for years when a case involves public records. Obtain frequent reports from one of the credit reporting agencies for about a year after the theft occurs, and then at less frequently in succeeding years.

SUMMING IT UP

Although it's important to communicate these steps to users of library computers, it's also necessary to let them know that library staff members are not experts. Identity theft is a serious crime, and victims require professional help. As librarians, we are not qualified to provide professional financial counseling; and patrons should seek additional help from the police, the Better Business Bureau, their local banker or other financial advisor. In Chapter 9, we will be taking a broader look at the library's Internet education program, an important part of which is protecting patrons from identity theft.

REFERENCES

Better Business Bureau. Information for consumers: what is identity theft? *BBB Online.* http://www.bbbonline.org/idtheft/consumers.asp.

Bray, Hiawatha. 2005. Let's focus on the theft, not the identity. *Boston Globe,* March 21. http://www.boston.com/business/articles/2005/03/21/lets_focus_on_the_theft_not_the_identity/.

Gowan, F. 2005. Don't get lured by phishing scams: avoid becoming a victim and reassure potential funders. *Tech Soup,* December 9. http://www.techsoup.org/learningcenter/internet/page4223.cfm.

Poulsen, Kevin. 2003. Guilty plea in Kinko's keystroke caper. SecurityFocus, July 18. http://www.security focus.com/news/6447.

Zeller, Tom. 2005. Breach points up flaws in privacy laws. *New York Times,* February 24, p. C1. http://www.nytimes.com/2005/02/24/business/24datas.html?ei=5088&en=1a34f1accdb516d9&ex=1267160400&partner=rssnyt&pagewanted=print&position=.

Zeller, Tom. 2006. Victims fight to clear their names after others' deeds. *New York Times,* September 4. http://www.nytimes.com/2006/09/04/us/04victim.html?_r=1&oref=slogin/.

CHAPTER 3
Privacy Threats
from the Business World

After reading the previous chapter, you might deduce that most
online assaults on our patrons' privacy are the work of criminals.
Unfortunately, many arise from perfectly legal activities, often ones
that have no more nefarious goal than selling a product.

MARKETING POTENTIAL OF THE INTERNET

As you may be aware, the Internet arose from what was once called
ARPANET, an early computer network designed to allow government
agencies to communicate with one another, even if the nation were
under attack. The idea was to have a "network of networks" each of
which could communicate with the others without going through a
central hub. That would mean that if communication lines were down
in one area, traffic could be routed around the problem. Although it
was initially meant for official use only, ARPANET quickly expanded
to research centers and universities. As it grew, informal use skyrock-
eted, especially e-mail and newsgroups. The business community
quickly realized its potential for marketing their products, and many
new businesses sprang up to service both their Internet needs and
those of the general public.

Today, most of us use the Internet in one way or another. The creation of an online world has revolutionized not only the way business
and government conduct their activities, but it has also changed the

way individuals communicate. One of the most unexpected surprises has been the extraordinary eagerness of computer users to share personal information with strangers. In fact, people may give little thought to the intrusive questions that pop up when they register to use a service or find themselves selected to complete online surveys. Psychologists tell us that human beings are inherently lonely and have deeply-seated needs to reach out to others, even total strangers. The anonymity of the Internet encourages them to be even more honest and more candid than they might be in face-to-face communication.

ECONOMIC VALUE OF PERSONAL INFORMATION

With the arrival of the World Wide Web, opportunities for recreational use of the Internet exploded. Many Online service companies took possession of cyberspace, providing search services, news, weather, classified ads, online maps, and driving directions. Many new retail businesses like Amazon.com, headquartered in cyberspace, prospered, and traditional, brick and mortar businesses like banks, bookstores, and clothing emporia opened web-based branches.

The most popular services allowed Web surfers to get together with other people or to express their views on every conceivable subject. Free e-mail was, of course, the most popular service of all, but it seemed as if every Internet service provider offered online dating, chat, and group discussion sites. No matter how unusual your interests, you could be assured that there were other people out there on the Net who shared them. At this writing, Yahoo! offers 324 groups devoted to the discussion of Voodoo, 2,256 devoted to divination, 431 to Gaelic football, 3,246 to heartbreak, and 50 to collecting lawnmowers. I have no idea what "potato guns" are but there are 104 Yahoo! groups that discuss them.

Capturing Limitless Information

What has occurred is, in a sense, a social revolution resulting in endless informal communication about an endless stream of topics. This means that vast quantities of personal information are exchanged and stored in untold numbers of computers. Millions of people interact daily with and through Internet service providers without considering that their messages and queries are almost invariably accompanied by their computer's identifiers and often by personally identifiable information as well. It quickly became evident that this information could be useful to Web site owners. They could use it to sell services to their own customers, and they could sell the data to marketers and newly established database brokers. Even law abiding Web sites collect vast quantities of information that can get into the wrong hands.

A Typical Library Computer User

Because we respect their privacy, we may not be fully aware of what our library computer users are doing while they're online. To better understand the dangers they face, let's invent a few more library customers. Let's look over the shoulder of a recently retired man named Steve who comes into the library almost every day. Steve's job required him to use e-mail but he never learned much about computers in general. Now he has quite a bit of time on his hands since he hasn't fully adjusted to retirement. He began using the library's public computers to check his e-mail account and has gradually extended his use to other Web-based services.

Yahoo!'s Popularity

Steve especially likes to "Yahoo!" because this Web-based service provider offers such a wide variety of interesting features. Since he knew he would soon lose the e-mail address provided by his employer, Steve signed up for a free Yahoo! account before he retired. Fortunately, the application form he completed was very brief. Required information included first and last name, gender, birth date, and ZIP code. These questions do not seem terribly intrusive, but if you ever access a site like Intelius, a background information/public records search site, you'll discover that this is enough information to match Steve up with his birth, marriage, real estate, bankruptcy, and motor vehicle records. A security question is also required but most of them like "What is the name of your pet?" cannot compromise Steve's privacy. The registration form, however, includes three questions about Steve's occupation that are very specific. The first question asks about the industry and by the time Steve answers the third question, he has probably entered his exact job title and area of specialization. Answering these occupation questions is not required, but a new member like Steve may not notice the very small asterisk before required questions.

A few years ago, the e-mail signup form was much longer. Yahoo! found it useful (and profitable) to collect as much information about its members as possible. When signing up for a new account, applicants were confronted with three long pages full of questions about practically every aspect of their lives. Some of this information, including home address, appeared in a publicly accessible profile, and still more information was added to members' profiles when they purchased a premium service or a Yahoo! product like a computer game. Fortunately, Yahoo!, like other large Web portals, learned that having all this information was not necessarily a good thing. Such vast stores of personal information attracted identity thieves, as well as subpoenas by government agencies. Yahoo! now requires significantly less personal information to sign up for an e-mail account, but it still collects considerably more information than its members are aware of. Some Yahoo! members have also complained loudly when they discovered online profile information they had not meant to divulge.

Yahoo! Member Profiles

Awhile back, Steve discovered that he could chat with his grandson using the Yahoo! instant messenger program. It's an unusually good one that allows Steve to screen incoming messages and even make himself invisible if he chooses to do so. Steve likes the online radio module that allows him to create his own station that plays all his favorite music through library headphones. Messenger users are encouraged to create their own personal profiles in the member directory so that they can get to know other people and other people can get to know them. Steve is a widower, and he's a little lonely. The idea of meeting people online appeals to him so he created a profile. Here is some of the information the profile asks for:

The information on the e-mail application form
- Location
- Age
- Marital status
- Sex
- Occupation
- Interests

It's easy to see that these questions were chosen with online romance in mind. Although they are not really very invasive, they contribute significantly toward the critical mass of information needed to steal one's identity.

Yahoo! Address Book

In addition, Yahoo! encourages its e-mail users to create an online address book. Since Steve frequently forgets the e-mail addresses of his friends and relatives, this seemed like a good idea. This way, he can access the information on any computer, either in the library or at the senior center he sometimes visits. Each time he adds a contact, Steve is presented with a form that asks for the following information:

- Name
- Nickname
- E-mail address
- Alternate e-mail address
- Instant messenger ID
- Home, Work, Pager, and Mobile phone numbers
- Fax number
- Alternate messenger IDs
- Home address
- Personal Web site
- Company name
- Job title
- Company address
- Birth date
- Anniversary

This is an extraordinary amount of personal information to collect. Remember that all of this data resides on Yahoo! servers and all of it may be available to government agencies, Yahoo! staff, data brokers, and marketing companies under certain circumstances. Yahoo! has a privacy policy, but Steve has never read it. It's quite long and Steve thinks he has better things to do with his time. Not only is Steve's personal information useful in itself, but it points out social relationships or networks of family and acquaintances. As we will discover in later chapters, both commercial data brokers and federal intelligence agencies are extremely interested in these interpersonal connections.

Yahoo! Calendar

Steve also likes Yahoo!'s calendar program. Computerized calendars are very convenient and many computer owners often use programs like Microsoft Outlook that provide a calendar, appointment schedule, to-do list, and virtual alarm clock on their own personal computers.

Steve doesn't have this particular option, but the Yahoo! calendar has most of those features. The problem with a calendar, however, is that if Yahoo! already knows Steve's name, birth date, and ZIP code, things are getting a little too personal. Steve's calendar tells a great deal about his life including where he goes, what he does, and whom he visits. When coupled with the information he's already provided to Yahoo, it's possible to discover his political beliefs, his mental and physical health, possibly even specifics of his love-life and some personal habits that Steve would not like to become public knowledge.

Jerry Kanga, law professor at UCLA and an expert on the impact of technology on privacy, believes that this is just too much personal information to leave lying around.

"What's going to be taking place over the next 10 years in the privacy space will have profound implications for how we relate to each other socially, economically and politically.... We shouldn't be too quick to turn personal data over to market forces" (Freedman 2006).

Yahoo! Briefcase and other File Storage Options

Another feature that Steve likes is the Yahoo! Briefcase. Since most libraries do not allow public computer users to save files to their hard drives, it is difficult for Steve to keep the interesting articles and other information he discovers online. He must bring his own floppy disks, which can be easily damaged. Since their storage capacity is very limited, he is often unable to save even a single Web page. However, if he signs up for a Yahoo! briefcase, he can take his files with him, easily accessing them on any library or senior center computer. This is possible because hard drive storage space has become very inexpensive in recent years; and it is possible for Web services like Yahoo! to offer their members what amounts to their own personal hard drives. Microsoft is planning to enter the fray with its "Live Drive," a service that reportedly will provide about two gigabytes of free storage space to its users.

Google will soon be offering GDrive, a service that is expected to give public computer users so much online file storage space that they can use public computers almost as if they were their own personal PCs. We as librarians are always happy to see our customers getting a good deal, and these services make up for many of the inequities between computer "haves and have nots." However, once again, all this information is, to some extent, available to commercial interests and government agencies; and there are dangers associated with them.

Financial Services

Soon Steve discovered Yahoo!'s financial services. Their "bill pay" service is especially helpful and easy to use. However, the service requires that Steve type in bank account, Social Security, and driver's license numbers. This is precisely the information needed to steal Steve's identity. When Steve divulges this information, he is opening himself up to danger from an incredibly large number of sources.

In one sense, this is no different from the situation that confronts computer owners. Yahoo! could be unwittingly sharing the information with hackers who gain illegal access to Yahoo! servers, or with dishonest Yahoo! employees. Library computers, however, pose additional dangers. Remember, for example, those criminals in the last chapter who loaded malicious software on library computers. An innocent patron may unwittingly download an e-mail message to which one of these programs was secretly attached. He or she clicks to open the attachment and voila! The malicious software installs itself and lays waiting for the next unsuspecting user and the next. If computer owners choose to share personal information with Yahoo!, they can do so in the privacy of their own homes. A library patron sitting at the next computer may be able to see Steve type into Yahoo!'s online forms. In all, there are literally dozens of ways in which Steve's information can get into someone else's hands.

Google and Personal Information

Another frequent user of her library's public computers is Susan, but she prefers Google to Yahoo! She has signed up for a variety of Google services including e-mail (Gmail). In addition, Google is moving rapidly into a market called software as a service. New Google software allows individuals and businesses and to obtain software delivered over the Web. Some of these products are free. In the case of the new Google Apps Premier Edition, a fifty dollar annual fee entitles customers to use a sophisticated software suite somewhat resembling MS Office and have ten gigabytes of storage space available for their personal files. While computer owners are free to select and purchase software to run on their own machines, library computer users have been limited to the software the library selects for them. Software as a service means that much like computer owners, they will be able to access not only library software, but additional online programs that meet their personal needs. Although Google Apps Premier Edition is, at this writing, newly arrived on the market, other Google programs have been in use for some time. Google users have been able to use a free spreadsheet program that stores user files at Google's datacenters and allows users to access them online. Your Domain is a free service that allows even the smallest fledgling business to create a Web domain of its own, develop a Web site, and send Google e-mail from that domain. This could be a lifesaver for out-of-work patrons or those interested in starting a home business.

Such free software, however, poses some new conundrums for the library. Although most of the computer code is stored on the Internet provider's computer servers, small parts of the programs are usually downloaded onto the user's computer for speed and convenience. It is possible to hide malicious software in almost any kind of file and so greater convenience may also mean greater danger.

The Google Subpoena

In May of 2006, Google announced that it would not comply with a subpoena issued by the U.S. Department of Justice which demanded a month of search requests. While Google refused to provide data on its users' searches, other online service providers had supplied huge quantities of similar data. Although in this instance, Google defended the privacy of its users and ultimately supplied only a fraction of the data demanded, the publicity surrounding the subpoena served as a wakeup call to privacy advocates. Google has been collecting far more personal information than anyone imagined.

Google is able to connect Internet queries to cookies deposited on user computers, even the computers of people who do not have Google accounts. When Google account IDs are available, so much the better. Not only is this information collected and stored for years, but is aggregated or linked to other information from the same computer. In other words, information from different Google services like e-mail, word processing, search engine queries, and Web site traffic analysis can be brought together to produce extensive personal profiles. Google encourages new users to agree to its "Web History" tracking system that lets them review all their past Google searches. This allows Google to review the searches as well. The Google Toolbar can capture the URLs of all the Web sites visited.

Privacy International is a British civil liberties organization that is best known for its Big Brother Awards. The group evaluated the privacy practices of twenty-eight online content providers including YouTube, Microsoft, eBay, and MySpace. Google scored at the bottom of their list. Simon Davies, Privacy International's director, explained the reasons why Google did so badly: "One of the points we are making is that Google is the new Microsoft. Five years ago, Microsoft was rightly perceived as the evil empire. But Microsoft has turned the ship around somewhat, and it doesn't require much tweaking to embed privacy infrastructure into planning processes" (Singel 2007).

Most people, including our library user Susan, are unaware that Google and other service providers store much of their data in other parts of the world where it is not protected by U.S. law. Other governments may not share America's views on privacy or human rights. Google's agreement with the Chinese government to censor its search results makes it clear that service providers are under the direct control of foreign governments when they do business in their countries.

Gmail Content Scanned

Service providers like Google encourage members to use their servers as extensions of their own computers. This allows users to access their data anywhere on any computer. Google offers Gmail, a very attractive free e-mail service that allows users to store up to one gigabyte of their old messages. However, Google scans the messages for specific keywords, and inserts content-targeted advertisements into the messages. When Susan sends an e-mail via Gmail, the subject matter is correlated to an all too relevant advertisement. Specifically, Google sends e-mail content to "DoubleClick," one of the more infamous pop-up advertisers.

Weak Privacy Protection

Most of the millions of people who use the library's public computers have signed up for Web-based e-mail accounts like Gmail, Hotmail, and Yahoo!. Competitors may not provide as much storage space as Google, but all encourage users to store a large number of messages online. In other words, messages are stored on the computer servers owned and maintained by these service providers. However, according to the provisions of the Electronic Communications Privacy Act (ECPA), messages and documents stored by Web mail providers are entitled to only weak privacy protection. In general, government agencies do not need a sub-poena to access Web mail. They may obtain online correspondence without notifying the person or persons whose mail is being read.

Computer owners usually keep up their online correspondence using e-mail clients, software programs that download messages to their personal computers and store them locally. Messages are usually deleted from the service provider's computer as soon as they are downloaded and so are not vulnerable to the same weak protection. Library users are at an unfair disadvantage since Web mail is often their only option. Chris Hoofnagle, a lawyer for the Electronic Privacy Information Center (EPIC), believes that the huge storage capacity e-mail service providers offer can seriously compromise the privacy of millions of innocent people. "Most people think it's just Tony Soprano whose records get seized," he says, "but in actuality it is anyone who has had contact with Tony Soprano" (Singel 2004). Depending on the scope of the investigation, the interest of law enforcement agencies may extend to contacts of contacts of Soprano contacts, in other words, almost anyone.

Ari Schwartz of the Center for Democracy and Technology (CDT) agrees. "Your e-mails are not protected under law the same way they are in your house. I hope Google, Microsoft, Yahoo! and all the other Web mail providers will fight for stronger protections" (Singel 2004).

Amazon.com

If there is any one Web site that both library staff and library users flock to in droves, it is Amazon.com. In my informal survey, I was unable to find a single librarian who had not perused the delightful attractions of Amazon.com. Whether or not you have actually made a purchase, Amazon knows an amazing amount about you and your patrons. Its patented technology tracks information about both its customers and the people for whom they purchase gifts, producing one of the largest and most personal troves of data on the Web.

Amazon.com's Partners

Amazon.com's intention is basically to build a large audience of loyal customers and knowing more about them is good for business. As Werner Vogels, Amazon's chief technology officer, puts it: "In general, we collect as much information as possible such that we can provide you with the best feedback" (Linn 2005). Privacy experts, however, believe that Amazon.com may have gone too far in its voracious acquisition of personal information. Chris Hoofnagle of the EPIC warns that "They are constantly finding new ways to exploit personal information" (Linn 2005). Perhaps the paramount danger is that Amazon.com shares personal information with businesses it buys or partners with. If one looks at the huge number of stores like Toys R Us on the Amazon.com site, it is easy to see that a substantial part of the retail world may have access to the information that Amazon. com collects. Once again, an ever expanding group consisting of thousands of honest and dishonest people—employees of dozens of companies and their Internet service providers, as well as criminal hackers—may have access to customer credit card numbers and other confidential information.

Targeted Services

Just what kind of information does Amazon collect? Although it is like other E-commerce sites in that it stores names, addresses, and credit card information, Amazon.com goes several steps further. Its sophisticated software tools are able to make uncanny inferences about their customers' interests. If John Doe purchases one DVD, for example, Amazon.com can accurately predict that he may be interested in several others.

Many customers turn to Amazon.com when they need to purchase a gift for a friend or relative because Amazon makes it so easy to choose the right gift. It thoughtfully encourages engaged couples to use Amazon for their Wedding Registry and expectant parents list preferred infant paraphernalia on the Baby Registry. In addition, everyone young and old, is encouraged to post their wish lists, the modern equivalent of all-season letters to Santa, and many users take advantage of the offer. From personal experience, I know of few teenagers who do not have five-page lists of sought after Christmas, Hanukkah, or birthday presents.

From Cradle to Grave

Although many E-commerce sites collect information about their customers, Amazon.com goes a step further and collects information about gift recipients. It has developed software that tracks their age and preferences. In theory, Amazon can follow a large segment of the population from the cradle, through adolescence, marriage, child-rearing, and into old age. Karen Coyle of Computer Professionals for Social Responsibility (CPSR) believes that such technology may actually violate federal law by collecting information on children under the age of 13 (Linn).

America Online

To round out our picture of library computer use, we'll invent yet another library computer user who happens to be a member of America Online (AOL). Brian is a college student whose family subscribes to AOL as its Internet service provider. The company provides both Internet access (dial-up and high speed) and a generous serving of very popular online content. Brian has his own AOL login and uses it when he visits both his university and public libraries. AOL's dating site is among the largest on the Net, and one of Brian's favorites. Since August 2006, many of AOL's most heavily used services no longer require a paid membership. That means that library computer users who do not own their own computers can now enjoy many of those services.

AOL maintains a publicly-accessible research Web site for the designers of search engines and other Web utilities. In August 2006, AOL posted on this Web site 19 million Internet search queries typed by more than 658,000 customers over a three month period. Somehow the AOL executives who approved this massive invasion of their members' privacy imagined that stripping off personal names would render the data anonymous. As was quickly discovered, this was not true. An individual member's searches were all listed under a single number. That means that since Brian used his AOL account during the period, all of Brian's searches were listed together under one number. Like most people, he frequently searches his own name, those of his friends and family, his hometown, his university, and many terms related to his personal interests. Some AOL members actually entered extremely confidential information like their Social Security numbers and home addresses, assuming that their searches were simply disappearing into cyberspace. Instead, the content of each and every search appeared online, grouped with the other searches performed by the same individual.

Wake Up Call

Privacy experts were appalled. "On AOL's part this is an absolutely, unbelievably stupid maneuver," complained chief executive of

PrivacyToday.com and information security consultant Rob Douglas. "For consumers this is a real wake-up call for them as they learn that this information is not only being maintained, but I think it's a great demonstration of how realistically you can track it back to a specific person" (O'Connor 2006).

New York Times reporters quickly demonstrated that the data were not anonymous. They took the search queries of one individual, supplemented by a telephone book and correctly identified the user as Thelma Arnold, 62, of Lilburn, Georgia (Barbaro 2006). They looked at her searches which included "numb fingers," "60 single men," "dry mouth," "bipolar," "landscapers in Lilburn, GA," and a number of people whose last name was Arnold. As it turned out, only some of this information really applied to Ms. Arnold. Like many of us, she sometimes looks up medical and other information to assist her friends.

Tracking Computer Users

Because America Online is a paid service, we might try to reassure ourselves that most library users are not involved in these disturbing revelations. Considering AOL's new generosity in making many services freely available, this is no longer a realistic expectation. Let's return, however, to the library computer users we met earlier in this chapter. You may recall that Steve is an ardent Yahoo! user and Susan prefers Google. Both of these services provide popular search engines and both offer free e-mail and other features that are particularly attractive to people like our library users. Steve and Susan have both completed application forms that request personal information, and both regularly sign into their accounts when they go online. Both service providers are known to store user data for long periods of time although recent news articles indicate that they are considering policy changes in the wake of government subpoenas and the AOL scandal.

Both services use "cookies" to identify users so that they can custom tailor content and advertisements to their preferences. Cookies are small files generated by a Web server and stored in user computers. They become embedded in the information flowing back and forth between the workstation computer and the Web site's server. Web servers automatically access cookies when the user establishes a connection.

Here's an example. Yahoo!'s server sends a cookie to the computer Steve is using when he signs in. Steve enjoys having his own "My

Yahoo!" Web page and has chosen the items he wants on his page from a list of suggested interests. This and other personal information about Steve is included in a cookie so Yahoo! can create the page to Steve's specifications. Steve is unaware of the cookie's existence, and he is also unaware that each time he clicks on a Yahoo! page or types a query into the Yahoo! search engine, the Yahoo! cookie accompanies his request.

This means that the major online service providers not only store the same information that was inadvertently divulged by AOL, but this information is also linked to individual names, birthdays, gender, ZIP codes, and other personal information already collected. Google stores information indefinitely, although this policy is under review.

Are Public Computers Really Anonymous?

In theory, library computers should be more anonymous than those of computer owners. After all, the computer's address is really the library. Terrorists have taken advantage of this anonymity to communicate with their organizations. My own interviews with library computer users, however, indicate that they are unaware of the information that is being collected during computer use. Patrons tend to use their real names when they sign up for an e-mail account and for the other services they use most often. Because they may be uncomfortable with computers, they are likely to have only one e-mail account and one service that they use on a regular basis. Steve says he tends to forget user names and passwords so he keeps things simple by using one account and search tool, reusing the same user name and password. Yahoo! has plenty of useful features, so he rarely strays to other online services.

Protecting Library Users

Although protecting our users from some types of privacy assaults can be complicated, this particular danger can be easily dealt with. If Steve's Yahoo! account contains personal information, he can simply close it and open an anonymous account under an assumed name. He can then continue to use Yahoo! for most of his needs, but stick to Google for his online searching. This way, it will not be possible to track his searches by connecting them with Steve's other online activities. Since he is using library computers, it will also be impossible to separate his searches from those of other library users.

As mentioned earlier, library patrons like Steve should be cautioned to complete online service providers' applications using assumed names, but they may need considerable encouragement. They may imagine that doing so is illegal; but the same subterfuge is used by millions of people to protect their privacy. These are very simple, easily implemented suggestions, but they require that we establish real communication with our users.

COMMERCIAL DATA COLLECTION AND DATA MINING

Private industry views the availability of huge quantities of personal information as a marketing bonanza. As we have already discovered, businesses like Amazon.com are convinced that the more they know about their potential customers (age, sex, income, personal likes, dislikes, and prejudices) the easier it is to market goods and services to them.

Online service providers and online advertisers can use the information they collect in two ways. First, of course, they can use it to sell their own products and services. They can make even more money, however, by selling it. Although they might sell information to other advertisers, personal information increasingly finds its way to large commercial data brokers (CDBs). When a library patron answers a long string of questions to get a free e-mail account or sign up for a luxury automobile drawing, the information will very likely find its way to a CDB like ChoicePoint, Inc. This CDB, however, does not depend entirely on the information that computer users divulge about themselves. It also stores purchases made on supermarket discount cards, telephone numbers, and government records like motor vehicle violations, Social Security numbers, court records, and marriages.

The Reach of Data Brokers

ChoicePoint, a company based in Alpharetta, Georgia, sells information and data services to businesses, insurers, government agencies, and direct marketers. ChoicePoint has purchased a number of other CDBs, like the VitalChek Network and DBT Online, absorbing the data that each has amassed, and gradually becoming one of the largest, if not the largest, repositories of official, personal, and consumer information. Insurance agents, law enforcement officers, and direct marketers can all obtain comprehensive, personal profiles of millions of individuals literally in seconds.

At the root of at least some of the evils of commercial data collection is the belief that you just can't have too much information. The corporate world collects and stores personal information, to some extent, just because it can. There is a widespread belief that you can't know too much about your customers. The more you know about people, the theory goes, the more likely that you can sell them your product.

You Just Might Need It

There is also a widely-held belief that you may need this or that bit of information at some future date. We in libraries are all too aware of this belief. When we set up a new library automation system and choose the fields in the patron record, many of the options sound useful. For example, if we can't get hold of patrons at home, wouldn't it be helpful to call them at work? Of course, we might get a wrong number so it would also be useful to know their place of employment. The names of spouses and children would also be helpful. When patrons first register, we usually ask for proof of identity and address, often a driver's license. Why not enter that number as well? That way, we might prevent one person from using another's library card.

The answer to all these questions is that we do not really need all this personal information, and we can't protect it. Library staff members have access to these records, as do work study students, high school pages, volunteers, employees of the company that maintains our automated systems, and possibly a few people who hack their way into the library database. The same answer applies to commercial enterprises; but in their case, the number of people who have access to personal records may be in the hundreds. In the case of large CDBs, the number of people who can view information may be in the thousands or even millions. It is almost inevitable that some of those people have both the inclination and the ability to misuse the information.

Personal Information in the Wrong Hands

Take, for example, the case of American International Group, Inc. (AIG), an insurer that provides supplemental medical insurance through 690 different insurance brokers. On March 31, 2006, a laptop computer and a file server containing 970,000 personal records of insurance applicants were stolen. The company waited nearly three months to alert these applicants that personal information like their Social Security numbers was in the hands of thieves. AIG spokesman Chris Winans passed the blame to the data brokers that provided the personal information. "While we had told brokers in the past that we didn't want this information—we don't need it—now we are saying: 'You are prohibited from giving us this information. Do not send us any files with this kind of information. We don't need it, and we don't want to be in possession of it" (Smith 2006).

Why then, if there was no need for AIG to collect Social Security numbers and other sensitive information, did they continue to accept it and enter it into their computers? Beth Givens, Director of the non-profit Privacy Rights Clearinghouse, states the issue clearly. "Obviously, they knew they were getting this kind of information from brokers, probably for years ... but they didn't do anything about it until they experienced this serious breach" (Smith).

Unfortunately, this is far from an isolated incident. Again and again, organizations that collect personal information fail to protect it. Employees ignore the danger to which they are subjecting their customers (or their customers' customers) and take risks that seem unbelievably careless in hindsight. Here are just a few incidents that took place over three months in 2005.

- In February 2005, the Bank of America lost a backup tape containing the financial records of 1,200,000 customers.
- That same month, a central computer of DSW Retail Ventures was hacked and credit card information on approximately 100,000 people was stolen. One would think that this incident might have encouraged the company to tighten its security. However, in April, an additional 1,300,000 customer records were illegally exposed.
- Also in April, the San Jose Medical Group lost 185,000 patient records in yet another computer theft.
- The library world's own LexisNexis inadvertently gave would-be thieves password access to 280,000 customer accounts; and clothing mogul Ralph Lauren exposed the credit card numbers of 180,000 customers to hackers.

Each time that confidential data is stolen, the victims become vulnerable to identity theft. In some of the incidents described above, data like

Social Security and credit card numbers were being sold on the Internet hours, days, or even weeks before the crime was reported.

SUMMING IT UP

Librarians offer public computers to their patrons because they know that everyone needs access to information. The Internet has become the most extensive information storehouse in history and, therefore, anyone denied its riches is unable to compete effectively in the modern world. Infrequent users, however, may be entranced by its pleasures and unaware that their mouse clicks and other responses are all being recorded by corporate entities. Since we cannot, in good conscience, provide a service that endangers our patrons, we must become more aware of the kind of personal information they are sharing and the uses to which that information is being put.

REFERENCES

Barbaro, Michael, and Tom Zeller Jr. 2006. A face is exposed for AOL searcher no. 4417749. *New York Times*, August 9. http://select.nytimes.com/search/restricted/article?res=F10612FC345B0C7A8CDDA10894DE404482.

Freedman, David H. 2006. Why privacy won't matter: Google, Yahoo and Microsoft desperately want to know every last thing about what you do, say and buy. *Newsweek*, April 3. http://www.msnbc.msn.com/id/12017579/site/newsweek/.

Linn, A. 2005. Amazon.com knows what you bought—and may know what you'll shop for next. *AP Worldstream*, March 28. http://www.alwayson-network.com/comments.php?id=P9500_0_6_0_C/.

O'Connor, Philip. 2006. Web queries offer clues to personal data. *St. Louis Post-Dispatch*, August 12. http://www.stltoday.com/stltoday/news/stories.nsf/stlouiscitycounty/story/0A3CC7AD1C7A1F21862571C8006B6FC0?OpenDocument/.

Singel, Ryan. 2004. Gmail still sparking debate. *Wired News*, April 24. http://www.wired.com/news/infostructure/0,1377,63204,00.html?tw=wn_tophead_2/.

Singel, Ryan. 2006. Poor privacy grade reflects Google's growing power. *Wired News*, June 12. http://www.wired.com/politics/onlinerights/news/2007/06/googleprivacyreport.

Smith, Blair. 2006. AIG: personal data on 970,000 lost in burglary. *USA Today*, June 18. http://www.usatoday.com/tech/news/computersecurity/infotheft/2006-06-18-aig-theft_x.htm?POE=TECISVA/.

CHAPTER 4
Protecting Children and Teenagers

Since so many books and articles have been devoted to the topic of children on the Internet and the dangers they face, this chapter will focus specifically on protecting their privacy. Of course, pedophiles and other unwanted lurkers invade the privacy of children and teenagers, but the more general topic of children's safety is an issue that cannot be fully addressed here.

THE NEED FOR PRIVACY

It is essential to make a clear distinction between protecting young people's privacy and protecting them from other dangers. This is particularly important because as ardent opponents of censorship, librarians have been at the forefront of the battle against Internet content filters. We may have become so sensitive that our hackles go up automatically when we hear someone talking about protecting the children who use library computers. Privacy, however, is another issue entirely.

Opposition to censorship and support of privacy protection go hand in hand. Children, even more than adults, share personal information about themselves and their families without understanding the implications of their actions. Our role is not to censor but to help them understand the good and bad aspects of the Web. It is entirely possible for children to participate in its pleasures and seek out its information resources while guarding their privacy.

Online Predators are not the Only Danger

Again, when most people think of online dangers threatening children, they immediately picture lurkers waiting to lure children into perilous situations. However, it is not just criminals who are interested in the personal information that children unwittingly provide. Marketing firms have discovered that this age group has enormous spending power, and is the demographic segment most readily influenced by advertising ploys. Young people are voracious consumers of the latest trends in clothing, music, sports equipment, and entertainment, so it is natural that marketers want to know more about them. They find it very useful to collect as much information as possible, storing it in huge databases. To obtain this information, they use strategies that take advantage of young people's natural need to feel important and to be accepted.

Self-Absorption

Both children and teenagers have a profound need to talk about themselves and to connect with peers to whom they can share their hopes and fears. All of us suffered through this period, and we should remember that they were frequently the loneliest years of our lives. We felt that we were not understood by our parents, and we were forever searching for someone who would really understand us. It is, therefore, easy to see why the Internet is so important to this age group. Somewhere out there in cyberspace is someone who will discover your blog, your MySpace Web page, or your web cam and reach out to you. Out there on the web, children and teenagers imagine, is a future friend who will say to himself or herself "this is someone just like me!"

The corporate world knows that young people want to talk about themselves and takes advantage of this golden opportunity by presenting them with a welter of sign up forms, questionnaires, personality tests, and other lures intended to persuade them to share personal information. Marketing surveys are easily disguised; children and teenagers are told by online marketers that their opinions are important while parents and teachers may inadvertently be sending just the opposite message, or at least that's how it may be perceived by the children.

CHILDREN AND TEENS AS LIBRARY COMPUTER USERS

Computers have become the chief point of access to information for most people in industrialized countries in the twenty-first century. As we discussed in the first chapter, most library computer users do not own computers. Some children have computers at home but it is more convenient to use their school or public library computers. Some are not permitted to use their parent's computer or their use is restricted. If school and public libraries did not make computers available on a limited basis, many of our younger users might be totally cut off from the information and social interaction that have become important to the well-being of most Americans.

Children's Online Privacy Protection Act

The Children's Online Privacy Protection Act (COPPA) was designed to protect the privacy of children under the age of thirteen by requiring parental consent for the online collection or use of personal information from children. The Act, which went into effect in April 2000, was passed in reaction to Internet marketing techniques that targeted children. It applies to commercial Web sites and online services directed at children. Web sites aimed at children must provide a detailed privacy policy describing the information they collect. Web sites must obtain verifiable parental consent before collecting personal information from children under thirteen, and must disclose to parents the extent of the information collected. Furthermore, parents can revoke their consent at any time and request that information on their child be deleted.

Pending Legislation

Children and teenagers are citizens entitled to the rights and privileges that status conveys. These rights include the freedom to read and the freedom to obtain the information they need to live successful and rewarding lives. COPPA does not limit children's access to information, but rather limits the information that corporate marketers can gather about children. It is totally unlike the Children's Internet Protection Act (CIPA), which limits children's access to much useful information. CIPA places both libraries and their users at the mercy of the producers of filtering software that censors a variety of religious, political, and lifestyle information.

At this writing, a new threat to the rights of children is looming on the horizon. It appears that the Deleting Online Predators Act (DOPA) will soon be enacted into law. The bill, as it was written when it was passed by the House of Representatives in 2006, requires libraries to remove access to all social networking and e-mail sites from their computers. The language of the law is so vague that it appears that other interactive sites, many of which are educational in nature, could also be banned. Like CIPA, DOPA may force some sexual predators to change their tactics at enormous cost to young people who depend entirely on the library for their Internet access.

It is true that there are sexual predators online just as it is true that there are sexual predators in the stacks of the library and lurking outside the elementary school. Children are, indeed, at risk; but taking away their access to both information and friendship is hardly acting in their best interests. Isn't this an exaggeration, you may ask? Aren't young people safer and better off with such restrictions? It might be helpful to begin by looking over the shoulder of a typical computer user in this age group. In fact, let's imagine an eleven-year-old girl whom we'll call Allison.

INTRODUCING ALLISON

Allison stops by the public library after school whenever she can. Her family does not own a computer and her school's computers are not available for personal use. Allison is experiencing all the angst that most girls of her age do. She wants desperately to be pretty and popular. She wants to have lots of friends and to be accepted by the movers and shakers of her sixth grade class. Large Web portals like Yahoo! offer many resources for children and preteens like Allison. For example, she's grown up with a feature called Yahooligans! It's lots of fun, and even includes educational features like "Ask Earl," an entertaining question and answer column that discusses Antarctica, grammar, "cool" books, mathematicians, and microchips. The site includes plenty of homework resources like encyclopedias, as well as rock, hip hop, and other music popular with Allison's age group.

Allison is making the transition from child to young adult and she frequently turns to the Web for help. She has recently started menstruating and many of her questions concern sex. Although she has a good relationship with her mother, she has many questions she doesn't feel quite comfortable asking her mom. Allison has recently found a site called *Teen Advice Online* that describes itself as "a team of non-professionals, ages 13 and beyond, providing suggestions for your problems." Because young people submit questions and other young people provide answers, sometimes in sexually explicit language, this is probably one of the sites that DOPA would restrict. In fact, many content filters deny access to the site, but fortunately, Allison's public library has not installed filtering software. Typical questions come from teens and preteens who wonder whether they are gay, worry about getting pregnant, or feel conflicted about reporting an abusive parent. Had Allison been unable to access the site, many of her questions would have gone unanswered and her understanding of relationships, sexuality, substance abuse, self-esteem, and depression would consist mainly of playground mythology.

Good Web Sites, Bad Privacy Policies

The Internet offers a vast array of sites that provide help to troubled teenagers. Most of these resources offer sound advice on common teen problems. The anonymity of the Web encourages young people to seek out solutions to their problems instead of letting those problems grow and fester, occasionally leading to clinical depression or even teen suicide. Fortunately, Allison's problems are relatively minor at this point, but much of the information she needs to make the transition to young adulthood is readily available online and she takes full advantage of her opportunities. From a privacy perspective, however, some of these sites are poorly administered. Some Web sites may publish e-mail messages from their readers without stripping off personally identifiable information. Young readers may imagine themselves writing only to the helpful advisor, but in reality, their words may be read by millions of people, some of whom could misuse the personal information included in these heart-felt messages. Adult predators may thus be provided with both a child's e-mail address and enough personal information to initiate a contact leading to sexual abuse and even abduction. However, what is probably more likely is blackmail by other teenagers who threaten to reveal the information to parents or friends unless the victim meets their terms. This is surprisingly common as is the possibility that a mentally unstable teen will inundate the victim with abusive e-mail messages.

E-mail Use

This is Allison's first year at a new school. When her family moved out of state, it was very hard for her to leave her friends. She still feels like an outsider at her new school and depends on e-mail and instant messaging to stay in close contact with her old friends. Allison has several free online accounts, even though most Web mail sites require parental approval for minors. When Allison and her friends sign up for an e-mail account or other service, they simply change their date of birth.

Because no one can see her when she's online, Allison thinks of herself as being anonymous, able to say anything without having to put up a front for parents, teachers, or those movers and shakers. She is not aware that Google scans her e-mail to select appropriate advertisements. Neither does she know that her Web mail remains stored in the computers of e-mail service providers. In the past, Web mail providers forced, or at least encouraged, new users to answer dozens of personal questions about themselves. More recently (as we saw in the last chapter), larger sites like Yahoo!, conscious of privacy implications, have reduced their questions to a more reasonable number. However, to participate fully in these sites (for example, use the Yahoo! Address Book and Briefcase features) users repeatedly encounter more questions.

Protection for Children Under 13

Because Allison is eleven, she is covered by the COPPA. Since the Act was passed, online service providers have generally reduced the amount of personal information they request when computer users sign up for their services. While it was once necessary to answer several Web pages filled with personal questions, service providers like Yahoo! and Hotmail have redesigned their registration forms to be much less invasive. Nevertheless, children continue to encounter offers of free services in exchange for answering "a few brief questions." Remember too that although our young surfer is only eleven, she often adds a few years to her age when she is online. She is not required to provide any proof of age, so there is really no way for Internet service providers and their advertisers to know that she should have parental approval.

Unprotected Teens

Thirteen seems like an oddly arbitrary age to end privacy protection. Considering that younger children frequently misrepresent their age and teenagers are rarely better informed about privacy issues than their younger siblings, COPPA may not go far enough. Privacy experts contend that the law's chief drawback may be its failure to protect older children. Additional protection has been discussed in Congress but nothing has yet come out of the discussions.

One wonders why this piece of legislation, which protects the privacy of children while only minimally intruding on their freedom, fails to cover teenagers, while other proposed legislation like DOPA is so draconian. It is difficult not to jump to the conclusion that COPPA limits the commercial exploitation of young people, thereby interfering with corporate marketing. One wonders if corporate lobbyists would be able to similarly limit the scope of DOPA if it had such market-driven consequences.

Allison's sister Tiffany is fourteen. She spends much of her time in front of a mirror, experimenting with cosmetics and hairstyles. Her school library is open after school. She uses library computers to search for opportunities to get free beauty products and finds many offers. A typical offer promises a coupon for some desirable product if she will just complete a brief marketing survey. Rarely are these surveys brief and some take as long as an hour to complete. Typical questions concern customer preferences and are fairly innocuous. Is Tiffany's skin oily, dry, or a combination of the two? What colors does she like? However, many surveys also ask questions about customers' lives. Tiffany actually enjoys completing surveys because they make her feel grown up and important. She answers every question. When she is asked whether she owns a car, walks to school, or spends time at the mall, the questions can eventually add up to a complete description of Tiffany's activities. None of this would matter if there were no way to connect Tiffany's survey responses with her personal identity. Unfortunately, this cannot be assumed. Even if the survey did not ask for her name, e-mail address or other personally identifiable information, the marketing firm probably deposited a "cookie" on Tiffany's computer. This is a small file designed to retrieve information from her computer and send it back to its originator. If the survey comes from an Internet content provider, it may be possible to connect survey responses to Tiffany's membership information.

SOCIAL NETWORKING SITES

Tiffany has also discovered MySpace, the focus of much DOPA-related debate. This is because MySpace is the largest and perhaps the most popular example of a social networking site for young people. Web sites like MySpace, FaceBook, and Friendster encourage users to create personal networks consisting of their real life and virtual friends. Friends connect to other friends and create an extended group. Users are connected via chains of mutual friends. To get started, they must first create their personal Web pages and personal profiles. They are encouraged to write at length about themselves, including information like their age, geographical location, interests, activities, as well as their feelings about their boyfriends, girlfriends, teachers, and parents. Most services allow users to upload pictures of themselves and their friends. Again, MySpace has an age requirement, but it is widely ignored.

Dangers of Social Networking

There is, indeed, evidence that sexual predators have taken advantage of MySpace to approach young people. Investigations into the murders of two teenage girls suggest a link between their deaths and men they met on MySpace. The FBI has estimated that possibly 20% of child Internet users have been approached sexually, and thousands of sexual predators are online. As an experienced surfer, Tiffany knows something about this threat and has even received occasional instant messages of a dubious nature. When she was even younger than Allison, a man invited her into his car, but she knew she should not talk to or accept rides from strangers. Another peculiar man hung around her playground, but children told their parents about him, and the last they saw of him, he was entering a police car.

No one would dream of closing playgrounds or keeping children or teenagers off the sidewalks because a predator might approach them. The outcry from angry parents and children would be enormous. However, libraries are vulnerable to pressure because their tight budgets make them dependent on E-rate discounts. Library computer users are vulnerable because they lack the resources to own their own computers. They do not have the power or control over their lives enjoyed by older and more affluent members of our society.

Young People are Wary of Outsiders

MySpace is one of Tiffany's most important links with her friends. Like Allison, she feels like an outsider at her new school and depends on MySpace to keep in touch with her old friends. It is also her primary source of information about what is cool, hip, and in with her generation. In such an environment, adults stand out like sore thumbs, no matter how trendy they may try to appear. Tiffany's need to make friends and to be accepted leads her to reach out to strangers, but the language spoken in chat rooms and the topics under discussion are unintelligible to many adults. Even at her young age, Tiffany is wary of outsiders who try to get her into private chat rooms, and she knows how to make herself visible to friends and invisible to strangers. She is part of a community that shares such information, a community that alerts members to suspicious visitors. Laura Barton writes in the *Guardian Unlimited* that "Sites such as these are almost a tribal war drum" (Barton 2006).

The Illusion of Privacy

Social networking sites create an environment in which users vie for attention and that may mean divulging confidential information about themselves and their families, the more shocking and titillating the better. Many users provide colorful misinformation about their drinking, drug, and sexual experience to make themselves look "cool." Perhaps not surprisingly, many employers and scholarship committees have started searching social networking sites to see what their applicants have to say about themselves. Many a job has been lost when the image an applicant presented at the interview was at variance with his or her MySpace, FaceBook, or Friendster image.

Although we may think of Web pages as fleeting, ephemeral things, this is not really true. Many adults have rediscovered bulletin board comments they made ten or more years ago. Most discussion lists are archived and older comments are still accessible. Web pages that were long ago removed by their owners are still available at sites like the Internet Archive. This means that the old-fashioned crime of blackmail is alive and well in cyberspace.

Imagine Tim, a high school student who bragged of daring exploits on an early listserv. There are still lots of these online discussion groups dominated by teen males, where bragging and gross exaggeration are the norm. Drinking, sex, drug use, and brushes with the law are the usual subject matter and an "I can top that" attitude permeates most posts. Tim got carried away one night and described a minor drug-related incident in such dramatic terms that he turned it into what amounted to a felony. He imagined that no one would read his messages except the group of boys who used the site. Years later, after he had graduated from college and was working in a bank, he received an e-mail from an anonymous source. He was directed to a URL he didn't even know existed, an archive of listserv messages. He was told that this account of his criminal activities would be sent to his boss if he did not pay $1,000 immediately. Ten years from now, similarly exaggerated boasts that were once posted on MySpace or Friendster may still be floating around the Web, and other enterprising blackmailers may discover them.

Security Risks of Networking Sites

MySpace has been accused of a variety of questionable advertising practices, including downloading adware and and spyware to members' computers. In July of 2006, an online banner advertisement on MySpace took advantage of a Windows security flaw to infect more than a million users with spyware. When users browsed the site with versions of Windows that had not been updated with the correct security patch, criminals took advantage of the opportunity to download keylogging programs, Trojan horse viruses (called Trojan because they hide in your computer, lying in wait to activate and wreak havoc), and some of the deadliest spyware programs yet devised

It turned out that the ad "Deck Out Your Deck" had been hacked months earlier and for all that time, the malicious software was downloaded each time surfers simply arrived at the page containing the hacked advertisement. There is no way to know how many library computers were infected, but it is a safe guess that some libraries do not regularly install each and every Windows update. If key-logging programs remain undetected, they can continue sending back credit card numbers, bank account usernames and other highly confidential information until their presence is discovered. Considering that a high percentage of library computer users fall into the MySpace age group, one can assume that a number of identity thefts have occurred as a result.

The FaceBook Protest

Another virtual place Tiffany hangs out when she's surfing the Web is FaceBook. FaceBook is a MySpace competitor that has about 9 million members. It was originally established by a Harvard student as a kind of photo guide to help orient incoming Harvard freshmen. Gradually, it expanded to over 2,100 colleges and universities and later high school students became eligible to join. FaceBook was unlike the other major social networking sites in that it required a mobile phone number and proof that applicants met other requirements. FaceBook also divided its users into many small networks based on their location and their academic institution, limiting access to personal profiles to other members of one's own network. Tiffany was able to remain connected with her old school friends; she assumed that they shared a private world of their own. Although it was not difficult for unauthorized people to become members or hack into the service, FaceBook offered a greater measure of privacy than the other services and was very popular for this reason.

In September 2006, FaceBook shocked members who clicked on "The Wall," the news page where members post messages that can be read by everyone in their school network. The Wall is perhaps the most popular public gathering place on FaceBook, and functions like a message board where members can post news and connect with friends. On this fateful day, however, members discovered the comments and photos they had posted on their own personal Web pages displayed for all to see. The information that Jack had broken up with Jill or that Tim had gotten stoned at a frat party had suddenly become headline news. FaceBook's search engine was deliberately scanning members' pages looking for recent updates and posting some of those updates as news. Thus the information was available to the entire school network. The outcry was immediate; members protested that FaceBook was invading their privacy.

Assessing Privacy Risks

Actually, member privacy had always been at risk though not to the same extent as other social networking sites. On MySpace, it was always possible for anyone to enter a name in the search engine, find that member's profile, and go on to their Web page. If you were looking for particular individuals, you would probably find them. Even MySpace members usually assumed that no one but their friends would be looking for them, an assumption that was clearly untrue.

FaceBook responded by making it possible for members to opt out of the news feed but continued to make photos public, as well as the events members were attending. Eventually, FaceBook backed down entirely, but the service also dropped its membership requirements. Anyone can now become a member without providing any proof of age or identity.

Some teachers and counselors think that the FaceBook protest was a very good experience for its members. Since the teen years are a period of intense self-absorption, teachers say that their students screen out everything but their friends and their own personal world as they type their FaceBook or MySpace entries. Seeing personal information highlighted on public pages came as a shock, they say, but a much needed shock. FaceBook teens are now more likely to realize that there isn't really such a big difference between sharing their private lives on the news page and displaying it on their own Web page. In the MySpace world, anyone who knows their name can keep track of them. In the only slightly more private FaceBook world, anyone who is part of their network can also intrude on their private lives. Commented one high school teacher: "When they really stop to think about it, they realize that this group includes bosses, teachers, would-be suitors, jealous rivals, and pedophiles. Kids aren't stupid." A counselor confirms that "they do care about privacy and they respond when something like this happens. It forces them to look around and grow up."

MUSIC DOWNLOADING

But we've strayed a long way from eleven-year-old Allison and her online interests. Allison loves popular music and is very interested in downloading music files. Since she is too young for a credit card, she is usually unable to download music from commercial sites like iTunes. Most of us are familiar with Napster, the pioneering music download program that has been the object of so much litigation. The basic idea is simple: young people copy sound files from one another's computers. Napster and other file share services keep track of their millions of members and the sound files each has to offer. Napster has now been forced to charge a fee for their services that goes to recording companies, but there are plenty of music download services that still operate under the radar.

Because they are so popular, file share software programs have become targets for hackers and identity thieves. The Kazaa Media Desktop is an example of a service that has become infamous for downloading unwanted and sometimes malicious programs. Although libraries can prevent downloads and keep most of this invasive software from taking root in their computers, it is not so easy to prevent young people from sharing personal information about themselves and their families on such sites. Enticing free memberships require that users complete long questionnaires, packed with questions that Web sites do not need to ask.

Digital Rights Management

Allison is typical of the children and teenagers who are avid users of music file-swapping software like Napster and Kazaa. The owners and distributors of the music that is so freely exchanged naturally seek ways to restrict illegal downloads of their copyrighted material. Their efforts to restrict illegal sharing, however, have led at least some of them to violate the privacy of many young people. Digital rights management (DRM) systems have been developed to monitor music fans who download copyrighted files. They collect personal information intended to prevent piracy and ensure that copyright holders are paid. Systems administrators then fill huge databases with the information collected. To identify illegal activity, they create profiles of typical miscreants and match the profiles against the individuals in the database. Profiling is far from an exact science and tends to falsely identify many innocent people. In the next chapter we will devote more attention to this subject.

DRM systems have the potential to store personal information about children indefinitely, even violating the under 13 rule. They can add information that identifies some of them as criminally inclined, and they can share this information with other businesses including truly vast data-mining operations like ChoicePoint.

Librarians believe that the First Amendment gives citizens the right to explore ideas anonymously, whether those ideas are found in books, music, or movies. Although we fully understand that intellectual property rights must be protected, we object to forcing young people to divulge personal information just to listen to a song that's available online.

RFID TECHNOLOGY AND PRIVACY

Many of the offenses perpetrated against children are intended to keep them safe and allow parents and teachers to keep track of them more easily. For example, children at Brittan Elementary School in Sutter, California were made to wear badges into which radio frequency identification (RFID) chips were embedded. The school introduced the system as a way to simplify attendance-taking, reduce vandalism, and improve student safety. It plans to extend the program to pay for cafeteria meals and check out library books. RFID readers currently can read tags within a range of about 3 feet. Readers currently in development will be effective within a much larger range, so soon they will be able to be installed anywhere in the school.

As we consider the idea of young children wearing RFID badges we might first imagine a kindergartener or first grader. That doesn't sound like such a bad idea. Young children are always getting lost or forgetting their lunch money. When the children forget to wear their badges, we might further think it's okay to prevent their removal, perhaps with wrist bands. Some parents like the idea of embedding chips under the skin of young children. It would most likely help the police find children more easily if they were lost or abducted.

RFID Badges

Initially, these decisions sound quite reasonable, but are they? To answer this question, we'll need to return to the school badges. The school requires that all elementary students wear them, even seventh and eighth graders. Nearing adulthood, they lead lives apart from their parents and teachers. Does anyone really have the right to "tag" them, to deprive them of their separate world and their privacy? Imagine yourself at this age. Imagine how you would have felt knowing that you were under constant scrutiny and that you couldn't even go to the restroom without the precise location and length of time being recorded on an administrative computer.

If school authorities decide the system works well with elementary school students, they may extend its use to high school students. Essentially, high school students are adults. In more traditional societies, fifteen-year-olds marry and enter military service. By the time you enter high school, you have a life of your own. You have opinions not shared by your parents or teachers; you choose friends and make decisions that they may not approve of, just as you will in the years to come.

Expanding the System

Is there any real reason why, if we can justify such a system in schools, it can't be extended to the adult population? Suppose your employer were to require you to wear a wrist band that you could not remove. Actually, it might be very convenient. The RFID tag could open locked doors, even when you forget your key. It could keep unauthorized people from entering your workplace and possibly endangering your safety. It could also, however, establish the exact moment when you arrived for work, entered the restroom, left the staff lounge, and visited other parts of the building. That means it could potentially allow a jealous suitor, sexual predator, or voyeur boss to stalk you without ever leaving his or her computer. At this point, I think that most of us would say "Absolutely not!"

If there really were such a progression from tagging kindergarten children to monitoring the every move of adults in the work place, there would be dozens of intermediary steps. As each next step was considered, some people might insist that it was no big deal. The small step being contemplated would not really change very much and it would be so much more efficient. This has generally been the way that privacy rights have been abused. Everyone must sacrifice some of his or her privacy to be part of a society so no one has an absolute right to privacy. The problem we face is exactly where to draw the line.

RFIDs in Library Materials

In Chapter 6, we investigate the subject of radio frequency tags in much greater detail. A number of libraries have begun inserting tags into books and other library materials in place of barcodes. Heated battles are taking place around the country and some are chronicled here. Essentially, the argument made by RFID supporters is that the tags do not represent an invasion of anyone's privacy. They are not attached to one's person and the tags can only be read by large pieces of equipment that are readily visible and unique to libraries.

When one looks deeper, however, it often turns out that the tags in use in libraries are those designed to be affixed to containers in the shipping industry. Such tags can be read by a variety of readers and were designed with no thought to privacy considerations. Although some types of tags are better than others, there is as yet no universally-accepted industry standard that would prevent nosy individuals or law enforcement agencies from learning what books are being checked out or tracking the library patrons carrying the items. Considering the widespread belief in the law enforcement community that reading habits reveal criminal tendencies, libraries could expect greatly increased attention from the FBI and other police agencies as the technology matures.

FINGERPRINT IDENTIFICATION AND PRIVACY

The tendency of children to be forgetful and occasionally irresponsible has been frequently cited as a reason to violate their privacy. Public schools on both sides of the Atlantic are finding it convenient to scan children's fingerprints, allowing positive identification for a variety of school functions including library use. For example, the town of Taunton, Massachusetts has installed fingerprint technology in six of its schools: the Edmund Hatch Bennett, Elizabeth Pole, Joseph C. Chamberlain and East Taunton elementary schools, and James L. Mulcahey and Joseph H. Martin middle schools (Schuler 2007).

To better understand the ways in which children are at risk, however, let's turn our attention to the other side of the pond, where school libraries are the focus of a major battle on the privacy front. Micro Librarian Systems is a company that has installed library automation systems in a large number of school libraries in Great Britain. Their product, called Junior Librarian, has been marketed in the U.K. since 2002, matches children's fingerprints against prints stored in a database (Roberts 2006). Children check out books and other materials by pressing their fingers on a glass plate. Like the RFID tags described earlier, there is talk of extending fingerprint identification to other school functions such as paying for meals in the cafeteria.

It is estimated that Micro Librarian Systems has fingerprinted hundreds of thousands of British children (Roberts 2006). In most cases, the prints have been obtained without permission from the children's parents. In fact, most of the schools involved failed even to notify parents of the existence of the new system. Privacy groups throughout Britain have expressed shock and outrage. Phil Booth, speaking for the group No2ID expressed the view of many parents: "Are we sending our kids to school or to prison? We wouldn't accept fingerprinting for adults without informed consent, so it is utterly outrageous that children as young as five are being targeted" (Roberts 2006). Reportedly those 3,500 Micro Librarian libraries described translate to approximately 700,000 children.

What seems to shock privacy advocates most is that librarians and school authorities accepted the new technology with so little consideration of the issues involved. The governor of a school considering installing the same system responded: "It's all internal so I can't see it's really any different from passwords giving computer access" (Roberts 2006)

Vulnerability to Misuse

Is it really just an internal method for keeping library records? Think for a moment about the many databases in which these fingerprints are stored. The Identikit module collects fingerprints from children and stores them in the form of a standardized numeric equivalent for each fingerprint. Most are probably stored in not very secure computer servers in individual school libraries or school administrative offices; some are probably stored in consortia computers as well. The vendor Micro Librarian Systems has access to all of these databases for maintenance purposes. It is known from past experience that vendors sometimes copy their customers' databases for indexing and other purposes. This means that quite a large group of people might be able to reproduce the fingerprints. Of course most of them would have no reason to do so, but fingerprints left at a crime scene could effectively misdirect police. They could also inflict endless misery on their owner. As fingerprinting becomes a more common means of identification, such a database could become a treasure trove for an identity thief.

Fingerprints are Forever

Fingerprinting children is not just a simple, practical procedure. Your fingerprints are what you are; you carry them throughout your life. Your passwords are temporary, issued for particular purposes, changed as needed, and deleted when you no longer have any use for them. When the privacy represented by your fingerprints is compromised, it's not a temporary problem. You can't simply change your password, close an account, or cancel a credit card. You are vulnerable to identity theft for as long as the fingerprints or their computer code equivalents are out of your control.

Terri Dowty, Director of Action for the Rights of Children, warns that "One of the worries we have is the rather casual use of biometric data. If children get used to thinking biometric data can be used for trivial purposes—and a school library is a rather trivial purpose—how do they learn to be careful where they put their fingerprints and iris scans? The more you use biometric data and the more casually you use it, the more scope there is to exploit it" (Grossman 2006).

In the United States, the Ultra Scan Corporation introduced the Touch and Go system in the Buffalo and Erie County Public Library. Other library automation vendors are interested in this new and possibly lucrative fingerprint market. To quote the Buffalo and Erie County Public Library Web site, Touch and Go works by "imaging a finger and looking at its unique characteristics, thereby eliminating the need for library cards or other ID" (Buffalo and Erie County Public Library). However, there is no indication that large numbers of American libraries have followed suit. If such a system became popular in the United States it would mean that the fingerprints of thousands or possibly millions of children would be available to law enforcement agencies under the Patriot Act. Those prints could remain indefinitely as part of the children's records, and even at some future date linked to DNA and other personal information. If one considers the number of recent database thefts, it is almost inevitable that some of these records will fall into the hands of criminals. Since it is anticipated that biometric information for identification purposes will become widespread, the prints will be available for all manner of illicit activities.

SUMMING IT UP

"I think many parents will be deeply shocked to learn that their children are being fingerprinted," says Scotland's First Minister Jack McConnell in response to the Micro Systems Librarian situation. "I cannot imagine any justification for such intrusive use of technology in schools—how many books would a library need to lose each year to even make this system save money? We should be encouraging children to value their civil liberties, but instead there is a danger we will be teaching the next generation to surrender them without question" (McLaughlin 2006).

Librarians have embraced computer automation because it allows us to provide many more services and frees staff from many routine tasks. We have come to see computers as the answer to many of our practical problems, but our patrons must come first. Some new technologies will undoubtedly be adopted by libraries which will make them both more efficient and more productive. However, the privacy implications of each new technical development must be carefully investigated before endangering the well-being of the very people we serve.

REFERENCES

Barton, Laura. 2006. Whose space? *Guardian Unlimited*, August 2. http://www.guardian.co.uk.

Buffalo and Erie County Public Library. Web site. http://www.buffalolib.org/events/touchngo.asp.

Grossman, Wendy M. 2006. Is school fingerprinting out of bounds? *Guardian Unlimited*, March 30. http://technology.guardian.co.uk/weekly/story/0,,1742091,00.html.

McLaughlin, Martyn. 2006. Civil rights row over school fingerprints. *The Herald*, September 12. http://www.theherald.co.uk/.

Roberts, Bob. 2006. Exclusive: fingerprint scandal of 700,000 kids. *Daily Mirror*, July 3. http://www.mirror.co.uk/news/tm_objectid=17324161&method=full&siteid=94762&headline=fingerprint-scandal-of-700-000-kids–name_page.html.

Schuler, Rory. 2007. Schools' high-tech future starts in lunch line. *Taunton Gazette*, February 8. http://www.tauntongazette.com.

CHAPTER 5

Government Surveillance, Data Mining, and Just Plain Carelessness

Why should librarians be concerned about the federal government endangering their patrons? After all, the government wants to protect us all from terrorists and other criminals who threaten our safety. Unlike marketing firms and cyber-criminals, whose motive is personal gain, the U.S. government has an important job to do, and as citizens, we have an obligation to help the government achieve its goals.

COMBATING TERRORISTS AND OTHER CRIMINALS

Largely in response to the fear that resulted from 9/11, we are experiencing a period when government leaders are willing to consider almost any strategy to fight terrorists. This is happening at a time when privacy law has not been substantially altered to deal with recent computer developments. Existing legislation reflects a world in which there were no databases containing billions of records, no Google, and no computer-enabled identity theft. In time, privacy law will probably catch up with technology, and technology itself will mature. But what's happening to our right to privacy right now?

There has long been a belief in government agencies like the FBI that learning what books people read can help to reveal subversive tendencies. For example, in the 1950s, New York police were trying to find a criminal they had dubbed The Mad Bomber. Much of their time was spent going through New York Public Library records, listing the names of all the people who had checked out books on explosives and demolition, and interrogating a number of them. No one so identified turned out to be the Bomber, but librarians around the country came to realize that throwing open their records to law enforcement agencies can do irreparable harm to their patrons.

When Reading Habits are a Matter of Record

Years later, John Hinckley attempted to assassinate President Ronald Reagan. When he was arrested, he was carrying a Jefferson County, Colorado Public Library card. Journalists leapt to the conclusion that there was a good story in Hinkley's reading habits and besieged the Jefferson County librarian for information about the books Hinkley had checked out. When the librarian refused these requests, the county attorney held that circulation records were public and could be viewed by anyone who wanted to see them. This decision was overturned, however, and library records remained private. It was a close call, and the incident further heightened privacy concerns of the library community, as well as the community at large.

At the center of a somewhat similar case was Library Director Janis M. Lee of the Swarthmore Public Library in Delaware County, Pennsylvania. She was forced to endure virulent personal attacks because she would not divulge the reading habits of a deranged murderer until she received a court order. As she described her ordeal with the local police, "they tried to get me to say things I didn't want to say. They asked me questions rapidly, one after another, hoping I wouldn't have time to think and would blurt out what they wanted to hear. At times I was treated with disdain and even animosity. They made me feel as if I was the one in the wrong. I was an obstacle" (Lee 1998). Fortunately, Hill had the support of her library board and a strongly worded state law protecting the privacy of library records. Other librarians in similar situations have not been so fortunate.

The Library Awareness Program

During the Cold War, library users who read a lot of books on international topics, especially Communism, became the focus of official attention. In the 1980s, this interest in the reading habits of library patrons gained official standing. The FBI established a program called The Library Awareness Program, the aim of which was to enlist librarians and other citizens in an effort to keep tabs on individuals thought to be reading subversive materials. The FBI assumed that librarians would complacently turn over their records; they did not anticipate the angry outcry of the library community. "The FBI's asking us to become vigilantes ... promoting an atmosphere of suspicion among co-workers" (Anderson 1989). Eventually the program fizzled out, largely because FBI agents usually did not have enough evidence to obtain the court orders librarians demanded.

This brings us to our present post-9/11 era. In the wake of the hasty legislation that followed the tragedy, there are few limits on the amount of personal data that can be collected by government agencies. As a result of the Patriot Act, the traditional or Constitutional standard for obtaining personal information, probable cause, need not be demonstrated. The basic principle of judicial oversight has been called into question. Lawsuits alleging that the government has violated numerous laws including the Foreign Intelligence Surveillance Act of 1978 (FISA) are being met with demands for dismissal on the grounds that state secrets would be divulged.

THE LIBRARY'S RESPONSIBILITY TO PROTECT ITS USERS

Over time, it will probably be understood that projects like the NSA's astounding failures, the Terrorist Futures Market and the Total Information Awareness Program, as well as more recent data mining projects, do not meet the standard imposed by the Fourth Amendment to the Constitution. Unless there are substantial improvements in the technology, we will learn that these programs are not very effective law enforcement tools. As has happened so many times in the past, hot heads will cool, and remember that judicial oversight is essential to a democratic government. Ultimately, we hope, it will be realized that there are more effective ways of finding terrorists and other evildoers than collecting personal information on millions of innocent people.

Careless Misuse of Personal Information

While the library community waits for the calm that we hope will follow the storm, we need to consider what is happening to all this data that the government is collecting. Take for example, the theft on May 22, 2006, of a laptop computer and external hard drive containing the Social Security numbers, birth dates, and addresses of 26.5 million veterans. It was stolen from the home of a career data analyst in the Veteran's Administration. As more information became available, it became clear that the data also included similar information about most military personnel currently in the reserves and on active duty. Because the files had been copied from a secure government computer to an insecure laptop for the convenience of the analyst, none of the information was encrypted or otherwise protected from misuse.

Internal investigation revealed that taking such information home was a common practice in the Veteran's Administration, and there is further evidence that similar practices are not uncommon in other federal agencies. The data analyst had apparently been taking home sensitive data for at least three years preceding the theft and the Veteran's Administration had been repeatedly cited for poor security practices. Senator Susan Collins (R-ME), chair of the Homeland Security and Governmental Affairs Committee, chastised Veterans Administration Secretary Jim Nicholson during testimony before her committee saying, "You seem to be saying it was just one employee. But it's not just one employee. You have a high-risk, vulnerable system that has been identified time and again as vulnerable" (Bazar 2006).

What makes the situation even more disturbing, though, is that the theft was not reported immediately. It is human nature to try to cover one's mistakes. In any workplace, employees are both hoping for advancement and fearful of losing their jobs. The average staff member may be essentially honest and upright, but may go the extra mile to cover up a mistake. In this case, it was thirteen days before the crime was reported to VA Secretary Jim Nicholson.

The Federal Government's Track Record

Unfortunately, the veterans' data incident is just one of many that have plagued the executive branch of the federal government. Here are just a few others:

- A hacker broke into the Agriculture Department computer system and obtained names, Social Security numbers and photos of 26,000 employees and contractors. (Bazar 2006)
- An insurance company employee loaded Department of Health and Human Services (DHHS) personal information for nearly 17,000 Medicare beneficiaries on a publicly accessible hotel computer and forgot to delete the file. (Bazar 2006)

- Another hacker gained entry to the Department of Energy (DOE) computer system and accessed the Social Security numbers and other data of nearly 1,500 National Nuclear Security Administration (NNSA) employees. This incident was not reported for almost a year after it occurred, providing more than enough time for the information to be circulated around the Internet. (Bazar 2006)
- An especially bizarre incident occurred when two Federal Trade Commission (FTC) laptops were stolen from the car belonging to an employee of the federal agency responsible for fighting identity theft, the FTC's Division of Privacy and Identity Theft Protection. Apparently the data, including Social Security numbers, bank account numbers, and other financial records belonged to individuals who were being investigated for identity theft. (Bazar 2006)

One would think that once a government agency is thrust into the spotlight and its careless procedures are exposed, it would be more careful of its data. After all, no political appointee actually courts bad publicity. That doesn't, however, appear to be true for the Department of Agriculture. The loss of the 26,000 Social Security numbers in 2006 described above was just the beginning. In April 2007, the Social Security numbers of approximately 63,000 people who received Agriculture Department grants were discovered to be posted on a government Web site. In fact, it turned out that they had been there since 1996 (Federal 2007). Have other government agencies slept through their wake-up calls as well? It certainly seems so based on the steady stream of newspaper articles about data breaches that continues without pause.

Do They Really Need So Much Data?

If you examined these incidents more closely and the work environment that made them possible, you could identify possibly a hundred or more careless practices and flawed assumptions. Although the names of the careless employees, like the data analyst in the veterans' incident, are not usually released, and we do not know the duties involved in their positions, it is probable that the data needed to do their jobs were actually a small subset of the data available in agency databases.

There is probably no one who needs access to all the veterans, all the reservists and active military, all the Social Security numbers and addresses at one time and in one place. Rather, it is the recent explosion of hard disk storage space and corresponding software improvements that have made it possible to create these vast collections of data. Bureaucrats have responded in precisely the same way as the corporate marketers we met in an earlier chapter. In other words, "if we *can* do it, let's do it!" They assume that the more information they have, the better. This mindset appears to be contagious and has spread throughout federal, state, and local government agencies.

Who Has Access to Personal Information?

When we speak of government, we rarely think of the individuals who carry out the millions of large and small duties that the huge federal bureaucracy requires. Rarely do we think of the many civil servants and young political appointees who make most of the daily decisions that ultimately impact our lives. Although there are many experienced career civil servants in Washington, there is also a plethora of young men and women at the beginning of their careers. Young lawyers vie for Congressional staff positions or spend a few years with the Justice Department before going into private practice. Enthusiastic, young political supporters accompany their candidate to the halls of power. Although their government salaries are meager compared to the sums they might earn in private industry, they are attracted by the power and excitement of the Washington scene.

Whether career civil servants or short-timers, both groups are composed of normal, and often fallible human beings. They have their successes but also their failures, and on a bad day they may make some very stupid and dangerous mistakes, such as the ones described.

Data from Library Users

Librarians, of course, had nothing to do with the privacy disasters previously described but they can learn a lot from the investigations that followed them. Library directors are experienced supervisors, and they have uncovered many small subterfuges among the library staff. We can assume that precisely these same instincts are at work among government bureaucracies. None of the data contained in the Veterans Administration database was amassed from public computers in libraries. However, we know for certain that much of the information contained in commercial databases like ChoicePoint was purchased from Web sites. We also know that the federal government purchases millions of dollars worth of data from ChoicePoint and other commercial brokers to support its data mining projects.

Librarians are citizens who support their government; but they are becoming increasingly aware that their patrons are, in a sense, guinea pigs who are less likely than other users to protect their own privacy. When a screen prompts them to type their names, addresses, occupations, consumer preferences, religion, and income, or possibly their views on abortion, gay marriage, and race relations, they do so without imagining that this information will ultimately be available to government agencies. If asked, they might wonder why government agencies would be interested in the minutiae of their lives.

Demands from Law Enforcement Agencies

Increasingly, when the FBI or other law enforcement agency wants information, their visit to the library results in the surrender of one or more library hard disk. Since hard disk capacity has increased rapidly in recent years, a single disk can store many gigabytes of information, most of which has absolutely nothing to do with an investigation. However, libraries have nevertheless been forced turn over information about hundreds or even thousands of library users. Much of the information stored on hard disks can be reclaimed, even when it's been erased, and that data can in turn be fed into the voracious government data mining projects.

Government Agencies Focus on Social Networking Sites

If you were to look over the shoulder of your younger users, you might discover that they are busily fine-tuning their MySpace pages. They can be found adding new friends, since listing a huge number of friends on MySpace, Friendster, and other social networking sites has become the ultimate status symbol. It turns out that the government is very interested in this information. New Scientist magazine reported on June 9, 2006 that the NSA is funding "semantic Web" research to combine data from social networking sites like MySpace with billions of gigabytes of personal information from airline, highway tollbooth, credit card, banking, retail, and property records.

In other words, each member of a social networking site may list twenty-five, fifty, or more of their dearest friends, together with extensive personal information about each one. At least some of those friends will have their own pages on the Web site and will in turn list their fifty best friends. Thus a vast and intricate network is created, often including highly personal information. The NSA plans to build up comprehensive personal profiles of individuals from all this data. In addition, the agency will be able to take the information gleaned from the millions of phone calls it logs and combine it with the acquaintance webs found at the social networking sites.

As Jon Callas of PGP Corporation, a producer of encryption software, writes "I am continually shocked and appalled at the details people voluntarily post online about themselves" (Marks 2006). Not only do the members of MySpace and Friendster freely share details about themselves, their parents, and their love life, but they provide similar information about their friends. Young people have a deep-seated need for attention. They anxiously check the Web site to learn how many people have visited their site and seek to attract more viewers by enticing them with almost any sensational piece of information they can think of. This is the kind of information that the NSA plans to mine and it is the very people who line up to use our computers who are at risk.

GOVERNMENT DATA MINING PROJECTS

What does your library have to offer intelligence agencies that they can't get from merely downloading Web pages? Your library card numbers and other patron data do an excellent job of linking MySpace or other social networking information to specific individuals, something that can be difficult when one of the thousands of Jennie Millers lists Joe Terrorist as her very dearest friend. Of course, if one could track down Joe Terrorist this easily, there might be a good reason to part with this information. What is becoming increasingly clear, however, is that such faith in data mining and other types of broad brush technology-driven intelligence is, at least at this point in time, largely unjustified.

Data mining was first developed for marketing applications and has been remarkably successful. As we discussed earlier, consumer profiles are relatively simple to create. For example, if a customer purchases certain products and the record of those purchases is linked with personally identifiable information (like the supermarket discount card that yesterday deducted $3.24 from your bill), that same customer will be more likely to respond to special offers for related merchandise.

History of Government Data Mining

The NSA has for some time included large numbers of mathematicians and computer experts on its payroll. Because data mining was on of the hottest new technologies, it found its way to the NSA in the late 1990s. One of the first projects was ThinThread, which sought to analyze large quantities of wiretap data for useful intelligence. Privacy protection was actually part of the design of ThinThread, but as fears escalated following 9/11, privacy concerns became much less important.

The Total Information Awareness (TIA) was one outcome of NSA's interest in data mining that initially received generous funding. This was a vast database that could follow American citizens in real time as they made credit-card purchases, initiated bank transactions, paid medical bills, and in other ways carried out the business of their daily lives. In 2003, Congress essentially broke up the program because of concerns over privacy and civil liberties. However, data mining research continued at NSA and the fruits of that research, complete with its privacy implications, have been absorbed into many newer but still closely-related projects. In other words, when NSA was told that it could not create one total or comprehensive system, it simply broke up the program into smaller ones with smaller databases that could be chained together (Turley 1996). An August 2006 report by the U.S. Inspector General indicated that the Department of Homeland Security (DHS) alone has twelve data-mining projects in development (Strohm 2006). Lee Tien, a staff attorney with the Electronic Frontier Foundation, described the situation: "We don't realize that as we live our lives and make little choices like buying groceries, buying on Amazon, Googling, we're leaving traces everywhere...We have an attitude that no one will connect all those dots. But these programs are about connecting those dots—analyzing and aggregating them—in a way that we haven't thought about. It's one of the underlying fundamental issues we have yet to come to grips with" (Clayton 2006).

The New "Big Brother"

The attention of the government data mining community is currently focused on a vast project called ADVISE (Analysis, Dissemination,

Visualization, Insight, and Semantic Enhancement), a venture of DHS. Its storage requirement (one quadrillion entities) boggles the imagination. The project uses mathematical algorithms to uncover hidden relationships in a vast sea of data. The idea is to troll this extraordinary mine of information, including business records, hotel and flight reservations, telephone calls and e-mail, as well as government and sometimes library records, to discover people, places, and other suspicious bits of information.

At this writing, ADVISE is being tested in several pilot programs, including one at the Office of Intelligence and Analysis. Many wonder if ADVISE is just a bigger, better TIA program. Although the project's budget is very large, the requests for proposals that appear to support the project include no mention of privacy technology (Clayton 2006). It was this resemblance to TIA that led Congress, in its 2007 Homeland Security spending bill, to require a Government Accountability Office (GAO) review of the program. GAO reported that while the system was being tested, numerous privacy violations occurred and some aspects of the testing appear to be illegal (Nakashima 2007). The testing should have been conducted with fake data; but real data, in other words citizens' private information, was used by ADVISE without proper notification to the public. Even though only preliminary findings are available, it appears that privacy breaches are numerous. "Undoubtedly, there are likely to be more," said GAO Comptroller David Walker testifying at a Congressional hearing (Nakashima 2007). It is clear that data is being used for a purpose that is very different from what was originally envisioned.

Anita Ramasastry, Associate Professor of Law at the University of Washington School of Law in Seattle, Washington and a Director of the Shidler Center for Law, Commerce & Technology, writes that privacy issues appear to have been largely ignored. "How much data about people would be compiled and from where? For how long will this data be stored? What happens if someone is flagged as potentially suspicious? Will he or she be flagged indefinitely? What if someone is flagged in error? Can that error be corrected?" (Ramasastry 2007). Most importantly, she wants to know what policies and procedures are in place to protect innocent people. "When programs are based on patterning, innocent people can easily be wrongly accused. A terrorist may use cash to buy a one-way plane ticket, but so may a broke college student who has just enough money in his account for an impulse trip to visit his girlfriend on the opposite coast. A terrorist may buy large amounts of fertilizer for a bomb; someone else may do so simply because she's bought additional farmland" (Ramasastry 2007).

Despite considerable pressure from Congress and negative publicity concerning ADVISE, it appears that other government agencies are still initiating their own data-mining projects. In July 2007, the Justice Department reported that The Federal Bureau of Investigations was developing a profiling system called "System to Assess Risk" (STAR) that assigns terrorist risk scores in the same way a credit bureau assigns their ratings based on consumer behavior. Senator Patrick J Leahy (D-VT), chair of the Senate Judiciary Committee, voiced the concern of many of his fellow legislators. "The Bush administration has expanded the use of this technology, often in secret, to collect and sift through Americans' most sensitive personal information" (Nakashima 2007). The STAR data mine, like the one at the core of ADVISE, consists of hundreds of thousands of names collected from the government, airlines, and commercial data brokers such as ChoicePoint. The information collected can then be run through the database of Accurint, yet another data broker that tracks addresses, phone numbers, and driver's licenses. David Sobel, senior counsel for the nonprofit advocacy group Electronic Frontier Foundation believes the system depends on potentially unreliable data. "If we can't assess the accuracy of the information being fed into the system, it's very hard to assess the effectiveness of the system" (Nakashima 2007).

Data Mining and Library Computer Users

As mentioned earlier, Attorney General Alberto Gonzales has requested a law to force Internet service providers (ISPs) to store customer information for one to two years. Representative Dianne DeGette (D-CO) has promised to introduce such a "data retention" bill in spring 2007. In discussing her intentions, DeGette has suggested making this information available not only to government agencies but also to civil litigants (Schmillen 2007). If actually collected by government agencies, it would be natural to add all this data to ADVISE and other data-mining projects. Such data could include all e-mail messages, instant messages, and histories of all sites visited by all Internet users. A substantial amount of this information would, of course be provided by library computer users. Remember the descriptions of typical library computer users in Chapter 1? Because they are less knowledgeable about computers in general and the Internet in particular, they would probably be less circumspect in their communications. Since they cannot store their e-mail messages on their own computers and must depend on Web mail, their words would actually be somewhat more likely to find their way into a database than those of computer owners.

The Poor Track Record of Computer Data Analysis

On February 5, 2006, the *Washington Post* reported on the warrant-less eavesdropping on thousands of Americans making or receiving overseas calls (Gugliotta 2006). You may recall that President Bush defended the practice by declaring "if you're talking to a member of al Qaeda, we want to know why," but apparently the program revealed few, if any, such conversations. The article reports that less than ten U.S. residents or citizens each year aroused enough interest for the intelligence community to obtain a warrant for domestic wiretapping. The NSA has also collected the records of millions or perhaps billions of telephone calls between American citizens within the United States. The justification for this program, like the international wiretaps, has been the hope of discovering social networks like those described. Again, the President purportedly wants to know who is calling al Qaeda, but the program is equally unlikely to produce useful information.

However, telephone and e-mail data (including library patrons' Web mail) can also be added to the mulligan stew of information already available in government databanks. Such treasure troves now include data from the Social Security Administration and other government agencies, bank records, credit card information, and airline flights. Armed with such a wealth of information, sifted and filtered by highly sophisticated software programs, government officials hope to obtain knowledge that will help the U.S. gain power over its enemies. It turns out, however, that there is one big glitch in this scenario. Whether they are working with telephone and e-mail records obtained from service providers like AT&T, flight itineraries from the airlines, or social networking webs downloaded from MySpace, programmers must first tell computers what to look for.

What Do Terrorists Eat for Breakfast?

Actually, there is little to distinguish the personal habits of a terrorist from those of millions of Arab-Americans or for that matter, from most other Americans. The results of electronic surveillance and data mining activities are, of course, secret, but the information that is gradually being amassed by newsgathering sources indicates that these techniques do not work as well as traditional law enforcement. Frequently called pattern analysis research, data mining studies are still highly theoretical. There appears to be no solid evidence that it can identify terrorists. However, government officials sometimes cite anecdotal evidence. For example, they assert that in 2003, data mining helped interrogators at the U.S. prison at Guantanamo Bay, Cuba, determine which detainees posed the biggest threats.

Here is the basic problem: when intelligence agencies begin with individuals, they can move outward, tracking their activities, tapping their telephones, and generally ensnaring the people and organizations that are part of a web surrounding the targeted individual. This is called link analysis and, when performed with more conventional law enforcement techniques, it has been very successful. Jeff Jonas is the Founder and chief scientist at Systems, Research and Development, a company that uses computers to expose casino fraud. He describes this approach clearly: "You start with a few bad guys, and you have to know where to look," he explains. "Phone records can give you that" (Gugliotta 2006). However, he goes on to explain that this is a task for good law enforcement officers. High tech solutions are not as effective. He advocates a deductive approach, going from the particular to the general—the opposite of data mining.

Data mining begins not with the one but with the many, in other words with a huge mass of unrelated data. It begins by identifying not individuals but patterns. If terrorists exhibit patterns that are different from other people, if they make telephone calls to different places, purchase different consumer goods, initiate different types of bank transactions, and/or check out different books from the library, then one might be able to construct a terrorist profile and mine or search a database for individuals who resemble the profile. At this point, however, there are few indications that this is possible.

One of the main reasons why NSA is interested in adding vast amounts of e-mail and telephone data to its databases is to identify social networking patterns. Valdis Krebs, a consultant for some of the largest technology firms in the world, is also one of the well-known experts on deriving social networks through data mining. He is not convinced that the government is on the right track: "It might not be a bad person you find; it may be that the soccer team and the softball team are calling the same pizza parlor ... I'm sure the NSA is excellent at finding patterns and motifs in the data, but what do they mean? Unless you start getting more information on the patterns, you're not going to be able to interpret them at all. Patterns alone won't tell you whether someone's good or evil" (Gugliotta 2006). Jim Harper, Director of Information Policy Studies at the Cato Institute agrees. "They will turn up hundreds of soccer teams, family reunions, and civil war re-enactors whose patterns of behavior happen to be the same as the terrorist network" (Nakashima 2007).

Data Mining and the Constitution

Just what happens when vast databases are mined? First a filter screens for specific pieces of information, eliminating from consideration the data that passes through the filter. Next the data is fed through a second filter and a third. At each stage, potentially interesting information is separated from the rest and an artificial intelligence system ranks the data in order of its interest to human analysts. Filters, however, are created by computer programmers, not intelligence officers. In the case of telephone data, for example, it is necessary for experienced human beings to test the computer judgments by listening to brief fragments of conversation. Just this brief human interaction results in eliminating most leads. More intensive follow-ups usually wash out all but a few, and even these leads will probably not produce a terrorist. Of course, the business of catching terrorists is shrouded in secrecy and there is little concrete information available. Insiders assert that successes have been few and the huge sums spent on data mining would have been far better spent on traditional intelligence techniques that require highly skilled government agents, especially native Arabic speakers.

Experts say that most of the leads produced by this process are false positives and the software programs currently available are essentially glorified search engines. The Fourth Amendment specifies that the only reason that Americans may be subjected to search or seizure by government agencies is probable cause. In Chapter 8, I describe my own experience with a death threat sent to Hillary Clinton from a computer in my own library. It was clear that a crime had been committed; in fact, the e-mail message provided an extraordinary wealth of data that confirmed the likely identity of the author.

Such a wealth of evidence is rare, but the Constitution and subsequent court interpretations make it clear that there has to be a good chance that the person who is the object of the search committed a crime. Of the thousands of supposed terrorist leads, whose personal lives are examined in minute detail by both computers and human eyes and ears, only a very small fraction of one percent turn out to be worthy of further investigation. It's hard to establish precisely what constitutes probable cause, but there certainly must be a fifty-fifty or better chance that someone is guilty of a crime. One in a thousand obviously doesn't meet that standard.

"A serious discussion on the implications of data mining programs is long overdue" argues Senator Russ Feingold (D-WI). "Many Americans are understandably concerned about the idea of secret government programs analyzing their personal information. Congress needs to know more about the operational aspects and privacy implications of data mining programs before these programs are allowed to go forward," Senator Feingold, along with Senator John E. Sununu (R-NH), is sponsoring a bill that would require the Bush administration to report to Congress the extent of its data mining programs. Congressional oversight is essential. Executive agencies have repeatedly shown themselves willing to violate the privacy of citizens and probably violate the law as well. The GAO report on the ADVISE program is a good example of responsible Congressional involvement. If other data-mining projects turn out to be as carelessly designed as ADVISE, major legislation is needed to stop such abuses.

Irresponsible Government Agencies

In the course of collecting and sifting through personal information, government agencies have sometimes entrusted personal information about millions of people to criminals. Take, for example, the commercial databases described in the last chapter like the ones maintained by ChoicePoint Inc. ChoicePoint sells data to government agencies that includes personally identifiable data like Social Security numbers, motor vehicle violations, marriage and divorce records, and liens or judgments against millions of people. It also includes the personal information that library computer users have submitted to various Web sites. That information is available to law enforcement agencies around the country. In fact, ChoicePoint developed what is probably the most heavily used Web site for law enforcement personnel.

Although such databases have streamlined the procedure for gathering information about suspects, the information has also been misused. FBI agents, DEA officers and local policemen have, on numerous occasions, endangered the very people they are sworn to protect. Such databases facilitate blackmail, identity fraud, and stalking crimes. The Electronic Privacy Information Center (EPIC) has gathered documents under the Freedom of Information Act showing that law enforcement agencies routinely misuse personal information provided by commercial data brokers. Because of inadequate internal controls, agencies failed to limit the individuals authorized to view information or regulate what uses could be made of information. The documents revealed that frequently, no audits were conducted to determine who used databases and for what purposes. Neither were there adequate controls to assure the accuracy of the information contained in commercial databases. In fact, it turned out that a substantial portion of the information contained in such databases had been obtained illegally.

This last point is of special concern. Federal, state, and local governments routinely purchase from commercial brokers information that was gathered illegally. Congressional investigators discovered that the U.S. government spent over $30 million in 2005 to purchase personal data from private brokers. The information requested from brokers included names associated with unlisted phone numbers, records of phone calls, e-mail aliases, and even the locations of cell phone signals.

Overdependence on Technology

Not only are the procedures for collecting and using data flawed, but the technology itself often fails. Technology has been developed by fallible human beings and it mirrors their limitations. Consider the case of Portland lawyer Brandon Mayfield, who was arrested in the 2004 train bombing in Madrid. The FBI matched Mayfield's twenty-two year old fingerprint to one found at the scene of the crime. Eventually, it was discovered that the print belonged to an Algerian terrorist.

Although there was nothing in Mayfield's past to point to terrorist activity, FBI investigators searched the database with magical powers. Its flawed information counted much more heavily than the traditional and often successful methods used by the FBI to identify criminals. It is possible that in a few years, just such a twenty-two year old fingerprint might have its source in a school or public library computer, perhaps used with the Junior Librarian library software program discussed earlier. Keep in mind that children's fingerprints change somewhat over time and the library staff members who take the prints, like those at the Buffalo and Erie County Public Library, are not trained in fingerprinting procedures.

Occasionally, the carelessness and lack of common sense displayed by government agencies is truly astonishing. Take the example of the personal data on 28,000 sailors that appeared on June 24, 2006 on the Navy's Web site. The information included the names, birth dates, and Social Security numbers, belonging not only to the sailors themselves, but also to their relatives. At this writing, the Navy doesn't know how the information got there. Lieutenant Justin Cole, a spokesman for the Chief of Naval Personnel, was stymied. "It was information you don't want on a public Web site but there was no indication it was being used for illegal purposes" (White 2006). This distinction may not mean a great deal to sailors who become victims of identity theft as a result of the blunder.

Terrorism Futures Market

The convergence of data mining developments with the events of 9/11 has encouraged frightened people to believe that technology can make them safe. They are told that it is possible to analyze billions of small pieces of information to automatically create a "tailored and logical" picture of a suicide bomber or other potentially dangerous suspect. Fans of Mad Magazine will recall a cartoon called "Spy vs. Spy." The two classic spy characters were forever leaving bombs for one another and otherwise satirizing the secret agent stereotype. A few years ago, the Defense Advanced Research Projects Agency (DARPA), as part of the controversial TIA program described above, attempted to implement a scenario that seemed to have come straight from the pages of the magazine. The bizarre idea was to conduct an online financial futures market to help predict terrorist strikes. It is hard to believe, but the scheme was to catch terrorists betting on themselves and attempting to make money by predicting events that they expected to have a role in. Congress quickly put an end to the project, but what is disturbing is that top-level decision makers including the attorney general participated in the planning of this enterprise. It is also disturbing that this same agency continues to be responsible for many of the larger data mining projects currently in development.

Soon after learning about the Terrorist Futures project, I began frequenting the DARPA Web site (http://www.darpa.mil), as well as the some high tech online bulletin boards. Although messages written after the furor took on a somewhat different tone, earlier ones focused on what a cool idea it was. Young people who had spent their adolescence playing computer games loved the idea of elevating their games to play an important role in the real world. When I read the descriptions of the program that were posted on the DARPA site, it was impossible not to hear in my head reverberations of the word cool. On neither the government site nor the techie discussion groups did I find any discussion about whether the project really should be implemented or what real impact it might have. Instead, both imagined cartoon villains like those in "Spy vs. Spy" or those who populated their own computer games falling into the trap and witlessly giving away their secret plans.

THE CURRENT STATE OF PRIVACY LEGISLATION

Privacy legislation is woefully behind the times. The Privacy Act of 1974 is the last comprehensive attempt by Congress to protect the privacy of American citizens. There have been numerous amendments over the last thirty years, but the act was hammered out at a time when the threats presented by inexpensive, immensely powerful computers had not yet been envisioned. Government computers could store only the data that agencies knew would be useful to them. They could not go on trolling expeditions in vast seas of personal data. Even with such limited capacity to store personal information, Congress rightly feared that there existed the possibility of misuse. After all, they were looking toward 1984, only ten years in the future, and the threat of "Big Brother" was very real. Over time, however, government agencies have become anesthetized to privacy risks, and the horror of 9/11 has all but obscured the very real fears that motivated legislators to draft the Privacy Act of 1974.

SUMMING IT UP

In the absence of current privacy legislation, our users are at risk every time they type any personal information into a library computer. Too often we put them at further risk by collecting more personal information about our patrons than is absolutely necessary. Information stored on both your staff and public computers is available to law enforcement agencies, sometimes without a search warrant. When a library uses a software program to manage its public computers, it often requires that users identify themselves by typing their library card number. By doing so, patrons forge the connecting link of the chain that joins their online activities with their library records. They inadvertently reveal, for example, the real owner of their anonymous e-mail account, the real source of their contributions to blogs and other online discussions. Whether information is obtained directly by law enforcement agencies or indirectly through data brokers like ChoicePoint, our patrons' privacy has been violated.

In practice, the amount of personal information so revealed varies with the security measures the library has put in place. However, it must be remembered that information erased from hard disks may be invisible to other library users, but it isn't necessarily gone. Even libraries that have secured their computers with the latest security devices need to look carefully at what information is being entered into their computers.

REFERENCES

Anderson, A. J. 1989. The FBI wants you to spy. *Library Journal* 114 (June 15, 1989): 37–39.

Associated Press. 2006a. VA employee improperly took data home for 3 years, investigators say. *USA Today*, May 25. http://www.usatoday.com/news/washington/2006-05-25-vets-id-theft_x.htm.

Associated Press. 2006b. Government hit by rash of data breaches. *ENT News*, June 23. http://entmag.com/news/article.asp?EditorialsID=7555/.

Bazar, Emily. 2006. Cost to tell veterans of data theft starts at $10M. *USA Today*, May 25. http://www.usatoday.com/news/washington/2006-05-25-veteran-id-theft_x.htm.

Clayton, Mark. 2006. U.S. plans massive data sweep. *Christian Science Monitor*, February 9, p. 1. http://www.csmonitor.com/2006/0209/p01s02-uspo.html.

Houston Chronicle. 2007. Federal Web site exposed private data. *Houston Chronicle*, April 21, p. A4. http://www.chron.com/CDA/archives/archive.mpl?id=2007_4329695.

Gugliotta, Guy. 2006. Data mining still needs a clue to be effective. *Washington Post*, June 19, p. A8. http://www.washingtonpost.com/wp-dyn/content/article/2006/06/18/AR2006061800524.html.

Lee, J. M. 1998. Confidentiality: from the stacks to the witness stand. *American Libraries* 19 (June): 444–53.

Marks, Paul. 2006. Pentagon sets its sights on social networking Web sites. *New Scientist*, June 9. http://www.newscientist.com/.

Nakashima, Ellen. 2007. Potential targets get risk rating. *Washington Post*, July 11, p. A8. http://www.washingtonpost.com/wp-dyn/content/article/2007/07/10/AR2007071001871.html.

Nakashima, Ellen, and Alec Klein. 2007. New profiling program raises privacy concerns. *Washington Post*, February 28, p. A8. http://www.washingtonpost.com/wp-dyn/content/article/2007/02/27/AR2007022701542.html.

New Scientist magazine. 2006. June 9, issue 2555, p. 30.

Ramasastry, A. 2007. Why the ADVISE data-mining program may be very ill-advised: reports of likely privacy violations point to the need to mandate specific privacy safeguards. *FindLaw: Legal News and Commentary*, March 8. http://writ.news.findlaw.com/ramasastry/20070308.html.

Schmillen, Achim. 2007. Opinion: Don't let Uncle Sam become a computer hacker and identity thief's best friend. *Detroit News*, March 8. http://www.detnews.com/.

Strohm, Chris. 2006. Lawmakers seek probe of Homeland Security data-mining project. *GOVEXEC.com*, October 3. http://www.govexec.com/dailyfed/1006/100306cdpm1.htm.

Turley, Jonathan. 2006. Americans let right of privacy slip away. *Albany Times Union*, July 2, p. C2. http://www.timesunion.com/AspStories/story.asp?ID=49643&category=OPINION&newsdate=7/2/2006.

White, Josh. 2006. Navy finds data on thousands of sailors on Web site. *Washington Post*, June 24, p. A11. http://www.washingtonpost.com/wp-dyn/content/article/2006/06/23/AR2006062301493.html.

CHAPTER 6

RFID Systems in Libraries

Perhaps the most controversial issue presently facing libraries is whether or not to implement library automation systems based on the use of radio frequency identification tags or RFIDs as they are usually called. Yet many librarians may be only vaguely aware of their existence. What are RFIDs and are they really something we should be worrying about?

UNDERSTANDING RFID TECHNOLOGY

A few years ago, the business community became aware of a new technology in use for tracking shipments and assuring that merchandise in transit reaches its intended destination. Radio frequency tags were attached to shipping containers, making it possible to identify the location of any shipment and substantially reducing losses. RFID use is slowly being expanded to include individual items of merchandise. Industry advocates say that when affixed to DVDs or shaving cream, they can reduce theft and speed purchase transactions. However, they have been condemned by privacy advocates because they have the potential to keep track not only of the materials to which they are affixed but also of the individuals who purchase them. The possibilities inherent in the new technology are so numerous that nearly every large business enterprise and government agency is considering ways they can be adapted for use. In fact, the U.S. State

Department is planning to insert the tags into passports and identity cards for legal aliens.

How is RFID Technology Currently Used?

At present RFIDs are used in industry primarily for supply chain applications. Large retail chains like Wal-Mart, Target, and Albertsons require their suppliers to use radio tags on containers and/or pallets so that any given shipment can be tracked while it is in transit, when it reaches a warehouse, and finally when it arrives at the retail store. Since tags are affixed only to containers, individual items can no longer be tracked once they have been unpacked and placed on the shelf.

The Department of Defense (DOD) uses RFID technology to monitor shipments of weapons and supplies to armed forces around the globe. This has proven effective in minimizing theft and making sure that shipments get to their intended destinations.

RFIDs in Libraries

RFID tags entered the library market in the late 1990s and are currently in use in several hundred libraries. The big difference between library use and most commercial applications, however, is that libraries use RFID at the item level, not at the container level. In other words, the tags are attached directly to books and other materials. It is not expected that item level use of RFIDs in retail will be common for several years since they are currently too expensive to use on all but high priced items. If and when RFID is widely used in retail, for example in security devices, it is anticipated that it will be possible to permanently disable tags after items are purchased. Once they've been scanned by the right device, tags can become "inert." IBM has developed other RFID tags that can be simply torn off, either by the consumer or at point of sale.

When used in libraries, RFID tags replace barcodes. Since they are scanned or read over and over, they must always be readable; they cannot be turned off or torn off. In other words, the library model is more like the supply chain container model. To a large extent, the concern over privacy arises from this difference. Although RFID tags are still too expensive for most retail applications, the expenditure can pay off for libraries since they circulate the same materials again and again. If you've ever worked in a library that used the more traditional CheckPoint radio-based security system, you will recognize the tags. They're about one inch square and can be attached to books in much the same way as any paper label. When patrons pass through security gates, the old CheckPoint systems emitted radio signals that could set off an alarm if materials weren't charged out. The new tags also emit radio signals but these can be interpreted by RFID readers as information about a book or other item. It is, therefore, possible to inventory a shelf in seconds or an entire stack range in just a few minutes. Checkout can be accomplished without even opening a book.

The Public Perception of RFIDs

Even though the year 1984 has come and gone, the "Big Brother" dominated society created by George Orwell is still alive and well in the public imagination. In that famous book, citizens had no privacy whatsoever. They were monitored in their homes, their bedrooms, and on the street. They could do nothing without coming under the watchful eye of a camera. To many people, RFID technology harkens back to this Orwellian society. Unfortunately, a few corporations have initiated ill-conceived experiments that seem especially designed to arouse negative public opinion.

Your Underwear is Sending Out Radio Signals

Take, for example, the Benetton Group, manufacturers of underwear for men, women, and children which was discovered placing RFID tags in their underwear. A joint press release from Benetton and chip manufacturer Philips Electronics in 2003, stating that the tags are "imperceptible to the wearer and remain in individual items of clothing throughout their lifetime" (Phillips 2003), further angered the public. Philips Semiconductor, a division of Philips Electronics, then announced that it would ship 15 million radio tags to Benetton for use in their Sisley line of clothing. Benetton finally stepped back and insisted that it was still analyzing and evaluating the new technology and had never actually put tags into any of their merchandise (Roberti 2003). As you can imagine, this was one of the public relations disasters of the year. What could be more reminiscent of 1984 than the idea that one's underwear is sending out radio signals that can identify the wearer? As former candidate for California Secretary of State Debra Bowen testified, "How would you like it if, for instance, one day you realized your underwear was reporting on your whereabouts?" (Gamboa 2007).

Hold it! You're on Candid Camera

The Gillette Corporation added fuel to the fire by not only inserting tags in the packaging of its shaving products, but using the tags to trigger hidden cameras. As the customer picked up the Gillette package, the RFID tag alerted a hidden camera that snapped a close-up photo of the customer. When the customer arrived at the check-out desk, another photograph was taken. It is unclear whether the digital photographs were connected with credit card and customer discount card data at the point of checkout. The Auto ID Center at the Massachusetts Institute of Technology (MIT) developed the system, and its documents indicate that it was intended to track customers through the store for security purposes. Security guards would be alerted when a tagged package failed to arrive at the checkout counter. Since the photos produced by the system were clear close-ups, they became known mug shots in the press (Kuchinskas 2003).

The most recent commercial RFID news concerns American Express credit cards. At a 2007 Consumer Federation of America Conference in Washington DC, discussions focused on an American Express patent application, titled "Method and System for Facilitating a Shopping Experience." The patent application described a plan for keeping track of consumers through RFID-enabled objects, like the American Express Blue Card. RFID readers called "consumer trackers" would be installed in store shelving to pick up "consumer identification signals" emitted by RFID chips embedded in objects carried by shoppers (American Express credit cards). These would be used to "identify people, track their movements, and observe their behavior" (American 2007).

These are just two of the horror stories to which the public has been subjected over the last few years. Typically, the company involved responds with misinformation, sometimes misrepresenting its own activities or insisting that safety concerns are groundless. For example, they may claim that tags are deactivated when they are actually using a type that is always active. They may insist that tag readers are too large to be hidden and too weak to read tags at a distance when smaller and more powerful tag readers are under development. Corporate executives are often surprised at the public outcry, having focused entirely on selling their products with no thought to wider implications. Later in this chapter, we will discuss a Cincinnati company that embedded chips in the arms of some of its employees. It is hard to imagine rational business executives focusing so narrowly on security issues (RFID chips were intended to unlock doors for authorized employees) that they failed to see the Orwellian potential for tracking employees twenty-four hours a day.

ONE LIBRARY SYSTEM'S EXPERIENCE

Perhaps the easiest way to become familiar with the many issues surrounding RFIDs in libraries is to take a close look at the controversy at the Berkeley Public Library in the San Francisco Bay area. The reason that this library system lends itself to examination is that it has been prominently featured in so many newspaper and journal articles. RFIDs are not the only reason the library has been news worthy. The many conflicts that existed in this library resulted in the forced resignation of its director.

When the Berkeley Library Board unanimously approved an RFID project several years ago, hardly anyone was even familiar with the acronym. Since then, however, opposition to RFIDs has grown rapidly and much of this discussion has focused on Berkeley. Librarians, local residents, vendors, and privacy experts have all voiced their opinions in the press and so this is where we will focus our attention.

The Project Description

By 2004, the Berkeley Library System was committed to a $650,000 project to place RFID tags in all of its 550,000 items. If labor and other costs were included, the figure would be substantially higher. Self-checkout stations equipped with RFID tag readers were being installed at all system libraries. Most library systems rely on barcoding to match information about library users with bibliographic data. The move from barcodes to RFID tags can be an expensive one since tags currently cost up to $1.00 each. However, cost is expected to drop quickly as the tags become more widely used in the retail industry.

Much of the controversy surrounding RFIDs in Berkeley revolved around the project's cost, in addition to privacy issues. The library system had been experiencing a budget crunch and had laid off a number of staff members, eliminated Sunday hours, and cut the materials budget by 25%. Both staff and local residents wondered why the RFID project was going forward when so many library services were suffering.

Cost Savings

Berkeley's library director claimed that the system would save $2 million in worker's compensation for repetitive motion injuries over a five-year period. Other enthusiasts promised that since the ability to inventory their entire collections in a few days would save so much staff time, savings would quickly exceed expenditures. Other libraries that have installed RFID systems agree that they were indeed time savers. Library Director Harvey Varent of Providence College reported that his library saved "hundreds and hundreds of hours of labor" after installing an RFID-based system (Heining 2004). It is never quite clear from the various testimonials, however, how these "hundreds and hundreds of hours" compare with system costs.

While Berkeley's library director praised the new technology, many others in the library community, as well as civil liberties organizations like the Electronic Frontier Foundation (EFF) and the American Civil Liberties Union (ACLU), opposed them. If RFIDs can reap such extensive rewards for libraries and if they are becoming widely used in the commercial sphere, why are privacy advocates concerned about them?

How Tags Work

The RFID tags currently in use in libraries consist of very small radio receivers, each with a microchip. The microchips store only a small amount of information, often a number similar to a barcode number, which is programmed into the chip just once. However, it is possible to store considerably more information in some chips and newer read-write chips allow information to be added or deleted any number of times. More correctly called transponders, tags can hold as much as 1,024 bits, so it is actually possible to store considerably more information if staff time and equipment were available to program them. Since they can be as small as a grain of rice or as large as two inches, RFIDs can be used on both books and smaller media items like CDs.

Most RFID tags, including those used in libraries, are what are called passive. In other words, they lack a power source and so are unable to transmit a signal. They depend for power on the radio signal sent by the reader. Active tags have their own miniature power source and can not only communicate with the tag reader but also, to a limited extent, function as tiny computers.

Public Meeting

In August 2005, the Berkeley Daily Planet reported on a meeting held at the South Berkeley Senior Center to debate the Library's RFID plan (Artz 2005). For the most part, the people who spoke at the forum were opposed to the project. The library staff was represented by their union, and many local residents also voiced their opinions. Lee Tien represented the EFF. He stated that although RFIDs do not pose much of an immediate danger, it is expected that tag readers will soon become common in many stores, malls, and airports. While antennae can now pick up the radio signal within a range of only a few feet, it is anticipated that more powerful antennae will make it possible to read tags over a much longer distance. Government agencies might find library RFID tags a very convenient way to track citizens. It is likely that hand-held readers will be available to government agencies, private detectives, and even criminals. "Big money wants to sell RFID chips to manage information.... And the government wants that information, too" (Artz 2005).

Libraries as Guinea Pigs

Tien is a vocal opponent of RFID technology and has frequently expressed his views in the news media. The week following the discussion, he and Peter Warfield wrote another article that appeared in the Berkeley Daily Planet. It was a follow-up to a point Tien had made at the meeting, to the effect that the book industry wants to use libraries as "guinea pigs to test a new technology that isn't really ready for public consumption" (Warfield). He quotes a letter from James Lichtenberg, chair of the New Technology Committee of the Book Industry Study Group (BISG) urging funding of an RFID project at the San Francisco Public Library, a project that was later abandoned. Lichtenberg suggested that libraries can "make a contribution to maintaining our free and open society as we embrace new and untested technologies." He continued: "For libraries to abandon the field now would leave the development of RFID essentially in the hands of commercial and defense interests where 'national security' and the profit motive often overshadow concerns for civil liberty" (Warfield 2005).

TECHNICAL ISSUES IMPACTING PRIVACY

It should be mentioned that the standard governing most RFID technology (ISO 15693) was developed specifically for use with containers and intended for supply chain applications like keeping track of inventory in a warehouse. Privacy issues were not a consideration. The newer standard, ISO 18000, which was designed for item-level tagging, does address at least some privacy concerns. At this writing, however, many library applications use the earlier ISO 15693 standards. It is anticipated that ISO 18000 tags will soon be available for libraries, but it is not easy or cheap to replace one generation of tags with another. Few libraries are going to be able to quickly advance to the new tags when they become available if they have already invested large sums of money on older systems.

Untested Technology

Although the term guinea pig is not an attractive one, there is a good deal of truth in the assertion that libraries would be among the first to explore an untested technology. Item-level RFID implementation is in its infancy, and at least some manufacturers of consumer goods have backed away because of concerns similar to those expressed at the Berkeley meeting. Lichtenberg is further quoted to the effect that future development "ultimately will make the technology itself stronger and safer as it matures and its implementation broadens" (Warfield 2005). Many library advocates wonder if this is a burden that any library should ever take on. Libraries, as it is clear from the Berkeley example, have very limited budgets, and RFID implementation can mean that other library priorities are sacrificed. Imagine a library that invests hundreds of thousands of dollars in a system, only to discover that, essentially, they did it wrong. The Cesar Chavez Library, described below, had just such an experience.

The Lichtenberg letter expresses the belief that libraries can mold and change the development of RFIDs if they "get in on the bottom floor" so to speak. When one compares the financial bargaining power of libraries with that of the commercial sector of the economy, it seems doubtful that libraries could ever be very influential, no matter how early or late they became involved.

Tracking and Hotlisting: Ease of Linking Titles to Tags

Getting back to the discussion at the Berkeley Senior Center, how-ever, another participant was David Mulnar, a University of California graduate student who had worked with the library to explore the privacy issues surrounding RFIDs. He made it clear that the library had been alert to privacy concerns and had avoided pitfalls into which other libraries had fallen. He mentioned the Cesar Chavez branch library in Oakland, where the identification number used for each tag was just the barcode number of the item written backwards. This made it relatively easy for a snooper to build a database of tag numbers and thereby keep track of patron borrowing habits with an inexpensive tag reader.

Many library privacy advocates believe the dangers posed by RFIDs can be divided into two broad issues: tracking and hotlisting. Tracking refers to the ability of someone with a tag reader to track the move-ments, not only of library books but also of individuals carrying library books. Multiple observations can be correlated to produce a clear pic-ture of the comings and goings of library users. Although readers at present can only pick up signals within about a three foot range, with a more powerful antenna, a reader could intercept signals over a wide area. Even the reader itself could be disguised in a variety of ways.

Hotlisting is a term used for building a database of books with their RFID tag numbers. Once the database has been created, it becomes possible to use unauthorized readers to find out exactly who is check-ing out which books.

Information Stored in Chips

CheckPoint representative Paul Simon tried to allay the fear that tags could be easily read by lurkers. A six-foot high antenna, he said, would be required to read a library tag from three feet away. He also assured the audience that CheckPoint's tags did not have enough memory to store any more information than the book code. To better understand this issue of information storage, it is important to be aware of a few basic points about the chips themselves. Chips are a little like CD-ROM disks in that they can be:

- RO (read only, usually with unique numbers preprogrammed into them)

- WORM (write once, write many. These are also preprogrammed but additional information can be added if there is enough space)
- RW (read write. These chips can be updated at any time)

There is another category of semi-active tags still in the development stage that have their own batteries to power their micro-circuitry, but they still require a radio signal from a tag reader. Tags operate on different radio frequencies. Most library tags operate on a high frequency (13.56 MHz) and have a range from approximately 16 to 39 inches.

In general, library tags hold data that remains unchanged until the book or media program is removed from the collection. As librarians are well aware from hosting innumerable used book sales, barcode labels remain attached to library materials long after they leave the library for good. Although some libraries mark through barcodes with magic markers, passive RFID tags can be read almost indefinitely unless the circuitry is damaged.

Potential Health Hazards

We are, however, getting a long way away from the Berkeley Library public meeting. Library staff had voiced their concern that the tags posed health hazards and might even cause cancer, but Simon assured the audience that the tags contained no heavy metals. Some residents were also concerned that long exposure to the radio frequency posed presented a health risk. A City Council member and former physician argued that the radio frequency is higher than AM radio but lower than FM. He insisted that studies showed no relationship between exposure to radio waves and health risks like cancer. However, more recent studies linking cell phone use to low sperm counts are causing scientists to reconsider the safety of radio waves.

Use of RFIDs in Passports

For some time, the U.S. Government has been looking into the use of RFID chips in passports. Other uses under consideration include the identity cards carried by non-citizens. In 2006, a privacy and security advisory committee to the Department of Homeland Security (DHS) issued a draft report concluding that for the time being, the government should not use chips in identification documents that can be read remotely. One of the reasons cited in the report is that hackers have demonstrated the ability to skim off information and clone chips, leaving the system vulnerable to identity theft. The second problem cited is the ability to track individuals. Passports are carried by American citizens when they travel in other countries. There appears to be no reason why foreign governments could not install readers to follow the movements of our citizens, possibly endangering their safety.

In summarizing the present state of technology, the report concludes that "RFID appears to offer little benefit when compared to the consequences it brings for privacy and data integrity" (Singel 2006). However, it appears that the report is being ignored by government agencies, which appear to be proceeding with plans to implement RFID use. Chip readers will be able to read the stored information from a distance of twenty feet.

Privacy advocates are concerned that the government is deliberately ignoring the report and postponing indefinitely the publication of a final version. Jim Harper, a member of the advisory committee, is afraid the report may never be completed. "The powers that be took a good run at deep-sixing this report ... There's such a strongly held consensus among industry and DHS that RFID is the way to go that getting people off of that and getting them to examine the technology is very hard to do" (Singel 2006).

RFID, THE LIBRARY, AND THE COMMUNITY

RFIDs had become a very emotional issue for local residents of Berkeley who associated its adoption with library director Jackie Griffin. A citizen group known as BOLD (Berkeleyans Organizing for Library Defense) expressed their opposition to Griffin's leadership and to what they saw as the adoption of the program in the face of community disapproval. "You came in here and got some cabal to do this and didn't even tell people about it," declared group member Nancy Delaney bringing cheers from the audience. "How do I take you to court? How do I make you give us our democracy back?" (Artz 2006).

RFIDs in Georgia

Berkeley is known for its dissenting citizenry. Controversial issues are somewhat more likely to result in public debate than in other communities. However, libraries depend on public support for their existence. Residents of Berkeley, at least those attending the meeting, viewed the RFID project as being responsible in part for staff layoffs and reduced library services. It is interesting to note that another public library director, who was fired within days of the Berkeley director, was also criticized for implementing an RFID system. Jo Ann Pinder, Director of the Gwinnett County Library System in Georgia was fired at an angry public meeting on June 2, 2006. Gwinnett County is culturally as distant from Berkeley as any two library systems can be, but the reaction of the two communities was quite similar. The issues involved in Pinder's resignation, included intellectual freedom and were more complex than those in Berkeley. However, a major bone of contention was the $1.2 million that had thus far been expended for an RFID system.

There appears to be strong feeling among the residents of many communities that bleeding edge technology is not appropriate in libraries, and high tech, ethically questionable experiments shouldn't be conducted at the expense of taxpayers. We would all do well to pay attention to the admonition in the article "Technology, Privacy, Confidentiality, and Security." "If your library proceeds with a new technology that does affect privacy and confidentiality, and you haven't addressed those issues in advance, there's a good chance someone else will address them for you" (Crawford 2005).

Exaggerated Claims

An important reason given for implementing the RFID system in Berkeley was a reduction in repetitive stress injuries. The article describing the Berkeley public meeting mentions that Library Director Griffin anticipates $2 million in workers compensation savings over a five-year period. The minutes of the December 2003 Board of Library Trustees meeting show that President Laura Anderson asked the director if an RFID system "would result in savings." Griffin responded that the library had spent about $1 million in direct workers' compensation claims for the past five years, for the most part resulting from repetitive motion injuries. "This technology should result in a significant decrease in injuries and associated costs" (Warfield 2005).

Warfield and Tien, however, questioned Griffin's figures. They wrote that in December 2004, the Library Users Association and the

EFF requested documents from the library relating to their Workers' Compensation payments (Warfield). The documents supplied by the library showed that in the five-year period ending June 30, 2003, the library spent $642,161 on all workers' compensation claims, of which repetitive stress injuries accounted for only $167,871 in claims. In other words, actual costs fall far short of anticipated RFID savings. It is extremely difficult to precisely estimate the cost savings that can result from an RFID system, and some library directors like Griffin have lost credibility in their communities by making such unsupported claims. Librarians considering the adoption of RFID systems should make a careful cost-benefit analysis before going public with a proposal.

PRIVACY ISSUES AND RFID TECHNOLOGY

In the same article, Warfield and Tien succinctly summarize what they consider the privacy issues surrounding RFIDs. They caution that they are not suggesting that the current generation of RFID technology can result in this massive invasion of personal privacy but rather that it constitutes an important building block. "The surveillance society will not be built in a day by evil people. It will be built because we accept privacy-invading technologies for supposed short-term convenience, ignoring the long-term social costs" (Warfield 2005).

Since the list reflects the concerns of the organizations that actively oppose library implementation, it will be useful to briefly enumerate major concerns here and then examine each in some detail.

1. RFID tags can be read through clothing, book bags or briefcases by anyone with a reader.
2. There are several ways to associate a book title and tag number, with and without access to the library's database.
3. Tracking an individual with a tagged item requires only the ability to read its tag.
4. Retailers, individuals, and government agencies with doorway or portable scanners can potentially identify one's reading matter.
5. The ability to do this also means that it is possible to track the movements of the same individual.

Let us look at each of these arguments in turn.

Tags Can Be Read through Clothing, Book Bags, and Briefcases

As mentioned earlier, Paul Simon of CheckPoint assured the Berkeley audience that a six-foot antenna was required to read an RFID library tag from three feet away. That would presumably make it possible for door-mounted readers to pry into briefcases but not portable readers that currently have weaker antennae. Of course, the snooper would have to disguise or conceal the antenna but this apparently would not be difficult. However, RFID readers now in development can be quite small.

Libraries use tag readers in a variety of ways and so they usually need several of them. For example, to use the technology effectively, they generally need readers at work stations in their technical services departments, at the circulation desk, at self-checkout stations, at bookdrops, and at exits. In addition, they need hand-held units for inventory and shelf-reading. At this point in the development of the technology, none of these readers would pose much of a threat to anyone's privacy because they are so large, cumbersome, and unable to read tags more than a few feet away. However, since readers are relatively uncomplicated radio receivers that are both inexpensive and easy to tamper with, the real problem is with readers specially designed to snoop.

Book Titles Can Be Connected with Tag Numbers

This assertion is, unfortunately, very true. Initially, libraries used barcode numbers as RFID tag numbers. Then they tried simply transposing barcode numbers. You may recall that the Cesar Chavez library transposed the barcode number, making the last digit the first digit. Once snoopers have figured out the technique, they can simply spend a little time in the stacks jotting down titles and barcode numbers (barcodes are usually still affixed to the material since removing them is a labor intensive task). Presumably, our snooper would not be interested in the entire collection, just a subset of items that supposedly fit the profile of a terrorist or other evil doer. Although it seems extremely far fetched, it is conceivable that an irate citizen, angry that the library purchases what they consider to be smutty books, might make a list of them so as to expose the reading habits of library users.

If the library uses tag numbers that cannot be easily discovered, snoopers would need to bring a portable reader to the stacks, as well as a laptop computer to store the information. This would be more cumbersome. It's hard to picture such an activity going unnoticed in a small library, but it would not be difficult in the vast, nearly empty stacks of a university library. And, if the snooper is interested in a relatively small number of items, he or she could simply check them out and "read" them at home.

To Track an Individual with a Tagged Item, Just Read the Tag

Warfield and Tien use the phrase "with or without access to the library's database." What would it take to get into the library's database? According to computer hackers, it would not be very difficult. Take, for example, reports of attacks on high school and university computer systems. Even sixteen-year-old students have successfully changed their grades and those of their friends in their high school's administrative computer system. The stakes are higher at the university level and such intrusions have occurred frequently. Library systems have also been hacked, but since the rewards are not as great, it has not been a big problem. Nevertheless, our computers are not very sophisticated compared to the high tech systems available to industry and government. Since our budgets are not generous, our technical staffs are also somewhat low-tech, and the other library staff members who daily interact with the system know little about computer security.

If someone, whether a government agent or a nosy neighbor, were to gain access to the library's system, he or she would probably have access to both patron and materials records. This would add a new dimension to the problem described above. Warfield and Tien cite the ease of associating a book with a tag. If one had access to the library data base, it would indeed be possible to associate a book with a tag with a patron.

Retailers, Individuals and Government Agencies Can Read Tags

For the time being, this assertion is not really correct. Most retailers have not yet implemented RFID systems, and so far government use of the technology is in its formative stages. But what specifically is envisioned in the near future?

Library Applications

The way in which libraries currently use RFIDs is called "Asset Tracking." In other words, a library software application keeps track of materials that are checked out and checked in. "Asset tagging and identification" is another term for these functions, which includes library shelving and inventory control. These tend to be the principle uses of the technology in both libraries and the retail sector, although tagging is occasionally used for access control. In other words, RFID tags provide a method of keyless entry and make it possible for staff to enter areas not open to the public.

Warfield and Tien were assuming that when RFID technology becomes widely used, many different people will have access to readers that could potentially interpret the library's tags. Would people really want to devote their efforts to reading library tags? It's hard to know when we are talking about a reasonable possibility and when we are just being paranoid. Security cameras have become ubiquitous, turning up in almost every type of public building and as part of many retail security systems. They can be so small or well disguised that they go unnoticed by the people who come and go under their watchful eye. RFID antennae will undoubtedly become smaller and more powerful within the next few years. This presents the possibility of security cameras and RFID readers associated with one another and mounted in a wide variety of public places like shopping malls and post offices.

Is there really any reason to go to all this trouble to find out what people are reading? The idea certainly seems farfetched. Yet the library community has been shocked at revelations that the National Security Agency (NSA) is collecting information on our grocery store purchases, our banking transactions, and other information seemingly of no interest to law enforcement agencies. Reading habits are certainly more indicative of an individual's interests and inclinations than toothpaste brands.

RFID and Surveillance

Earlier in this chapter, a distinction was made between tracking and hotlisting. Tracking focuses not on the item but on the individual. In other words, RFIDs can make surveillance possible, even when the observer has no interest in the content of books and other library materials. As long as library patrons are carrying tagged items, or keeping them in their cars, there may be a way in which their movements can be tracked. If you couple tracking with security cameras, you have the basis for a plot like 1984 or other movie thrillers featuring a totalitarian government. Where does reality leave off and fantasy begin? Is this scenario possible or is it the product of an overactive imagination?

RFID Tags in Borrowers' Cards

Library privacy advocates worry that the next phase of RFID system implementation might be putting RFID chips into borrower's cards. This would speed up circulation transactions even more since patrons checking out their own materials would no longer need to scan their library cards. In fact, Karen Schneider, in her position paper presented to the California Committee on Energy and Utilities, asserts that one California library currently stores patron information in RFID tags (Schneider 2003).

Librarians intent on speeding up the checkout process might assert that just putting chips in library cards doesn't really compromise anyone's privacy. The identity of the borrower is safely stored and protected in the library's database. However, we have already noted that there are a variety of ways to associate a number with an item or individual.

RFID AND LIBRARY ORGANIZATIONS

As one might expect, the library community is hungry for information about RFID technology and its implications. A number of conferences have considered various aspects of the topic. The American Library Association (ALA) has been especially active in seeking out answers, and numerous vendors have shown their wares at ALA's annual and midwinter conferences. To some extent, because larger library systems like those in San Francisco and Berkeley have adopted or seriously considered RFID systems, the California Library Association (CLA) has also been active in bringing together experts in the field.

Following a seminar on RFID conducted by the CLA, panel moderator Lori Bowen Ayre of the Galecia Group summarized her conclusions:

"In closing the panel, I decided to ask what seemed to be to be the obvious question: why would ANYONE get into RFID at this stage? I asked this question because throughout the discussion, it became clear that the technology is so new that many of those tough questions couldn't be answered authoritatively.

- Standards are still being developed (data communication).
- Some standards (data model) haven't even BEGUN to be developed.
- Health effects (radio exposure, RSI) studies haven't been done.
- The [return on investment] isn't documented.

- The cost is very high to get started and once you commit to a vendor (at this point), you are really committed to the vendor" (Ayre 2005).

Establishing Standards

Ideally, librarians would like to see the development of RFID tags that could be read only by library readers, but at this writing they have not been developed. Libraries constitute only a very small part of the potential RFID market and future development will probably be driven by the retail industry.

On June 27, 2006, ALA's Intellectual Freedom Committee adopted a set of privacy and confidentiality guidelines for the use of RFIDs in libraries. At this writing, this is by far the best thought-out statement on the subject. Because the document is so important, I will summarize it below, but the complete document is available on the ALA Web site (www.ala.org).

Selection and Procurement Process

"Use the RFID selection and procurement process as an opportunity to educate library users about RFID technology ... A transparent selection process allows a library to publicize its reasons for wanting to implement an RFID system while listening to its users."

It seems clear that libraries that implement RFID systems without first consulting their users do so at their own peril. Bear in mind that no library MUST implement an RFID system. At this point in their development, it is accurate to say that such systems would speed and simplify some routine library functions. Claims that they revolutionize libraries, however, do not appear to be well-founded. There are currently defensible reasons both for adopting RFIDs and steering clear of them. Future advances in technology may alter the balance in one direction or the other. Although librarians can be expected to have a better grasp on technical considerations than the general public, they need the input of both their users and of local and national privacy groups before reaching final decisions.

Allow Users to Opt Out

"Consider selecting an 'opt-in' system that allows library users who wish to use or carry an RFID-enabled borrower card do so while allowing others to choose an alternative method to borrow materials."

RFIDs should never become a reason for library users to abandon their library. At present many privacy experts are speaking out against RFIDs and so protesting patrons, who refuse to check out books carrying RFID tags, should never be viewed as cranks. By trying to force all library users to accept the system, the library would be opening itself up to a barrage of bad publicity that it can ill afford.

Consider Library Privacy Policies and Practices

"Ensure that institutional privacy policies and practices addressing notice, access, use, disclosure, retention, enforcement, security, and disposal of records are reflected in the configuration of the RFID system."

In other words, analyze the privacy implications of any system under consideration. Do not depend on the vendor to do so. RFID systems were not originally designed for library use. They have been adapted for this purpose and may not fully meet the library's requirements. Just as RFID tags designed for shipping containers are not really suitable for library use, other future adaptations may be similarly flawed.

Personally Identifiable Information

"Delete personally identifiable information (PII) collected by RFID systems, just as libraries take reasonable steps to remove PII from aggregated, summary data."

There is plenty of evidence that libraries hold on to too much personally identifiable information. Whether because of carelessness or a failure to fully understand what data is stored, library hard drives are filled with transaction logs and other files that librarians may assume are deleted on a regular basis. RFIDs offer yet another opportunity to amass quantities of personal information and because systems are so new, vendors may not have fully addressed the problem of purging it.

Full Disclosure

"Notify the public about the library's use of RFID technology. Disclose any changes in the library's privacy policies that result from the adoption of an RFID system."

Ideally, the public should be kept informed throughout the process. There should be no surprises that could provoke a public uprising. Elsewhere in this book, I describe the unexpected revelation that 700,000 British children had been fingerprinted to streamline the school library checkout process. The damage done by the ensuing public relations disaster cannot be calculated.

Staff Training

"Assure that all library staff continue to receive training on privacy issues, especially regarding those issues that arise due to the implementation and use of RFID technology."

The library tasks for which RFID technology is appropriate are those performed by the clerical staff. Often these staff members receive only enough training to physically perform the repetitive tasks to which they are assigned. They understand few of the library's policies and may have no idea why patron privacy is important to the library. No library should implement an RFID system without extensive staff training that includes not only the rote procedures, but the related philosophy, and potentially controversial issues involved. They must understand that users who object to the system have legitimate concerns. They are not weirdos or crackpots. Their concerns should be heard with courtesy and understanding.

Database Security

"Librarians should continue their longstanding commitment to securing bibliographic and patron databases from unauthorized access and use. [They should] use the most secure connection possible for all communications with the Integrated Library Systems (ILS) to prevent unauthorized monitoring and access to personally identifiable information."

Because most librarians are not computer experts, they may not be fully aware of the computer attacks that are occurring daily in business and government. They might assume that no one would want to monitor their systems; but this is far from the truth. Even though we may not collect Social Security numbers or driver's license data, there is ample information contained in our library systems to be useful to identity thieves. Information acquired through an RFID system is presently more accessible than the patron records stored on library servers.

A few years ago, I worked in a library that employed an attractive female student. Over time we became aware that a young man seemed overly interested in her. Once he obtained her full name, he repeatedly attempted to learn her address and telephone number from library staff members. He began to follow her to classes and when she left the library, it became necessary for a security guard to escort her to her car. The young man was soon arrested as a stalker.

Imagine, however, that an RFID chip was embedded in her library card and stored in her purse or backpack. Many young people have a talent for rigging up electronic gadgets, and a radio receiver is a relatively simple device. Depending on the power of the radio antenna, the stalker would probably have been able to read whatever personal information was stored on the chip. This might include student ID or library card number. More sophisticated systems might even include enough personal information to track her to her home address. If he could obtain her address so easily, staff members might never have noticed him. He might conceivably have arrived on her doorstep before his behavior attracted any attention.

"Protect the data on RFID tags by the most secure means available, including encryption."

Although vendors are somewhat unclear in their literature, it appears that most information contained in library RFID tags is not encrypted. There is really no reason for this. Vendors can and should make sure that all personally identifiable information used by the library, whether it is stored in RFID chips or on computer servers is encrypted.

Limit and Protect Information

"Limit the bibliographic information stored on a tag to a unique identifier for the item (e.g., barcode number, record number, etc.). Use the security bit on the tag if it is applicable to your implementation. Block the public from searching the catalog by whatever unique identifier is used on RFID tags to avoid linking a specific item to information about its content."

This recommendation now seems dated since it suggests barcode numbers as an acceptable identifier. Libraries are accustomed to using barcode-based systems, and in many cases, have looked on RFID as merely an upgrade. When barcode numbers are publicly accessible, for example when barcode stickers remain affixed to materials after RFID implementation, they make it easy to track materials using unauthorized readers. Ideally, the number in an RFID chip should be a new number never before publicly accessible.

"Train staff not to release information about an item's unique identifier in response to blind or casual inquiries. Store no personally identifiable

information on any RFID tag. Limit the information stored on RFID-enabled borrower cards to a unique identifier."

Once again, barcode numbers have always been publicly accessible. RFID tag numbers are very different. They have the potential to compromise the privacy of library users, and therefore must be considered highly confidential.

RFID AND GOVERNMENT

Even though you may carefully observe these guidelines, you must also consider existing privacy legislation, as it has been enacted into law by your own state and local governments. In addition, consider the provisions of the Patriot Act and other federal legislation as they affect library patrons and library records. Although you can take steps to make your system as safe as possible, you cannot control what happens outside the library. It seems fair to say that if librarians are going to support the development of RFID, they have an obligation to support legislation to protect their users when they step outside the library. In most states, however, privacy statutes date back to a time when almost no one understood the dangers posed by massive collections of data. Technical developments like RFID were still in the realm of science fiction.

A few states, however, have begun tackling the problem and there are a number of bills coming before state legislatures. Perhaps the most interesting is California's "Identity Information Protection Act of 2006."

The California RFID Bill

The bill approved by both the California Senate and Assembly then vetoed by the governor in 2006 was one of the most comprehensive pieces of RFID legislation in the nation. Although it may not be perfect, it contains some important provisions that other states would do well to include in their own upcoming legislation. Here are some of its most important provisions from the Legislative Counsel's Digest:

- The bill covers the act of intentionally remotely reading identification documents using radio waves without the owner's knowledge and prior consent. It also includes knowingly disclosing the information or causing to be disclosed. The punishment for such acts includes imprisonment in a county jail for up to one year, a fine of not more than $5,000, or both that fine and imprisonment.

- This bill would require the California Research Bureau (CRB) to submit a report to the Legislature on security and privacy for government-issued, remotely readable identification documents.
- The CRB would be required to establish an advisory board, consisting of specified government officials and representatives from industry and privacy rights organizations, who would make recommendations to the Bureau (Identity 2006).

It is significant, however, that the bill was intended as an interim measure to control RFID use until the legislature could study the subject further and obtain more complete information. In fact, the governor cited this paucity of information as his primary reason for vetoing the bill. Legislators, like librarians, are having a difficult time grasping the full impact of the new technology. However, they are aware that personally identifiable information is already vulnerable. They can't afford to ignore the potentially dangerous implications of RFIDs just because the technology is in flux.

The Ohio Bill

In other states, legislators are also beginning to grapple with the dangers of RFID technology. As one would imagine, it is the implantation of RFIDs into human beings that has captured the public imagination. Other potential problems, not being so dramatic, are often left unaddressed.

In Ohio, State Senator Robert Schuler proposed a bill that would make it illegal for employers to require that employees implant RFID tags under the skin. Sound fantastic? Think again. He proposed the bill in response to a very real incident. Some workers at a private video surveillance company in Cincinnati had tags implanted in their arms that allow them to access a secure room. Schuler is concerned that "This same stuff could be used to track people when they're not at work ... Maybe they'll say you have to go to church on Sundays and you can't go out to the bar" (Cain 2006). State Sen. Ron Amstutz, co-sponsor of the bill agrees. "It's the government's role to prevent the abuse of technology. It's very powerful. It could be used for great good or great evil" (Cain 2006).

SUMMING UP

Karen Schneider writes that "RFID is an inevitable technology in libraries both for financial and humane reasons" (Schneider 2006). It is attractive to libraries for many reasons but there is no question that it brings up privacy issues that have not yet been resolved. Like so many technology issues relating to the privacy of library users, RFID is not inherently bad, but it is in its infancy and standards that would prevent its misuse are yet to be developed. At this writing, the Hitachi Corporation has just unveiled a new .05 mm RFID chip. This means the chip is smaller than a grain of sand and it's ultra-small size means that it could be embedded invisibly within almost anything or anyone without their knowledge. The case of the RFID tags implanted in the arms of Cincinnati employees is one that librarians should take to heart. It is doubtful that the video surveillance company intended to invade its employees' privacy. They had a security problem and this seemed like a good way to solve it. Libraries have inadequate staffing, and RFIDs might help to solve that problem.

Although universally accepted industry standards are essential, legislation is also needed to prevent RFID-related privacy violations. Congress must update privacy legislation to include RFID and other new technologies. However, the RFID industry has been lobbying Congress to delay any and all RFID legislation. "Technologically prescriptive legislation is inappropriate and likely to be ineffective and likely to hamper technology with enormous promise," argued Ari Juels, principal research scientist at RSA Laboratories (Westervelt 2007). The occasion for his remarks was the 2007 RSA Conference panel discussion entitled "Do We Legislate or Do We Innovate?" To delay legislation would mean that Congress will be dealing with a fait accompli, a generation of technology already in widespread use. Instead of guiding technical developments in a safe and ethical direction, legislators would be in the position of having to back up and undo years of development and huge investments in research and marketing. Naturally, Congress would be reluctant to impose what would amount to sanctions on the industry and so unsatisfactory compromises would be inevitable.

In time, universal standards will be established for RFID systems, legislation will be enacted, and most of the knottier questions will be answered. Because libraries have so much to gain from the technology, they should be spurring the industry on to solve its problems and encouraging Congress to do its part. Meanwhile, libraries that adopt RFID-based systems may be risking their well-deserved reputations as protectors of personal privacy. As previously described, RFID vendors are looking to libraries to partner with them in expanding the uses of the technology. It is in the best interests of libraries to make their concerns known to industry and support the integration of strong privacy protection.

REFERENCES

American Express addresses RFID people tracking plans. Press Release, March 9, 2007. Spychips.com. http://www.spychips.com/press-releases/american-express-conference.html.

Artz, Matthew. 2003. City library adopts controversial RFID chips. *Berkeley Daily Planet,* October 10. http://www.berkeleydaily.org/article.cfm?issue=10-10-03&storyID=17547/.

Artz, Matthew. 2005. RFID: library's new technology sparks controversy. *Berkeley Daily Planet,* March 4. http://www.berkeleydailyplanet.com/text/article.cfm?issue=02-15-05&storyID=20728/.

Artz, Matthew. 2005. Library workers, patrons denounce RFID system. *Berkeley Daily Planet,* August 5. http://www.berkeleydailyplanet.com/text/article.cfm?archiveDate=08-05-05&storyID=22017/.

Artz, Matthew. 2005. RFID detractors gather for protest. *Berkeley Daily Planet,* June 24. http://www.berkeleydaily.org/text/index.cfm?archiveDate=06-24-05/.

Ayre, Lorie Bowen, L. B. 2005. RFID systems in libraries. Position Paper, Galecia Group, august 30, 2004. p. 6. Later included in *Wireless Privacy: RFID, bluetooth and 802.11,* Boston: Addison-Wesley: 2005.

Berkeley Public Library. Berkeley Public Library: Best practices for RFID technology. http://berkeleypubliclibrary.org/BESTPRAC.pdf/.

Cain, Patrick. 2006. Bill would bar mandatory ID implants: Ohio companies could not put chips in workers' skin. *Akron Beacon Journal.* July 21. http://www.ohio.com/mld/ohio/news/15089670.htm.

Crawford, W. 2005. Technology, privacy, confidentiality, and security. *Library Technology Reports 41.2 24(7).*

Gamboa, John P. 2007. Micro RFID chips raise some privacy concerns. *The Daily Aztec* February 22. http://media.www.thedailyaztec.com/media/storage/paper741/news/2007/02/22/ScienceTechnology/Micro.Rfid.Chips.Raise.Some.Privacy.Concerns-2735515-page2.shtml.

Heining, Andrew and Christa Case. 2004. Are Book Tags a Threat? *Christian Science Monitor,* October 5. http://www.csmonitor.com.

Identity Information Protection Act of 2006. California Senate Bill SB768.2006.

Kuchinskas, S. 2003. California scrutinizes RFID privacy. *WiFi Planet.* August 15. http://www.wi-fiplanet.com/news/article.php/3064511/ /.

Molnar, D. and Wagner, D. Privacy and security in library RFID: issues, practices, and architectures. In *Proceedings of the 11th ACM Conference on Computer and Communications Security,* October 25–29, 2004, Washington DC.

Ozer, Nicole. 2006. Very disappointing news. ACLU of Northern California Web site. October 4. http://aclunc.org/isues/technology/bytes_and_pieces/very_disappointing_news.shtml.

Phillips Electronics and Benetton Group. For immediate release," news release. March 11, 2003. http://www.boycottbenetton.com/PR_030407.html.

Roberti, Mark. 2003. Benetton on RFID and privacy worries, *eWeek.com*, September 15. http://www.eweek.com/article2/0,1895,1269295,00.asp/.

Schneider, K. 2003. RFID and Libraries: Both sides of the chip. Committee on Energy and Utilities, California Senate, November 20. http://www.ala.org.

Singel, Ryan. 2006. Feds leapfrog RFID privacy study. *Wired News*, October 30. http://www.wired.com/news/technology/0,72019-0.html?tw=wn_technology_1/.

UN Observer. 2007. American Express addresses RFID people tracking plans: promises full patent review, tracking notice, and chip-free option. March 9. 2007. http://www.unobserver.com/layout5.php?id=3265&blz=1/.

Warfield, Peter and Lee Tien. 2005. Industry's gain, library's pain. *Berkeley Daily Planet*, May 10. http://www.berkeleydailyplanet.com/article. cfm?archiveDate=05-10-05&storyID=21365.

Westervelt, R. 2007. RSA Conference panel says privacy legislation too premature for RFID. *SearchSecurity.com*. http://searchsecurity.techtarget. com/originalContent/0,289142,sid14_gci1242602,00.html.

CHAPTER 7
The Challenge of Library Records: What to Keep and How Long to Keep It

If we were to board a time machine and return to the days when library records were kept manually, we could watch library users checking out their books. Each book had a pocket that held a card on which borrowers wrote their names or library card numbers. Some old timers will fondly remember the high tech Gaylord charger which stamped this information on the card. This handy little machine constituted a huge improvement over the illegible scribbles that turned us into unwilling cryptographers. Whether stamped or hand-written, the card was filed until the book was returned. This was the only record of the transaction. If an overdue notice was sent out, the information was probably written on a postcard and the postcard went to the tardy borrower. In addition to the book card file, the library also kept a borrower's file. These were also three by five cards, usually handwritten by patrons, and containing little more than their names, addresses, and phone numbers. Children's cards included the names of parents.

THE FBI'S INTEREST IN LIBRARIES

My own library memories go back to the Nixon era and I have a vivid memory of an FBI agent visiting our small public library. I was still in library school and the most junior member of the staff. One day, an agent came up to the circulation desk holding a book about

Communism and demanding to know the name of the patron who held card number 2345. The library director, my boss and my hero at the time, simply said no. The agent would need a warrant to obtain that information. As I recall, he attempted a bit of intimidation, but my boss held firm.

Although we saw the agent skulking in the stacks from time to time, he never produced a warrant. That was probably because it would have been much too much trouble to get the name of just one person who checked out one book about Communism. Even if, as in some smaller libraries, patrons wrote their names on cards, there was no list of library patrons coupled with the books they checked out. In other words, there really wasn't enough information in the library's files to do much damage to anyone's personal privacy.

The Arrival of Computers

All this changed with the arrival of computers. Computerized circulation systems automatically identify each book that is checked out by each library user. One of the things computers do best is to keep records, and they will record nearly every bit of information to which they have access. Unless they are commanded to forget, they will retain the information as long as the magnetic impulses survive. Even when records are deleted, they continue to exist and remain readable if you know how to look for them. Only when hard disks are scrubbed is the information really gone. The challenge that libraries face is, therefore, how to keep computers from doing what they do best.

Computers have proven themselves a wonderful gift to libraries, and none of us would ever want to go back to the days of card files. When we think of the vast collections of resources that even the smallest library can now access, we would never willingly go back to the old days. However, libraries have not made a clear distinction between patrons and resources. On the one hand, we have every right to revel in the joys of vast collections of resources. On the other hand, we do not need and cannot protect vast collections of patron information.

PERSONAL INFORMATION IN LIBRARY COMPUTERS

Librarianship as a profession rests on an ethical commitment. We believe that access to information is essential to every citizen. We believe that our role is to provide authoritative information regardless of personal prejudices or public pressure. Like physicians taking the Hippocratic Oath, we also make a commitment to do no harm. Because we believe that people need libraries, we must be sure that in seeking us out and availing themselves of our services, our users do not endanger their personal privacy.

Let us be very clear about patron information: we need only enough of it to get our books and DVDs back. This means essentially home address, home telephone number, and possibly an e-mail address if patrons prefer that we contact them electronically. We do not need workplace information or the other three telephone numbers at which the patron can sometimes be reached. We may also need a child's birth date and the name of a parent or guardian, but that's about it. We don't really need to know whether patrons own or rent their homes. We don't need driver's licenses, former addresses, citizenship information, employers, or mother's maiden names. Libraries may reasonably require proof of identity and home address when patrons are registering for new library cards. However, a staff member should review whatever documents are required, return them to their owner, and then forget them.

The Content of Circulation Records

If we are to protect the privacy of our library users, we must limit the information we collect. We must also delete the records of circulation transactions just as soon as our materials have been returned safely and accounts settled. Whenever we have the choice of collecting or not collecting information, we must decide in the negative. That means limiting the information we place in the notes fields of patron records because those notes are likely to become permanent. Even when the library system dies of old age and is replaced by a new system, that note you wrote, suggesting that you really don't believe Mary Smith returned a book as she claimed, has the potential to follow Mary from middle school through old age. For example, if one assumes that Mary is a public library user and remains in her hometown, it is likely that her library will simply update her patron record from time to time, leaving most of the data unchanged. If the libraries in Mary's region are members of a consortium and share a library automation system, Mary can move from school library to academic library to public library, all of which can access her centrally-stored patron record.

Many new technologies are at such an early stage of development that standards have not yet been established that will ultimately protect personal privacy. We have already discussed radio frequency identification tags (RFID), and later in this chapter we will be turning our attention to biometrics, especially fingerprinting. Keep your resolve. If you do not need information, do not collect it. Since we can keep track of most of our patrons most of the time, we will not invade their privacy by maintaining a database containing their fingerprints. The dangers involved would greatly outweigh the advantages. However, protecting patron privacy is not just about the things you won't do. We must be proactive, as well. If we see our patrons voluntarily surrendering information about themselves, we must let them know that they are placing themselves in danger.

The Proliferation of Library Records

Until the Patriot Act expanded the government's access to library records, it never occurred to most librarians just how many library records were available for their inspection. Times have changed since we kept only card files. Although the scope of this book is generally confined to electronic records, the line between paper and electronic library records is a very thin one. Once printed out, electronic records continue to exist, and a paper file copy comes into existence. For this reason, this section addresses the retention of library records in general and not exclusively electronic files. Let's look at some of the records that you may be keeping.

Patron Records

Patron information is typed into database forms that have fields for far more personal information than any library needs. When we see all those blank fields, our instinct is to ask the question and collect the information. After all, someday we may want to know where patrons work or when they were born. However, unless the patron is a child, there is absolutely no reason why any library needs to know their date of birth.

Checkout Information

Once an item has been returned, the library no longer needs to know who checked it out. Of course, fine records must be kept until fines are settled and sometimes libraries wait a few days in case other questions arise. This is reasonable since materials may be returned damaged or the patron used his credit card as a bookmark. Unfortunately, however, a number of systems do not erase a circulation transaction until the item is checked out again. Since many items do not circulate for years on end, this can mean that the information is available almost indefinitely.

It is important for you to see your library system, especially the circulation module, through the eyes of the people who use it. Who is permitted to view patron information? Can a student worker view the address and phone number of a fellow student or faculty member? Is this information available to anyone who works at the circulation desk, or is a special password required? If a password is required, is it known to all? Is it taped conveniently to each computer workstation? This is certainly not a good idea.

Other Circulation Transaction Records

Automated library systems maintain transaction logs of many different circulation activities. Library staff may not be aware of such logs, like the record of the times when a staff member overrides the system to allow an item to be checked out. Long after items are returned and the circulation record is erased, the override file may contain information on both the borrower and the items checked out. Library fines are another source of data for transaction logs. The amount of the fine is usually accompanied by the name or card number of the patron paying the fine and the items for which the fine was incurred. Make it a point to identify these logs and set up a schedule to regularly purge them from the system. Unfortunately, some systems do not alert you to the existence of these logs and thus make it difficult to delete them. Check your system manual for a list of log files and instructions for removing unwanted data. Other circulation records can include:

- **Records of access to electronic reserves.** These may be similar to other checkouts or they may be stored separately. Records may also be created when users access electronic resources stored in online subscription databases.
- **Records that support personalized circulation services.** Library systems usually allow patrons to access their own accounts, see which items are charged out and renew their own materials. They may also allow them to customize screens for their particular needs. Such customization may involve the creation of records that are identified with personal information.
- **Circulation usage statistics.** Most library systems keep track of the number of items patrons check out this month or this year.

It's not especially useful information but can't do much harm. However, this recordkeeping should never be linked to the actual items being counted.

Online Public Access Catalog (OPAC) Search Histories

Many OPACs include a feature that maintains a history of searches performed. It may be convenient for a user to be able to return to a search, but there is certainly no reason why the next user should have that search available. It is important to learn how many previous searches are kept available and what prompts the system to delete them.

Personalized OPAC Features

Newer OPACs allow users to personalize their searches and save them for future use. They can also help users fine-tune their searches by profiling their interests and providing other automated readers' advisory functions. Users can establish accounts that allow them to save search results and other information they discover, usually under their name or library card number. They should be informed; however, that there are potential privacy issues involved in leaving these breadcrumbs and it is a good idea for the library to delete them after a period of time.

Vendor-Readable Files

Some information can be read only by the library system vendor. Most of the information in these log files is generic and is not associated with specific patrons. However, it is important to find out exactly what information is contained in them and what is done with this information. Sometimes these log files are needed for statistical calculations and are important to the operation of both the circulation and report-generating modules. It can be very difficult to find out precisely what is in these files, but most library vendors are and all should be sensitive to library privacy concerns.

Backup Files

Every automated library system has a procedure for backing up data. In the event of a hard drive crash on the server, we naturally want to be able to restore the system without losing information. What we need, however, are yesterday's tapes, not backups made last year. Some libraries amass large collections of backups, each of which can provide vast quantities of circulation data. It might be argued that you should keep one older backup just in case the crash was due to a computer worm gradually eating away at disk contents, but this is about all you'll ever need.

Patron Reserves

Also known as holds, these records alert the staff that a patron is waiting for a book. In the case of bestsellers, dozens of patrons may be waiting for the same book. Once a waiting patron has checked out the item, the record of the hold should be deleted. Each automation system has a different way of treating these records and a few default to maintaining the information indefinitely. Again, it is essential for you to understand your own the system, and that you know how to change the settings.

E-mails to and from the library

Your library system probably has the capacity to generate e-mail messages. For example, it may be able to notify patrons that the books they requested are being held for them. Some libraries also e-mail overdue notices. Patrons may suggest new titles for the collection and these may be stored in the system as well. Libraries also make extensive use of e-mail unconnected with the automated library system. Since these messages contain personally identifiable information, it is important to have a procedure in place to purge them on a regular schedule. If e-mail messages are printed out, those paper files should be purged as well. All library records are available to law enforcement officers on fishing expeditions and paper records may be even more vulnerable than electronic ones.

Internet Sign-up Sheets

Many libraries maintain an informal system for determining who is entitled to the next available public access computer. Users simply write their names on a pad of paper. Each morning, a staff member begins a new page and writes the date at the top of the sheet. Used sheets are stored for later statistical tabulation. There is no need to list the last names of users on such a list. A stalker would have little difficulty discovering the name of an individual, since patrons simply draw a line through their names when a computer becomes available. Some libraries also keep the old sheets indefinitely. It is perhaps a five minute job to total the number of names on a sheet, record it, and discard the list. Yet, many libraries have hundreds of these sheets on file.

Public Computer Management Software

Many libraries require that public computer users have library cards. To enforce this policy, keep track of time limits, and otherwise manage computers more efficiently, they install special software programs. Computer management software can authenticate library computer users, facilitate reservations, and keep track of time, as well as manage security programs, printing, and statistical reporting. Patrons must usually type their library card numbers to be recognized as authorized users. Software programs vary but most retain a great deal of information about library users' computer habits. Although some argue that these are library records and therefore entitled to protection under state and local confidentiality legislation, this interpretation is not widely accepted. For this reason, settings should be configured to delete user information daily. If you are using such a software program, be sure that it is able to produce statistical reports without retaining personal data.

Employee Records

In your enthusiasm to protect your patrons, don't forget yourself and your own library employees. In a sense, library employees are twice as vulnerable as patrons because the library keeps track of them in two different ways. First, library staff members are almost always library users as well, and are enthusiastic consumers of library services. In fact, they have often chosen to work in the library because it has been part of their lives for so many years.

Additionally, libraries maintain personnel files on all their employees. These may be stored electronically or in traditional file folders. Often, the same information, the detailed record, not only of personnel actions but of private lives, is stored in both formats, resulting in much larger collections of information than existed before the computer age. Library staff members tend to be somewhat older than the average worker; in fact, many staff members have been working in the same library for twenty or even thirty years. It is not uncommon to find library personnel files that go back to the hire date. Each and every document has been retained, no matter how trivial. Although medical records should always be kept in a separate locked file, they are jumbled with all the others. Even the files of staff members who haven't worked in the library for years may still be gathering dust in the back of the drawer.

In a sense, personnel files can provide nearly complete biographies of the library's present and former staff. They might tell tales of financial crisis like bankruptcies and garnishments or chronicle battles with alcohol and drug dependency. They might reveal family problems, including ugly divorces, custody battles, delinquent children, or non-payment of child support.

The most personal aspects of individual lives often find their way into personnel files. Informal notes written by supervisors and colleagues may include unproven accusations or even character assassination. Although leave policies are somewhat less intrusive now than in years past, employers may require highly personal admissions to justify even brief absences. Although law enforcement agencies have sometimes demanded personnel records, a very real privacy threat is careless gossip. Clerical staff members could enjoy wiling away an otherwise boring afternoon by going through their colleagues' files. And they may not think twice when they receive an official sounding phone call asking about a staff member's sick-leave record. One reason that library administrators tend to hold on to personnel files is that, in the current litigious climate, they want to be prepared for possible employee lawsuits. While it is true that you must be prepared for such eventualities, it is often better to keep less, rather than more information. In general, very few personnel records should be held for more than three years, and those that are retained should be limited to formal or official documents like applications, compensation, pension and retirement records, tax forms, and formal evaluations. Library administrators should regularly purge files of the odds and ends that accumulate over time like absence excuses, memos, and staff conference notes. Medical information contained in electronic files should be purged regularly and, if necessary, converted to hard copy that can be kept in a separate locked cabinet. Most personnel files can be destroyed three years after the end of employment, but attorneys usually recommend that if a staff member's employment is terminated, his or her personnel file should be retained for seven years.

Other Data stored on Public and Staff Computers

At this point, it is unclear exactly what constitutes a library record. This term is important because most states have passed one or more statutes protecting the confidentiality of library records. Since library information is stored on both staff and public computers, it can be argued that everything on those computers meets the legal definition of "library record." Despite the existence of state and local laws, however, most library information is available to law enforcement agencies as a result of the Patriot Act. Remember, when you delete a file, it isn't really gone. The computer ignores it, but the FBI may not.

RECORDS THAT ARE NOT STORED IN THE LIBRARY

Since most library computers are able to communicate with remote servers and networks like those maintained by library consortia and database vendors, patrons may be unknowingly leaving electronic trails containing personally identifiable information. Their home libraries may be unaware that such trails exist, and may have little or no control over what information is stored in off-site computers. For example, library users searching the commercial databases to which their library subscribes probably leave behind a record of their search strategies and results, as well as the exact dates and times they conducted their searches.

Subscription Databases

If users log on to use these resources, that information is stored as well. It is available in log files and some vendors store a surprising amount of such data. Users may also be authenticated by going through a proxy server. Again, personal information is retained on these servers and librarians rarely know what is stored. In most cases, log records include IP addresses, patron types, and the databases that are accessed. However, vendors store data from actual searches as well. Public computer users are often required to login by typing their library card number or their student ID number. These numbers can easily be stored and associated with whatever information is sent and received including e-mail, word processing documents, and online conversations.

Databases may be available from large commercial vendors like ProQuest or directly from individual publishers. It's a good idea to check the privacy policies of any service that may be keeping data about your patrons. Vendors should display a link to their privacy policies on their Webs sites. Both database vendors and publishers collect information using cookies deposited on the library's computers. As we discussed in earlier chapters, cookies are small files sent out by websites and stored on the recipient's hard disk. When library users enter information into a search screen, the cookie attaches a small packet of identifying information to the query before it is transmitted to the database provider.

Extended Networks

Academic library computers are often part of a campus-wide computer network, and so network administrators are in a position to see what Web sites have been visited and what information has been sent and received. Public library computers may be part of local government networks, and once again, network administrators who know nothing of library privacy polices are in a position to regulate what information is stored in the system. Since the library is part of the network, you have a right to know how your county or campus IT department protects the privacy of computer users. Ask to see their privacy policy. If none exists, it's probable that little or no thought has been given to protecting user privacy.

If you were to peek into the inner sanctum of your IT department, you would probably find a number of young people who are quite new to their jobs. On a university campus, many would be student workers. In county and city government, relatively low salaries assure that most technical employees have little previous experience. These young people have been trained to maintain and troubleshoot computer hardware and software. However, it is probable that little effort has been made to acquaint them with the ethical issues that are a very real and very important part of their jobs.

Unless IT managers fully understand the importance of protecting the privacy of their users, you can reasonably expect frequent privacy violations. Some employers attempt to save money by hiring inexperienced young supervisors who are no more aware of the ethics of their profession than their young staff members. Talk with your IT manager and make it clear how important you consider the privacy of your library computer users. Stress that the personal information contained in library records should not be available to the young student worker who wants to see how many overdue books his roommate has checked out. Like hacking into other computers, attempts to gain access to library records should be punishable by suspension or even termination.

Choosing Security-Conscious Vendors

Libraries spend large sums of money on automated library systems and periodical databases. This means that they can exert their power of the purse when dealing with vendors. It's a good idea to find out about your vendors' privacy policies. In fact, they should be readily available on their Web sites. If you don't see them, e-mail the vendor and request a copy. Each policy will be somewhat different, but it should be clear that the vendor collects only the information needed for statistical and billing purposes. It should be clear that personal information like a login ID is not associated with searches.

Personal information stored in library records may be at risk for a variety of reasons. It may be accessed by government agencies or it may be vulnerable to hackers who break into the system illegally and extract data. In the case of such intruders, the library itself may be at fault because it has not taken adequate security precautions. However, library automation vendors can also be at fault if they do not keep up with current security issues and protect their systems with state-of-the art technology. When choosing a library system, be sure to talk with both sales representatives and their library references to determine whether security is an important concern. Ask how often the system is updated since new threats are constantly appearing on the horizon. Vendors should be prepared to respond to emergencies with frequent security updates.

LIBRARY RECORDS AND NEW TECHNOLOGIES

In every business and every government agency, it is important that people are who they say they are. In libraries, we daily encounter patrons who have borrowed someone else's library card. Perhaps they have overdue charges on their own card or possibly an outstanding fine. A resident of a neighboring town may not want to pay a nonresident fee and so uses her friend's card. A child borrows a card from an older brother so he can use the Internet. In general, such subterfuge is not a big problem for the library. However, it can be frustrating when a tearful teenager pleads innocent to losing half a dozen library books and DVDs. She was sure the friend who used her card would return them.

Fingerprinting

As we mentioned earlier in this book, a few libraries are so determined to identify their patrons that they have installed systems that substitute fingerprints for library cards. This means that they produce a different kind of patron record, a record that is intimately and permanently connected with the patron. When patrons check out items, their fingerprints are scanned. The resulting image is converted to a numeric equivalent, and matched against other fingerprints stored in a large database. For example, Micro Librarian Systems, providers of the Eclipse integrated library system, has developed IdentiKit, a product that replaces library cards with fingerprints. Ultra-Scan Corporation sells the Touch & Go! system, which also substitutes data from patron index fingers for library cards. The U.S. Biometrics Corporation is still another library vendor of fingerprint recognition technology. At this point, only a few libraries in the United States have adopted these systems, but they are widely used in Great Britain. Some libraries have installed fingerprint scanners at the checkout desk; others mount them at each public computer workstation.

Weighing the Arguments

Arguments rage about precisely how large a threat these systems pose to personal privacy. Vendors say that data cannot be used to reconstruct fingerprints (as, for example, a Hollywood-style evil doer who wears rubber gloves embossed with someone else's fingerprints). They also say that library fingerprint data cannot be used in data mining projects, or matched with prints in FBI or other law enforcement databases. However, experts say that recreating actual fingerprints from numeric information would be difficult but possible. And matching numeric data against biometric files in other databases is both possible and not especially difficult.

Experts also agree that almost any computer system, no matter how sophisticated, can be hacked. Take, for example, the credit card companies from which thousands of credit card numbers and other personal information have been stolen. Their annual computer security budgets are staggeringly large, and yet neither the money nor the high-end technology they buy can prevent break-ins. Library budgets are comparatively meager; we can never hope to buy the kind of protection that large businesses enjoy. We are, therefore, more vulnerable to intrusion and even the tech savvy high school student who wants to erase his overdue fines stands a good chance of breaking into the system.

The best way we can keep our data safe from intruders is simply to limit the data we collect.

Current Limitations of Biometrics

Experts point out that fingerprinting is not 100 percent reliable. Accustomed as we are to the kind of super technology found in Mission Impossible movies, we assume that technology can do things that are impossible at present. Although computers are at their best when it comes to massive calculating projects, they can be easily confused and thwarted by simple complications easily understood by humans.

Earlier in this book, we mentioned the case of Portland lawyer Brandon Mayfield, who was arrested in the 2004 Madrid train bombing. The FBI matched his twenty-two year old fingerprint to one found at the scene of the crime. It was later discovered that the print belonged not to Mayfield but to an Algerian terrorist. Probably, a combination of circumstances including the age of the print, differences between two generations of biometric technology, and the limitations of crime scene investigation, were responsible for the error. However, it is important to remember that law enforcement officials did not consider any of these possibilities when they arrested an innocent man who had nothing in his past to point to terrorist interests or activities.

Imagine a school or public library collecting fingerprints. Perhaps little Johnny's hands are dirty or Sally Green has a paper cut on her index finger. Both situations can confuse scanners and result in failures to read prints correctly. Fingerprint recognition technology is not a magic bullet that can eliminate the problem of patrons misrepresenting themselves. It is a tool that is effective in some situations but not in others—and it threatens our users' privacy. We have other tools at our disposal that are also flawed but they don't threaten privacy. When faced with a decision, we must choose to do the best we can under the circumstances, using the most effective tools. Even more important, however, we have an obligation to "do no harm."

People First, then Efficiency

Enthusiasm over new technologies seems to give rise to a kind of one-track thinking. If computers are so powerful, we assume they can fix everything and, in fact, they do fix a surprising number of problems in our world. Just because it is possible to do something, however, it may not be necessary to do it. In fact the real question may be why are we doing this at all? Compromising the privacy of all our patrons because some do not follow our rules just doesn't make sense. It is clearly overkill. We are not law enforcement officers, and playing Dick Tracy in our libraries is not consistent with our professional ethics.

Libraries are places where anonymity is highly valued. We have always understood that our users have a right to carry out some parts of their lives in private. We caution staff members that they are not to discuss the Alcoholics Anonymous book that Mrs. Jones checked out or Mr. Brown's sudden interest in bankruptcy law. Yet these bits of gossip cannot begin to compare with fingerprinting as an invasion of one's private self.

Knowing Our Limitations

Libraries have very tight budgets. Our staffs are always struggling to keep up with current trends and we generally do not have funds to hire highly sophisticated technicians. Most library staff members are somewhat skilled at Microsoft Word, have created a spreadsheet or two with Excel, and can perform most of the important tasks in the library automation system. We lack the technical expertise to fully understand the weaknesses of our systems. We are vulnerable to vendors who tell us that their solutions are foolproof, that they have solved all the problems. Yet, we know that this is never the case. Library systems continue to have "bugs" and since libraries are a relatively small market, vendors themselves are unable to pay top dollar for technical expertise. If the NSA, which can contract for the most sophisticated technical projects ever designed, can make such drastic errors as the one previously described, certainly our vendors and our staffs can't be expected to do better.

SUMMING IT UP

As you make decisions about what kinds of personal data your library will collect and how long it will be kept, it's a good idea to keep the following basic guidelines clearly in mind:

- Know exactly what information you are collecting. What about those old file cabinets in the basement? Why are you keeping those old interlibrary loan forms? Do you really need those old e-mail messages?
- Find out how personally identifiable data can be associated with your customers' information-seeking activities. What does your OPAC do with patron searches?
- Retain the least personal information necessary to meet your goals. The library needs contact information and little else.
- Don't keep any information in case you may need it down the road. Of course, we occasionally become confused when we have two patrons named Mary Smith, but the confusion can be resolved

without collecting more personal information about each and every library user.

- Be specific about how long you will keep data and delete data; set up a schedule. As we all know, tasks don't get done if they are not clearly assigned.
- Restrict access to all library records and be sure all library staff members know the rules. Even pages and work-study students need to understand basic privacy issues.
- Tell your customers what information the library keeps about them and their information-seeking activities. It is helpful to keep a brochure or fact sheet readily available at the circulation desk.

Most of the information that libraries retain about their patrons is related to circulation functions. Because the circulation staff may consist of clerks and students supervised by a paraprofessional, they may understand less about privacy issues than other staff members. They might think that nobody would want this information and wonder what all the fuss is about. Library administrators should find ways to put privacy issues into terms that the circulation staff can understand. Give them concrete examples of people who are hurt when their personal information is shared. Stalkers, of course, make more dramatic examples, but privacy may mean your nosy neighbor who has no right to know how old you are or that your marriage is on the rocks. You're not a terrorist because you read a book on terrorism, nor are you a pervert for reading a sexually explicit book. Privacy may be a complex ethical, philosophical, and political concept, but basic issues can be understood by everyone.

CHAPTER 8

The Patriot Act Quandary: Obeying the Law and Protecting Library Users

In March 2006, just before some sections were about to expire, President George Bush signed into law the Reauthorization of the USA Patriot Act, which fell far short of the expectations of librarians and other defenders of civil liberties. All sixteen sections that included sunset clauses, (sections scheduled to expire in 2005), were renewed. Although some small changes were made to the sections affecting libraries, the Act continues to limit the library's ability to safeguard the privacy rights of its users. At this writing, it remains possible for federal law enforcement agencies to obtain library records without meeting the traditional standard of probable cause, or obtaining court orders as required by the Constitution.

As you may be aware, Attorney General John Ashcroft referred to librarians who were concerned about the provisions of the Patriot Act as hysterics. At a speech delivered to the American Restaurant Association, he quipped that "According to ... breathless reports and baseless hysteria, some have convinced the [American Library Association] that under the bipartisanly enacted Patriot Act, the FBI is not fighting terrorism; instead, agents are checking how far you've gotten in the latest Tom Clancy novel. Now, you may have thought with all of this hysteria and hyperbole that something had to be wrong. Do we at the Justice Department really care what you are reading? No. The law enforcement community has no interest in your reading habits. Tracking reading habits would betray our high regard for the First Amendment, and even if someone in government wanted to do so, it would represent an impossible workload and a waste of law enforcement resources" (Ashcroft 2003).

Unfortunately, though the Attorney General got a laugh at the expense of the library community, the accuracy of his comments left much to be desired. Former ALA President Carla Hayden expressed her concerns when she responded "We are deeply concerned that the Attorney General should be so openly contemptuous of those who seek to defend our Constitution. Rather than ask the nations' librarians and Americans nationwide to 'just trust him,' Ashcroft could allay concerns by releasing aggregate information about the number of libraries visited using the expanded powers created by the USA Patriot Act." Hayden stressed that the danger to libraries and library patrons is very real. "The Patriot Act gives law enforcement unprecedented power of surveillance-including easy access to library records with minimal judicial oversight" (American Library Association 2003).

UNDERSTANDING THE PATRIOT ACT

Officially titled "The Uniting and Strengthening America by Providing Appropriate Tools Required to Intercept and Obstruct Terrorism Act of 2001," the Patriot Act was first signed into law on October 26, 2001, following closely upon the national tragedy of 9/11. Many members of Congress freely admitted that they did not have time to read the voluminous text, but the climate of public opinion propelled the Patriot Act through the House, the Senate, and the White House with almost unprecedented speed.

The Foreign Intelligence Surveillance Act of 1978 (FISA)

Since the provisions of the Patriot Act that affect libraries are amendments to or reinterpretations of FISA, it may be helpful to summarize FISA's key provisions. Perhaps most importantly, it authorizes the government to conduct surveillance activities against foreign powers in certain situations without first obtaining a court order. By "foreign power," the Act means foreign governments, or any factions of foreign governments not substantially composed of U.S. persons. Activities that do not require court orders may only be conducted when there is no substantial likelihood of intercepting communication to which a United States person is a party.

The Patriot Act amended FISA in order to extend the authority to conduct electronic surveillance and physical searches to what are referred to as lone wolves, individuals who are not necessarily under the control of a foreign government. A lone wolf is a non-US person who engages in or prepares for international terrorism. The FISA court is authorized to issue electronic surveillance and physical search orders without being required to find a connection between the lone wolf and a foreign government or terrorist group.

FISA specifically prohibits surveillance activities on U.S. persons (in other words citizens, lawfully admitted permanent resident aliens, and corporations incorporated in the U.S.) without a court order obtained from the FISA Court. This court, located within the Department of Justice (DOJ) headquarters building, is staffed by eleven judges appointed by the Chief Justice of the United States to serve seven-year terms. The Act directs the FISA Court to issue a warrant only when federal police agencies can meet the standard of probable cause. This means that the recent wiretapping of U.S. citizens and interception of e-mail messages constituted a clear violation of FISA. The government never approached the FISA Court for a court order, and it could never have met the "probable cause" requirement.

Few Changes in the Reauthorized Act

The Patriot Act of 2001 eliminated much of the privacy protection Americans enjoyed under FISA. However, many librarians believed that when legislators had an opportunity to look at the Act more closely under less stressful conditions, they would see that some of its provisions violated basic American values, and were at odds with the Constitution as it has long been interpreted. Unfortunately, the changes in the reauthorized Act are so few and so limited that the predicament that librarians face remains essentially unchanged.

Of the sixteen sections that included sunset clauses, fourteen were made permanent. Section 215 (Access to Records and other Items) and Section 206 (Roving Surveillance Authority) were extended. Before looking into the ways in which the Act has been interpreted by law enforcement agencies and the impact that those interpretations have had on libraries, it is important to understand what the Act now includes.

Almost all discussion within the library community focuses on three sections. The word library was never actually mentioned in the original 2001 USA Patriot Act. This does not however, lessen the threat. Library records come under the definition of business records and as such are fully covered. Although there are other issues that concern librarians, these three sections of the Patriot Act clearly impact the ability of libraries to carry out their missions.

USA Patriot Act Section 206: Roving Surveillance Authority

This section discusses the government's right to intercept communications in a FISA investigation. It allows investigating agencies to obtain a single court order to monitor the communications of a person at any location or using any device, including e-mail and other Internet communications. Such an order is so broad that it may be presented at any time and to any provider of electronic services. Since libraries provide public computer access to their patrons, they fall under the Act's definition of an Internet service provider (ISP).

In the 2006 revisions to the Patriot Act, libraries were excluded from the definition of "service provider" under certain circumstances. To quote from the Act "A library ... is not a wire or electronic communication service provider for purposes of this section, unless the library is providing the services defined in section 2510(15) ('electronic communication service') of this title (S. 2271)." Although the exact meaning of this section will have to be defined in future court opinions, it would appear that when public Internet use is involved, the library may become a service provider as defined in Section 2510(15). (USA PATRIOT and Terrorism Prevention Reauthorization Act of 2005).

Patriot Act Section 215: Access to Records under FISA

This section focuses on the business records provision of the FISA. It allows FBI agents to obtain "any tangible thing" in carrying out a search, including books, records, papers, floppy disks, data tapes, computers, and hard drives. Under FISA, agents were only permitted to obtain car rental records, hotel records, storage locker records, and common carrier records for a foreign agent. The Patriot Act expands the scope to include virtually any records of any business or organization. FBI agents may request the FISA Court to issue an "ex parte" secret court order when the records requested are part of an investigation into terrorism or foreign espionage. The agent only needs to specify that the records are sought for an authorized investigation without providing any further particulars.

The Demise of Probable Cause

This clause is of particular concern to civil libertarians because the standard for obtaining court orders prior to the Patriot Act was always the probability that the target was an agent of a foreign power, a condition usually referred to as probable cause. Section 215 requires only a vague and undefined relationship to an investigation.

In addition, federal agents may target U.S. citizens, just as long as the investigation is not based exclusively on their First Amendment-related activities. Again, the new standard goes far beyond FISA. Despite considerable discussion in both the House and the Senate, this standard remained unchanged in the 2006 reauthorization. The FISA court may not require any more justification than the fact that there is an ongoing investigation. The revised wording of the 2006 Reauthorization does, however, require that the FBI describe the items it is demanding under Section 215, so the library can limit the records it surrenders to those listed on the warrant.

Gag Order

The recipient of a court order, in our case the library, may not notify anyone that a warrant has been served. This means that the library may not notify the patron under suspicion, or the press. Neither may the library reveal the nature of the records surrendered. Since only FBI agents and authorized U.S. attorneys were able to appear before the FISA court, this meant that neither the library nor anyone else served with a FISA order could challenge the order.

The 2006 revision includes a clause giving recipients of court orders the right to consult their attorneys. This solves one major problem for libraries since the original Act was unclear and the gag order could be interpreted as including legal counsel. In addition, it allows recipients of Section 215 orders limited opportunity to challenge them. Although libraries and other recipients may not appeal to the FISA court directly, they may appeal to the Petition Review Panel of the court. However, the panel can only rule on whether the order is lawful, not on whether it is overbroad or otherwise in error. The revisions passed in 2006 also allow recipients to challenge the gag clause after one year has passed, unless there is reason to believe that such a disclosure could endanger national security or otherwise endanger an individual or investigation. The government's certification that such a situation exists is all the proof that is needed.

Patriot Act Section 505: Miscellaneous National Security Authorities

The focus of this section, as far as the library community is concerned, is the power of the FBI to issue National Security Letters (NSLs) to communications service providers. These NSLs are administrative subpoenas that can be used to compel service providers to turn over subscriber information, billing information, and electronic communication transaction records.

National Security Letters and Libraries

Because libraries provide Internet access to the public, the 2001 Act could be interpreted as applying to libraries; and there is evidence that libraries have been served with NSLs. Unlike FISA court orders, however, NSLs can be issued with no judicial review. The FBI is permitted to issue them on its own authority and need not seek approval from the FISA Court. Agents are *not* required to demonstrate probable cause, and the records being sought need not be evidence of a crime. All that is needed is a vague statement that the records sought are relevant to an ongoing investigation into international terrorism or espionage.

In various public statements, the Bush administration has implied that the issuance of NSLs is not a common occurrence. Like the Attorney General's put down of the library community described at the beginning of this chapter, the government would like to make it appear that the letters are issued only in extraordinary circumstances and ordinary citizens have nothing to fear. However, a 2007 audit by the Justice Department's Inspector General discovered that FBI offices did not even generate accurate counts of the national security letters they issued, omitting a large number of letters from their reports. Those inaccurate numbers, in turn, were used as the basis for required reports to Congress (Solomon and Gellman 2007, A01). The Inspector General found that in 2003, 39,000 letters were issued. The number rose in 2004 to about 56,000 declined in 2005 to 47,000. In all, 143,074 letters were issued over the three-year period. However, the FBI told Congress in 2005 that the combined total for 2003 and 2004 was 9,254 (U.S. Department of Justice 2007).

Libraries served with NSLs may not even disclose their existence or the fact that records were surrendered in response to them. Patrons may not be told that their records were given to the FBI or that they are subjects of an FBI investigation. Instead of softening requirements, the 2006 Patriot Act revisions establish a penalty of up to five years in prison for violating a NSL gag order.

What are Traditional Library Services?

The 2006 revision of Section 505 was, to some extent, an attempt to appease librarians and library supporters. However, when one looks closely at the new wording, it is unclear whether the changes will have real impact. The revised wording appears to protect libraries from the issuance of NSLs under some circumstances, but not others. It makes a distinction between traditional and nontraditional library services, stating that libraries cannot be served with NSLs if the records in question were created in the course of the library's traditional activities.

Judges, attorneys, and juries are already busy attempting to interpret this wording. Does it mean that records of circulation transactions may not be obtained through an NSL, but patron e-mail may? If the patron e-mail is a reference question addressed to the library, is it exempt because reference is a traditional service? One might reasonably answer yes to all of the above questions. However, with gag orders in place for at least one year, libraries will have little or no voice in defining what traditional services are.

One might even wonder whether the word traditional excludes the use of computers altogether. As we have discovered, some members of our communities still harbor objections to computers in libraries. Circulation and interlibrary loan (ILL) are certainly traditional library services, but they are no longer performed in the traditional manner. Most library transactions, as well as those of library consortia, occur electronically. If an FBI agent interprets electronic ILL records as nontraditional, there seems to be no provision for disputing this assumption.

Challenging NSLs

In the event that libraries are served with NSLs, the 2006 Patriot Act revisions allow them to challenge requests in a U.S. District Court. These courts are authorized to set aside letters if they determine that they are unreasonable, oppressive, or otherwise unlawful. Indeed, many of them do appear to be unlawful. Despite the relative ease with which the FBI may legally issue NSLs, there is mounting evidence that the agency has repeatedly violated the law.

The 2007 Justice Department Inspector General's audit, described above, was limited to just 77 case files in four FBI field offices. Sixty percent of files examined contained one or more policy violation (U.S. Department of Justice 2007). In a sampling of 293 national security letters between 2003 and 2005, auditors found 22 possible breaches of internal FBI and Justice Department regulations, some of which constitute potential violations of law. The FBI itself had already identified 26 additional violations in this group of letters (Solomon and Gellman 2007). FBI agents failed to cite an authorized investigation, claimed "exigent" circumstances that did not exist, and did not have adequate documentation to justify issuing some letters.

In some cases, the FBI obtained full credit reports using letters that could lawfully be used to obtain only summary information. In other cases, third parties such as telephone companies, banks, and Internet providers supplied detailed personal information about customers that could not legally be released (Ibid). In addition to the sample group, the audit found 700 letters that were signed by officials at FBI headquarters who were not authorized to sign NSLs, many of which were sent to three telephone companies. Furthermore, the report complains that, because the FBI does not retain copies of signed NSLs, the Inspector General's office was unable to conduct a comprehensive audit (U.S. Department of Justice 2007). In other words, the FBI retains the information it collects in response to national security letters—in some cases information to which it has no legal right—but deliberately obscures the record of its own involvement.

Let's return, however, to the powers of U.S. District Courts when responding to challenges. A court is not permitted to set aside an order if by doing so, it would affect national security or interfere with an ongoing investigation. All the government needs do is to certify that this is the case, and the letter stands. The government may declare that the letter affects international relations or endangers human safety. Again, there is no recourse. If a recipient violates the terms of an NSL, the government can go to a U.S. District Court to get an enforcement order, the violation of which is punishable as contempt of court.

THE LIBRARY'S RESPONSE TO THE PATRIOT ACT

Government demands for library records arise from a variety of situations and are not always related to the Patriot Act. For example, local law enforcement officials may demand library records when investigating local crimes that have nothing to do with the war on terror. Take, for example, the case of Library Director Michele Reutty of

Hasbrouck Heights, New Jersey, who demanded that the police obtain a subpoena before she would release the identity of a patron who supposedly borrowed a particular book. The patron in question had allegedly threatened a twelve-year-old child. Although the allegations had nothing to do with terror and no emergency situation was anticipated (providing ample time to obtain the statute-mandated paperwork), Reutty was threatened with suspension by members of the Hasbrouck Heights Borough Council, and was ultimately pressured to resign her position. The Patriot Act reinforced the belief that failing to comply with demands of local law enforcement agencies is un-American.

The Post-9/11 World

We are currently living at a time when respect for personal privacy is at low ebb. The warnings of our founding fathers and the Constitutional safeguards against unwonted government intervention in the private lives of citizens are going largely unheeded. Heightened fear levels following 9/11, the perceived dangers of the Internet, and a generalized sense of insecurity have caused people to forget the dangers of a big brother government. It is ironic that the 9/11 Commission Report equates literacy with freedom. The report states that "the United States should rebuild the scholarship, exchange, and library programs that reach out to young people and offer them knowledge and hope" (Airoldi 2006). Achieving the library's mission requires open access to information, while post-9/11 legislation may threaten that access.

Libraries and Law Enforcement

Because the line between Patriot Act-related pressure on libraries and more traditional demands from law enforcement agencies has become such a thin one, this chapter discusses the relationship of libraries to all law enforcement agencies, even when suspected terrorism may not be involved. We also limit our discussion of the Patriot Act to those sections that are of special concern to libraries. It is important to remember that neither libraries nor most librarians oppose the entire Act. Since it addresses the very real need to halt international terrorism, most of us support our government's intent, but object to specific methods of implementation.

An FBI Visit Before 9/11

Perhaps the clearest way of describing our present dilemma is to imagine a library visit by an FBI agent before 9/11 and before the passage of the Patriot Act. Such visits did occur, and those occasions are written indelibly on the memories of some experienced librarians. In most cases a law enforcement agency, frequently the FBI, was investigating an individual who was thought to be involved in illegal activity. During the Cold War era, that activity usually revolved around fears of Communists. An agent usually arrived with a subpoena or search warrant. If one or the other was not produced, we were coached by the ALA to remain adamant; most of the time we got our way. Although fishing expeditions were not unknown, the FBI was usually interested in one particular library user and the library materials that he or she had checked out.

Fortunately, during those years libraries kept very little information that could be useful to such inquiries. The old card systems made it possible to begin with a book and identify the patrons who checked it out. However, it was usually not possible to begin with the patron and discover his or her reading habits. Libraries have always been reluctant to part with any patron records but, in general, official visits produced very little information of value.

The Role of Technology

Even before 9/11, technology was taking center stage in intelligence work. Traditional surveillance work was being replaced by satellites and computer applications. In the last few years, however, we have witnessed government agencies spending more and more money on the still unproven data mining systems that analyze or mine vast quantities of personal data to identify the bad guys. The rationale goes something like this: if the government just had access to all the bits and pieces of information that are out there waiting to be harvested, it would be possible to track down any number of miscreants who now go free.

Consider for a moment Eliot Ness, that nemesis of organized crime. How much more efficiently he could have tracked down mobsters like Al Capone if he had access to their telephone conversations, their e-mail correspondence, and the clear trail they blazed as they were moving about the country, paying by credit card for their meals, transportation, and machine guns. Certainly, had Ness been able to obtain a court order for such records, his job would have been a lot easier. A problem arises, however, when no distinction is made between the records of suspected criminals and those of thousands of innocent citizens. When FBI agents visit today's library, they are likely to want much more data on many library users, even entire hard disks.

The Connecticut Connection

In the past, the law enforcement agency tracked down individuals when there was probable cause that they had committed crimes. Probable cause is no longer the usual standard for demanding information. Because both FISA orders and NSLs are accompanied by gag orders, we know very little about the libraries that have been required to comply with Patriot Act-related demands. However, we do know about one group of librarians who decided to fight back.

It was alleged by the government that on February 15, 2005, in a small, un-named public library in Connecticut, a patron used a computer to send some kind of terrorist-related threat. The FBI tracked the message to what it believed to be its source, a particular library computer. It then sent an NSL to the library and to the Library Connection, Inc., the Connecticut library consortium to which the library belongs.

The Challenge

It has recently been revealed that the use of National Security Letters was far more extensive than the public was led to believe. In 2005 alone, more than 19,000 letters were issued seeking 47,000 pieces of information (Solomon and Gellman 2007). In June 2007, an internal FBI audit conducted by the Justice Department's Inspector General Glenn A. Fine sampled just 77 case files. The audit found 48 violations of regulations, some of which violated the law. Most of the letters targeted telecommunications companies, and the audit report did not single out libraries (Solomon and Gellman 2007).

When an NSL letter is received, the recipient is prohibited from publicly discussing its existence. When Librarian George Christian received one such letter, he brought it to the executive Board of the Library Connection, which in turn contacted the American Civil Liberties Union (ACLU). This act required considerable bravery, since the Patriot Act, as it was approved in 2001, was unclear as to whether recipients of NSLs could seek help from attorneys. In August 2005, the ACLU filed a request to lift the NSL gag order on the grounds that it violated the librarians' First Amendment rights.

In September 2005, a judge ruled in favor of the librarians; but the decision was appealed by the FBI. The gag order was, therefore, left in place until a higher court ruled on the case. A stand-off between the librarians and the FBI followed, while the government continued to investigate the case, and the Library Connection continued to refuse to surrender its records. Because the librarians were still gagged, they were unable to testify before Congress when the Patriot Act was up for renewal. They were also unable to accept the University of Illinois's annual Robert B. Downs Intellectual Freedom Award. Judith Krug, Executive Director of the Freedom to Read Foundation, accepted the award in their stead saying "I am rather appalled that our country's laws silence John Doe and require him to remain anonymous for standing by his professional ethics, for standing up for the principle that it is nobody's business what you read, or listen to, or look at in the library but yours" (Cowan 2006). It was only in April 2006 that the government dropped its case against the gag order. Since the identity of the librarians had actually been revealed some time earlier on the District Court's Web site, this had little meaning. It was not until May of that year that librarians were allowed to publicly discuss the details of the case.

Eventually, the government closed the investigation entirely, having concluded that the case was without merit. On August 2, 2006 the Supreme Court ordered that court records related to the case be fully disclosed. In interviews with the press, George Christian made it clear that the intention of the Library Connection was not to hinder the investigation, and records would have been turned over immediately had it received a search warrant or subpoena. "As an American, I am embarrassed that our government would go to such extremes to stifle free and open debate and keep non-sensitive information from the public. It undermines the trust the public has in libraries when government agents can force librarians to turn over private patron information without any kind of court order or evidence of wrongdoing" (Supreme Court 2006). However the final word on the case may have been spoken by Ann Beeson, the ACLU lawyer representing the librarians. "The revised law provides almost no protection whatsoever for libraries; It's virtually meaningless" (Cowan 2006).

The Deming Case

Joan Airoldi recounts another encounter with the FBI in her article appearing in *Library Administration & Management* (Airoldi 2006).

While reading the book *Bin Laden: The Man Who Declared War on America*, by Yossef Bodansky, checked out from the Deming branch of the Whatcom County Library in Washington state, a patron experienced a shock. In the margin of one page was written "If the things I'm doing is considered a crime, then let history be a witness that I am a criminal. Hostility toward America is a religious duty and we hope to be rewarded by God." The patron immediately placed a call to the FBI.

In June 2004, an FBI agent visited the Deming library and asked the library to provide the names of the patrons who had borrowed the book. What apparently had not occurred to the FBI was that the passage was almost a direct quote from a statement made by Bin Laden in a 1998 interview. The FBI request was forwarded through the library's management to the library district's attorney, who told the FBI that the information could be released only in response to a court order.

The Board of Trustees

At a special meeting of the Whatcom County Library System Board of Trustees, attended by their attorney, the board passed a resolution to quash the subpoena based in part on the fact that "There was no substantial connection between the information sought and the subject of the grand jury proceedings, because of an inadequate foundation for inquiry." The Board used the opportunity to restate its right "to disseminate information freely, confidentially, and without the chilling effect of disclosure" (Airoldi 2006). The resolution also made it clear that the information being requested was stored not by the County Library but at the Bellingham Public Library. In response, the grand jury ruled to withdraw the subpoena and dismiss the motion to quash as moot without prejudice.

When the Library System released the information to the public, the response was generally positive. One patron wrote, "Know that there are many 'senior citizen' library card holders like me with an interest in world developments as well as multicultural, political, and social commentary including dissent, who, sadly have not used their cards for same since the Patriot Act was passed. I applaud your going public with the incident you described" (Airoldi 2006). Again, the library system made it clear that it was not trying to hinder government officials in the performance of their duty. Attorney Deborra Garrett explained, "it's not that privacy rights can never be invaded, but if the government seeks to invade them, the government has to show that it's absolutely necessary to do that." (Airoldi 2006).

Public Library Computers

Yesterday's FBI visit was usually confined to library circulation records, few of which were useful for anything but tracking down borrowers with overdue books. Today's library offers far more attractive pickings for law enforcement agencies. Of particular interest are our public computers, which are used by millions of library patrons every day. Depending on how computers are set up and protected, law enforcement agencies may discover a bonanza of e-mail messages, Web site visits, cookies, chat room conversations, search strategies, and personal information submitted to a variety of Web sites and Web portals.

If we are being honest, we must admit that library computers can be very attractive to terrorists and other criminally-minded individuals. During the Clinton era, I worked in a library that maintained hundreds of public computers. One day, several agents wearing black raincoats arrived with the news that someone had sent a death threat to Hillary Clinton from one of our computers. This type of situation presents a terribly difficult judgment call for librarians. Is someone, in this case Hillary Clinton, actually in danger? Is it reasonable to demand a search warrant under such circumstances? As it happened, the message had been quickly intercepted by the authorities, and there was time to obtain a warrant during normal business hours. Still, the library was made to feel obstructionist and unpatriotic for asking for a warrant.

The Profusion of Personal Information

As it turned out, the library had an amazing collection of information for the FBI. The e-mail included data that precisely identified the computer on which the message was composed and the precise second it was sent. Library surveillance cameras time-stamped video footage, once again precisely to the second. It was actually possible to watch a young man sitting at a public computer, calmly typing the very message that was sent to the White House. Both hard drive and video tape were confiscated; and it took quite a bit of convincing to prevent the agents from removing the computer on which the message was typed, the hard drive on the network server, and components of the surveillance system.

State vs. Federal Authority

Many states have passed laws that protect library records, but the federal Patriot Act trumps state law in most cases. Legal authorities disagree on whether or not state laws protect data stored on public computers. It has not been clearly established whether this data can be considered an extension of the library's registration and circulation records. Some librarians and attorneys argue that personally identifiable library information is stored in public computers, and this information can be used to link patrons' online activities with data in library records. This is especially true in libraries that use computer management software that requires patrons to type in their library card numbers. So far, however, it appears that the Patriot Act carries considerably more weight than state and local legislation.

Libraries will continue to oppose the provisions of the Patriot Act that endanger the privacy of the millions of Americans who depend on them for information and recreation. In the words of ALA President Michael Gorman, "Although most of the moderate, reasonable, and Constitutional reforms we sought were not included in the reauthorization bill, our work on restoring privacy and civil liberties to library users is not over. We will continue to argue for a more stringent standard for Section 215 orders—one that requires the FBI to limit its search of library records to individuals who are connected to a terrorist or suspected of a crime. We will also seek the addition of a provision allowing recipients of Section 215 or 505 orders to pose a meaningful challenge to the 'gag' order that prevents them from disclosing the fact that they have received such an order" (Gorman 2006).

PREPARING FOR THE WORST

No librarian wants to be caught unprepared in the event of a Patriot Act-related demand. This can become the beginning of a nightmare that continues for months and even years. What should librarians do to prepare themselves for a visit from the FBI or their local law enforcement agency? The following is a good list, though by no means a comprehensive one, to get you started.

Discuss the Patriot Act at Staff Meetings

The whole staff should be regularly updated on privacy procedures. Remember that any law enforcement visitors will arrive at the circulation desk. Too often library administrators simply instruct clerical and paraprofessional staff to turn the matter over to them. However, this formulaic response is not enough. From a practical perspective, the demand may come at night or on a weekend when no administrators are on duty. Even more important, staff members need to understand the issues involved and why it is important that they play their parts correctly. We are all better able to do our jobs when we know why we are doing it. Staff members may also wonder why the library is being unhelpful to law enforcement agencies. They may even think the library's response is un-American and communicate their concerns to community members. To be effective, the library must speak with one voice.

Work Closely with the Library Board

Be sure your board has a good, firm grounding in the privacy issues that concern libraries. Be sure they understand that concerns about the Patriot Act are a logical outgrowth of other library issues. It's a good idea to begin with your state law governing the confidentiality of library records (such laws exist in forty-eight states). Since they are complex, board members will need time to digest and discuss the information, and it is important that such discussion occupy a high priority. Of course, they must approve budget expenditures and get through their other routine business, but they also have an obligation to become fully informed if they are to protect the privacy of the library's users. If there are differences of opinion on the board, it is a good idea to resolve them before the FBI arrives at your doorstep. As new board members are appointed, make it clear to them that they may be in a position in which they must make critical decisions. The arrival of new board members is a good opportunity for the rest of the board to revisit the topic.

Pay a Visit to Your Library Attorneys

Your library probably shares attorneys with your city, county, university, or school district. They have little time to delve into the issues of particular concern to libraries, so make sure that they are aware of the library's concerns about the Patriot Act. Forewarn them that libraries across the country are receiving demands for records and explain your reservations about responding to such requests. Encourage them to review the case law surrounding the Act and become familiar with the legal issues involved. Use your reference skills to put together a packet of articles for them. To make sure that they do their homework, you might suggest that one or more attorneys make a brief presentation to the library staff and/or the board of trustees.

Attend Programs and Workshops to Obtain New Information

The law surrounding the Patriot Act is very complicated and the revision has brought a number of changes. National, state, and even local library organizations are able to bring together experts who are qualified to provide guidance. Don't assume that because you or other staff members have attended one meeting, you've done your duty and needn't pursue the issue further. Each time you attend a presentation or participate in a discussion, you will learn something new. Confusing legal points will gradually become clear and new case law will further clarify issues.

Read about the Laws Affecting Libraries

Don't stop with the Patriot Act. Take a good look at the other laws that impact libraries and their patrons. Obtain copies of your state's library confidentiality laws. It is fortunate that this is such a hot topic on the Internet. Many highly informative articles are available. The ALA Web site is also a real treasure trove of information, as is the FindLaw (findlaw.com) Web site.

Learn More about the Government's Perspective

Librarians are patriotic Americans, and we care about the safety of our country. It is essential that we understand both sides of the issues. As was clear from the derisive comments of Attorney General Ashcroft quoted above, librarians are sometimes viewed as "fluffy little women" who don't really understand the big, bad world of international terrorism. To a large extent, it is the librarian's responsibility to interpret the Patriot Act to the local community and this requires a balanced, informed outlook. What makes this task more difficult is the tendency to lump all library services together. As I mentioned earlier, library computers are occasionally used by criminals and it does appear that the 9/11 terrorists sent e-mails on library computers. There is no justification, however, for assumptions that if you read certain books or view certain DVDs, you are more likely to be a terrorist. The public needs to know that librarians live in the real world and are just as concerned about terrorism as their neighbors. Their aim is not to protect terrorists but to protect the Constitution. The FISA court is prepared at any time of the day or night to issue a court order. Citizens certainly have the right to demand that law enforcement agencies request one before demanding library records.

Communicate with Library Patrons

The negative publicity that often surrounds a conflict with law enforcement agencies can do irreparable harm to a library. However, it can also be an occasion for the library and the community to speak and act in unison. A demand for library records can lead to the forced resignation of the library director as happened in Hasbrouck Heights or it can become an opportunity for both the library and the community to reaffirm their democratic values as occurred at the Deming Library. It's important that library patrons understand that the library's goal is to protect them: their freedom to read, to gather information and to be left alone. It's a very good idea to prepare handouts or brochures and keep them readily available. Don't wait until a problem arises. When patrons ask questions, be sure they receive well-thought-out answers, framed in terms of how the library protects their personal information.

Update Library Policies

Most libraries have a confidentiality policy that was written long before the passage of the Patriot Act. Take a good look at yours. What more is needed to make it current?

- Does it pertain to all patron information including registration, circulation, ILL, electronic services, reference and other public services?
- Does it make it clear that both paper and electronic records are covered?
- Does it identify the persons who are authorized to release patron information?
- Does it state that a court order is required to release patron information?
- Does it state that the library will retain only the records it needs to function effectively? (It's a good idea to accompany the policy with a records retention schedule)

- Does it state that the library automation system will be configured to delete all unneeded patron information and public computers will be wiped clean of all data that has not been provided by the library?
- Is it sufficiently clear and concise that staff confronted with a demand from a law enforcement agency will be able to respond appropriately?

What other policies need to be changed or added? Go over these new and revised policies with the library staff, helping them understand how the policies impact their work. Discuss possible situations that might arise and how the policies should affect their actions. Don't forget to keep library boards, local government heads, and school administrators in the loop.

SUMMING IT UP

There is ample evidence that the kind of crises that divide the community and hurt the library's credibility can often be avoided. Libraries that develop effective policies and use them to educate staff and stakeholders will usually emerge from a painful encounter with the fewest possible bruises.

REFERENCES

Airoldi, Joan. 2006. Case study: a grand jury subpoena in the Patriot Act era. *Library Administration & Management* 20 (1): 26-9.

American Civil Liberties Union. 2006. "Supreme Court Unseals Documents in Patriot Act Case," news release. August 3.

American Library Association. 2003. "American Library Association responds to Attorney General remarks on librarians and USA PATRIOT Act: A statement by ALA President Carla Hayden." Press Release, September 16. Available from http://www.ala.org/ala/pressreleasesbucket/pressreleases2003sep/ameri canlibraryassociation.htm. Accessed on August 9, 2007.

American Library Association. 2006. "ALA President Michael Gorman Responds to Senate PATRIOT Act Reauthorization Vote," news release. March 1. http://www.ala.org/Template.cfm?Section=presscenter&template=/ContentManagement/ContentDisplay.cfm&ContentID=118686.

Ashcroft, John. 2003. Address to the National Restaurant Association's 18th Annual Public Affairs Conference. Washington, DC.

Cowan, Alison Leigh. 2006. Librarian is still John Doe, despite Patriot Act revision. *New York Times*, March 21. http://select.nytimes.com/search/restricted/article?res=F60F1EF634550C728EDDAA0894DE404482.

Solomon, John and Barton Gellman. 2007. "Frequent errors in FBI's secret records requests: Audit finds possible rule violations. *Washington Post*, March 9. p A01. http://www.washingtonpost.com/wp-dyn/content/article/2007/03/08/AR2007030802356_pf.html.

U.S. Department of Justice Office of the Inspector General. 2007. "A Review of the Federal Bureau of Investigation's Use of National Security Letters" (Unclassified). http://www.usdoj.gov/oig/special/s0703b/final.pdf.

USA PATRIOT and Terrorism Prevention Reauthorization Act of 2005, HR 3199.

CHAPTER 9

Protecting Electronic Privacy: A Step-by-Step Plan

Protecting patron privacy is a complex task that requires an understanding of technology and our fellow human beings. In this chapter, we focus more on the technical and policy-related aspects of privacy protection. In the next chapter, we turn our attention to our patrons and the ways in which the library can prevent them from endangering their own privacy. These aspects of privacy protection must go hand in hand; neither the technical nor the administrative, nor the educational side of the library's responsibility can be ignored.

POLICY REVIEW

The best place to begin a program to safeguard patron privacy is to take stock of your library's current situation. For example, does your library currently have a privacy or confidentiality policy? If you have such a policy, when was it last revised? Did the library staff create the policy from scratch or did it borrow a policy from another library? When you borrow, you tend to make a few minor changes and file the recycled policy away. Though it may be well-written, it is not really yours. It has not stimulated the mental exercise or discussion that result in an informed library staff and a sense of common purpose. Of course, you don't want to waste time reinventing the wheel, but it's important that you closely examine any policy you adopt. Be absolutely sure that your policy will be able to stand up to future legal tests and be an effective instrument for educating both the library staff and the library community.

What Should Your Policy Include?

Many libraries have had patron confidentiality policies in place for years. They may precede the computer era and be simple statements affirming the obligation of the library staff to safeguard personal information. The wording of such policies is often similar to the state laws that establish library confidentiality. Such policies can be expanded to encompass more complex technology-related issues. However, in this post-9/11 era, it may be preferable to start from scratch and create a carefully-crafted, technically-savvy policy that will provide solid backup and guidance in the event of a legal challenge.

Librarians have sometimes found themselves in uncomfortable positions when they cite policy to patrons or law enforcement officials. They may, for example, state that library records cannot be surrendered without a court order. Then, when they produce their policy, they discover it consists only of ringing phrases about intellectual freedom and First Amendment Rights. A good policy comfortably merges the philosophical and the practical. It is usually unwise to go into elaborate detail, but a privacy policy should be more than a lofty statement. Neither should it be merely a to-do list, since the procedures that will be used to implement the policy should be stored in a separate library procedure manual. Likewise, it is important to include the ethical basis on which the policy rests, but contents should be specific and practical enough that violations and responses to them are obvious. Although good policies come in many shapes and sizes, yours should at least include the following topics:

- Notice to users of their right to privacy and the library's responsibility to protect them (First Amendment and intellectual freedom).
- Types of information the library gathers, how and for how long it is stored, and the ways in which it is protected.
- Right of patrons to opt-out of providing some personal information.
- Right of patrons to view their own information and verify its accuracy (including parent's right to view and verify children's information)

- The library's obligation to maintain data integrity and take appropriate steps to insure the accuracy of the information it collects about its patrons.
- Statement regarding public computers. This should assure patrons that the library will not track or log their online activities. It should, however, also make it clear that it is not safe to entrust confidential information to public computers.
- Restrictions on library personnel having access to data and other data protection measures (e.g., encryption).
- Staff training to ensure privacy protection
- Records retention statement making it clear that records will be destroyed when they are no longer needed (refer to a records retention schedule included as an appendix to the policy or in a procedure manual)
- Statement concerning shared data. With whom will the library share information about its patrons (consortia, university business offices, vendors, etc.), and how will the library assure that the data remains accurate and up-to-date?
- Statement about the role of computer security practices in protecting patron privacy (again, actual security procedures should be listed in procedure manual).
- The library's response to law enforcement demands including how and by whom the decision is made to surrender library records.
- Plan for publicizing the privacy policy and interpreting it to patrons.

Once your library's privacy policy has been adopted, do not simply file it away and forget about it. Instead, use it in a variety of ways to educate the library staff and library patrons. Since it concerns patrons' rights, patrons must have access to it. Many libraries publish the policy in a brochure that also includes interpretation. The policy should also be posted on the library's Web site and in other prominent locations.

PRIVACY AUDIT

In the last chapter, we discussed the importance of a privacy audit to identify all the different types of records that libraries create both manually and electronically. Such an audit is also useful in identifying other privacy threats. For example, it's important that you review both your library's privacy policy and procedure manual to determine whether access to personal information is properly controlled. Have decisions been made concerning who will have access to the personal information stored on library computers? Have computer user accounts (rights, passwords, etc.) been reviewed to confirm that these decisions have been implemented? Have procedures been written for updating firewalls, and anti-virus and anti-spyware programs?

Do training procedures for technical staff emphasize privacy issues? In other words, when new staff, especially computer technicians, are hired, is patron privacy an important part of their training? Is it part of circulation training? You can adapt the principles of the privacy audit to include all library policies, procedures, training, and in-service programs that directly or indirectly impact patron privacy. Current, written procedures should be in place to support the privacy policy, including a records retention schedule and computer maintenance routines. Such procedures should go beyond obvious sources of personal information, identifying and purging information that is inadvertently stored on staff and public computers. This can include:

- Saved searches and sets. Technical staff have a responsibility to investigate both the information that is saved by the library's own system and that saved by online database providers.
- Browser histories saved after session is ended. Are browsers set to delete histories after each user?
- Web server logs, including proxy servers. Proxy servers are in a sense "go betweens" that authenticate users. They can easily be forgotten since they are all but invisible.
- Mail server logs. This is especially important in colleges, universities, and other institutions that provide e-mail accounts for their users.
- Cookies and certificates. Certificates are a way that online services identify you as being entitled to use the service. Cookies, as we already know, can send back information about you and your computer.
- Operating system logs. The computer's operating system keeps track of everything it does. This record can include personally identifiable information.
- Browser bookmarks.

PROTECTING THE LIBRARY'S COMPUTERS

Policies and procedures are essential in the effort to protect patron privacy, but the library's computer system must be configured and maintained to support them. Without a comprehensive computer security plan, your library may be playing unwitting host to hackers and identity thieves.

In some libraries, there is a great divide between the traditional library staff and the technical staff. They rarely meet together, and they tend to dismiss the concerns of one another as unimportant. This kind of environment provides a breeding ground for problems. The only way to effectively protect your patrons' privacy is to bring these two camps together and focus their attention on the patron, not on their grievances. As the technical staff installs software, erects firewalls, and limits access to potentially dangerous parts of the system, they must consider the impact their changes will have on the ability of other staff members to do their work, and the extent to which public computers can meet the needs of your users.

Both traditional and technical staff members may fail to understand the connection between computer security and patron privacy. Why, they ask, is remembering to update the anti-spyware program such a big deal? The answer is that privacy threats so often come from the Internet. They may come in the form of small programs that remain undetected, capturing personal information and sending it back to identity thieves. Computer security and privacy protection inevitably go hand in hand. There is no longer any way to fully protect your patrons without understanding and implementing a computer security plan.

Because technical issues can be complex, let's break the job down into small but important tasks that are not so formidable. Although it is impossible to completely avoid complex technical information, we will keep it to a minimum. You may want to use the more technical sections of this chapter as a draft outline for a discussion with your library's technical staff. A library director need not know the differences between WEP and WPA to discover whether library technicians have given adequate attention to privacy/security issues on a wireless network and made informed choices.

Security Systems for Public Access Computers

Computer owners make many, many changes to their systems in the course of their routine activities. Most of these changes are intentional and serve to customize settings to meet their own particular needs. Computer owners may not be aware, however, that their computers are automatically recording most of their actions including user names, passwords, and the Web sites they visit. Files are being downloaded constantly without the permission of the owner. By the time a personal computer is a few months old, it has been customized to the point that its innards, including software, desktop design, and user preferences, are unique. In the library environment, this is neither possible nor desirable. You must set up your computers in a way that works best for most of your users and you must not permit changes. Otherwise, user settings would conflict with one another and chaos would ensue.

Additionally, we have a responsibility to make sure no personal files are left behind. Otherwise, we would be allowing some users to invade the privacy of others, reading and copying their files. If they are also allowed to download and save files, they might install unwanted programs that would conflict with library software or they might download malicious programs or malware.

How is it possible to freeze your computers at a specific point in time and keep them exactly the same? How can you prevent users from downloading games or changing the Web browser's homepage? How can you prevent Web sites from depositing cookies that send back personal information about your users? This can be an extremely difficult task but fortunately there are a number of hardware and software solutions on the market designed specifically to address the problem. They can either prevent changes from being made to computers or return them to their original condition at the end of each user's session.

Security systems range from inexpensive, basic software programs to costly hardware/software solutions. When considering the various options available, it's important to look carefully at your library and its needs. For example:

- How many public computers does the library maintain?
- Are your public computers in constant use, or is usage light to medium?
- Are public computers distributed throughout the library or are they close together in a computer-lab type of configuration?
- Are your public computers configured in a client-server network or are they stand alone workstations? Are you using thin clients (stripped-down computers that depend mostly on a server for

processing activities) or some other configuration that makes your situation unusual?

- Who will install and configure the security system? Do you have more than one staff person qualified to administer the system?
- How technically sophisticated is your information technology (IT) staff? Are you dependent on outside contractors for some of your technology needs? Do you have any fully trained technicians or do they tend to be college students?
- Do you have enough staff to maintain your public computers or has finding time for maintenance been a serious problem?

Beyond the limitations imposed by the library and the staff, consider the needs of your patrons. How do they use the library's computers? What kinds of things do they do frequently? In general, library patrons tend to spend most of their time on the Internet, but there may be ways in which their usage differs from other libraries. If your library happens to be located in a popular tourist area, your visitors may want to upload their digital photographs to Web sites. Understanding these differences is important because any security system you choose will place some restrictions on public computer users.

Take for example, Centurion Guard, a combination of hardware and software that is used in many libraries. The package, marketed by Fortres, is intended to lock down desktop computers and prevent users from performing actions that might be considered dangerous. It works well, but like many of the other products on the market, it can sometimes prevent users from performing necessary tasks like burning CD disks and saving files to flash memory drives. Each library should carefully balance the needs of its computer users against the need for computer security. It will undoubtedly be necessary to prevent users from doing some of the things they enjoy, but no security system should make it impossible for them to carry out basic and necessary tasks like saving their own work to their own disk.

Some security systems are designed to prevent users from engaging in unsafe practices. Others allow them more freedom and then reset computers at the end of the session, thus returning all files and settings to their original state. The first option may interfere with the quality of the user's experience and the second may permit viruses and other infections to take root during a session. It is often necessary to choose between these two basic system types, but one can sometimes achieve a compromise. The packages currently on the market range from inexpensive to costly and from simple to highly sophisticated.

Security Systems for Public Access Computers

Centurion Guard and CornerStone
Centurion Technologies, Inc.
512 Rudder Rd.
Fenton, MO 63026
(800) 224-7977
http://www.centuriontech.com
andrea@centuriontech.com

Clean Slate and Clean Slate Snap-in
Fortres Grand Corp.
P.O. Box 888
Plymouth, IN 46563
(800)331-0372
http://www.fortresgrand.com
sales@fortresgrand.com

FoolProof Security
Riverdeep Inc., LLC
100 Pine St., Suite 1900
San Francisco, CA 941 1 1
(415) 659-2000
http://www.riverdeep.net
info@riverdeep.net

Folder Guard
WinAbility Software Corp.
244 W. Main St.
Rockville, UT 84763-0272
(801) 303-7310
http://www.winability.com

Full Control and WinU
Bardon Data Systems
164 Solano Ave. #415
Albany, CA 94706
(510)526-8470
http://www.bardon.com
info@bardon.com

LockDown Rx, and RollBack Rx
Horizon DataSys, Inc.
1685 H St. #846
Blaine, WA 98230
(604) 324-0797

http://www.horizondatasystem.com
sales@horizondatasys.com

Secure Desktop
Visual Automation, Inc.
403 S. Clinton St., Suite 4
Grand Ledge, MI 48837
(517) 622-1850
http://www.visualautomation.com
sales@visualautomation.com

WINSelect and Deep Freeze
Faronics Technologies USA, Inc.
5241 I Old Crow Canyon Rd. Suite 170
San Ramon, CA 94583
(800) 943-6422, ext. 4081
http://www.faronics.com
shaun@faronics.com

It's a good idea to find out which of these systems are in use in libraries in your area. Visit some librarians who have a system in place, or at least discuss their experiences on the phone. Ask their technical staff about ease of installation and maintenance. Ask public service staff about any inconvenience to users. Centurian Guard and Deep Freeze are in use in most libraries that have received Gates Foundation Grants so they'll be easy to investigate. The market is changing rapidly, however, so you may discover that other systems are now more competitive.

In-Depth Defense

In general, overkill is a good thing when it comes to computer security. Two antivirus programs are better than one. Two anti-spyware programs will almost always produce somewhat different results. Unfortunately, many software producers require that customers remove other programs before installing their software. In other words, the Norton Antivirus program may require that you remove the McAfee program before it can be installed. There are many good security software programs on the market and it is a good idea to find out which ones can coexist peacefully before making expensive purchases.

Least Privilege

Most systems analysts recommend giving users the fewest privileges possible. When setting up user accounts, they often recommend starting by denying all rights and then turning on just the privileges that users really need. This advice, however, should be tempered with good judgment. Restricted privileges should never interfere with the library staff's ability to perform their jobs effectively. In general, public computers need fewer rights than staff computers, but all users must be able to carry out basic tasks without hindrance. Entrust such decisions to a small group representing different library departments and consult with staff members before restricting computer rights.

Detection before Protection

It's essential to know your system from top to bottom, or be certain there is someone else on staff who does. The following is information that the library's technical staff needs to know, and also needs to understand in terms of its privacy and security implications:

- What ports are exposed to the Internet at the router?
- What network ports are physically available to patrons? Which are available for laptop computer plug-in?
- What rights or privileges do different logons give users?
- Do users have only as much authority as is needed to do their jobs or to perform basic tasks on public computers?

Older Operating Systems

In general, it's best not to keep older computers or accept them as donations (some libraries rotate computers off the network after two years, some after three if funds are scarce). Not only will they slow down your network, but their operating systems may have few security features. The newer the operating system, the more security is programmed into its design. You will definitely want to discard any operating systems that predate Windows XP, and this system will be replaced by Microsoft Vista. Libraries tend to purchase computers a few at a time. Unlike corporations and other large organizations, they rarely have funds available to purchase hundreds of computers at once. Yet most librarians are surprised to learn how many computers are really connected to their systems. Each year, they may purchase a few new computers for the library functions that demand the most computing power. This frees up other computers that can be reassigned to less demanding tasks. Computers are often shifted to less and less demanding jobs, but those at the bottom of the priority list are rarely discarded.

As you know, there is always a demand for more computers. Maybe your Friends of the Library group has requested a computer. Maybe you can relieve some of the pressure on public computers by designating an older computer for e-mail or word processing. Loading plain vanilla Web browsers like Opera on such computers can speed them up and allow them to perform acceptably, but this doesn't remove the security risk. Computer management becomes much more difficult when some computers are equipped with older, less sophisticated software and others have the latest versions.

Hard Drive Safety

What do you do with your library's old computers? When a staff computer is no longer powerful enough to perform library functions but can still be used at a public work station, do you simply erase or delete the library files and programs? Remember, those files are not gone, they are still available to anyone who has the technical know-how to find them. In fact, they are equally available to inquisitive high school students, identity thieves, and government agencies. Before you discard any library computer or make it available to the public, you must scour, or wipe the hard drive clean. A number of free and inexpensive disk washing utilities are available for this purpose. The following is a sampling of them:

- Blancco Data Cleaner (http://www.blancco.com)
- Kill Disk (http://www.killdisk.com)
- BC Wipe (http://www.jetico.com/download.htm)
- Darik's Boot and Nuke (http://dban.sourceforge.net)
- Data Eraser (http://www.ontrack.com/dataeraser/)
- Eraser (http://www.heidi.ie/eraser/)
- PGP Wipe Utility (http://www.pgp.com/products/desktop/index. html
- R-Wipe & Clean (http://www.r-wipe.com)

Privacy Screens or Filters

To put it in technical terms, privacy Filters are sheets of thin, plastic, light-control film containing closely spaced black micro-louvers with a polycarbonate cover material. The micro-louvers serve as barriers when screens are viewed from an angle, preventing nosy patrons at neighboring computers from seeing one's screen. Privacy screens or filters are available in different sizes to fit both desktop and laptop computers. They can be an excellent investment for public desktop computers, but costs vary widely. Although even relatively inexpensive screens can be effective, some are nothing more than ineffective, tinted, easily-scratched plastic. Products marketed as glare screens may or may not offer privacy protection, so read the description carefully. It's also important to examine the way they attach to the computer. Some can fall off of their own volition, and others can be easily removed by mischievous teenagers. Most library supply catalogs include privacy filters, and they are also available directly from 3M Corporation (http://solutions.3m.com/en_US/).

Antivirus and Anti-Spyware Programs

Most security software can be set to run automatically, but computers sometimes forget. They may download updates at the same time every day or every week, and so we grow complacent. Don't trust your updates to chance. All sorts of small changes can affect software settings and interfere with the ability of the program to do what it has been told to do. We can make inadvertent changes like scheduling a virus scan at a time when computers are shut down. Be sure a real live human being checks all computers on a regular basis to assure that updates are current and that full scans are performed daily.

Occasionally, an error message appears that doesn't seem to make sense. It is generated by one of your security programs and is written in classic computerese. An error message means that something is wrong; it may be something unimportant or it may mean that the program has ceased to function. Although you may have become accustomed to ignoring such messages in some other programs, this is definitely not a safe practice when it comes to the programs that are safeguarding your computers. Some viruses are designed to disable antivirus programs. Since the antivirus program is disabled, it won't be able to notify you of the problem. Instead, you may simply be aware of a larger than average number of error messages.

Signature File Updates

New computer viruses and predatory spyware programs appear daily and libraries are in a constant race to download the fix or signature file that will deactivate the bug before it can do its dirty work. Most antivirus and anti-spyware vendors have a schedule for releasing these updated files. It's important to check online and find out when your antivirus vendor updates its signature files. Since even a delay of a few days can leave you vulnerable to attack, it's a good idea to synchronize your security software programs to get the new updates as soon as they are available.

MS Office Updates

Some libraries are very careful to update their firewall, antivirus and anti-spyware software on schedule, but they may forget about updates to other programs. Because it dominates the industry, Microsoft is targeted by hackers more often than almost any other software producer. Microsoft Office in particular is very vulnerable to attack, and these specialized attack files that take advantage of specific program features may go unnoticed by antivirus programs. Microsoft releases its updates the second Tuesday of every month. To be fully secure, download updates for all your software programs as soon as they are available. Once again, you will probably want to download them automatically, but follow up to be sure that updates are really being installed.

Strong Passwords

Computer users, whether library staff members or the general public, prefer easy to remember passwords. They choose the names of their cats, their telephone numbers, or even their own names. Since forgetting a password can be a frustrating experience, this is understandable but very dangerous. Hackers use password-breaking software that makes it easy to discover common passwords. Once one account is compromised, it's easy for hackers to install spyware that collects additional passwords. A careless user with an easy-to-break password can make the whole network vulnerable.

Passwords should be at least eight characters of mixed lowercase, capital, and numeric characters. It's a good idea to include some of those special characters like exclamation marks, pound signs, and asterisks as well. In general, the longer the password, the more difficult it is to crack. This means that staff and public computer users might create a whole phrase or sentence. "Fluffyisacutecat" is a whole lot better than just "Fluffy." Lengthening the pass-phrase, even if it's just lowercase, makes it stronger than a cryptic eight-character password. If this technique creates a password that has more characters than allowed, just leave off the ones on the end.

Both library users and library staff members hate to change their passwords. They believe, often with good reason, that they will get confused with all their different passwords and be unable to do their work or get into their e-mail account. Computer technicians have good intentions when they force staff to change passwords before they can log onto the system, but they may be fanning the flames of conflict. Staff members need to understand that they never know if or when their password has been compromised. If a hacker has cracked their password, the only real way to stop him is to change the password. Experienced computer users often create patterns for changing passwords, patterns that make sense only to them. For example, all their passwords relate to their pets or to their hobbies. Even a small internal change can often deflect a hacker.

Blocking Sensitive Ports

Just as ports connect land and sea, network ports connect the library system to the Internet. Ports, however, are a common way for hackers to gain entry to the library. Our in-house networks are comparatively small and uncomplicated, so many of the available ports go unused. Some ports should be used only within the library and should not have access to the outside world. Ports 135, 139, and 445 are not intended for use beyond your local area network (LAN) and should definitely not be able to access the Internet. These are ports used for communication between Microsoft platforms on a LAN. There is no real reason for anyone outside your LAN to access these ports, so they should be blocked at the router to stop both incoming and outgoing traffic. Hackers frequently gain access to computers through these ports; the act of blocking them will protect your system from many attacks.

Blocking Fake IP Addresses

The library's computer server recognizes the computers that are part of the library network because they identify themselves. When data is

Protecting Electronic Privacy: A Step-by-Step Plan

sent from one computer to another, it is sent in packets identified by
the IP (Internet protocol) address of the computer that sent it out.
Attackers sending files to the library system frequently disguise packets as internal library traffic. You will need to block packets coming
from outside the library when they purport to be from an IP address
in the address space used by the library. In other words, a packet of
data that purports to come from a library computer must be bogus if
it is coming from somewhere outside the library. The IP address has
obviously been tampered with, or in hacker jargon, spoofed.

Your Router's Default Password

A router is the piece of equipment that passes packets across your
computer network. In other words, it routes them to their destination
computers. When you purchase and install a router, it comes with a
default password. You need to change that password immediately.
Obviously, hackers know that many people, including qualified technicians, are so focused on installing the router and resolving the problems they encounter that they put off changing the password until
some later date. Of course, good intentions are soon forgotten and the
password will likely remain the same throughout the life of the router.
This is one of the many problems to which the Microsoft Baseline
Security Analyzer alerts you. This tool, intended to analyze MS
Windows problems, is perhaps your most valuable defense against
attack. It generates a list of items that affect your system's security,
and awards your system a score or grade for each. Problems are color-
coded red and yellow and are accompanied by descriptive information
and directions for repair. For more information about this tool, go to
http://www.microsoft.com/technet/security/tools/mbsahome.mspx.

Manually Configure Host IP Addresses

Each computer in your network must have its own IP address. The
computer can ask the network server to assign an address or a techni-
cian can manually type in the new address. The problem with allowing the server to do the assigning is that it uses the same set of rules
each time it makes an assignment. Naturally, experienced hackers
know these rules and can make educated guesses about the probable
address of any computer in your network. For this reason, you
should *not* use what is called Dynamic Host Configuration Protocol

(DHCP). Instead, you should assign addresses manually. This makes it difficult for either library computer users or outside hackers to sur-reptitiously use one of your network ports.

Limit Laptop Privileges

Of course, it's important to accommodate patron laptops whenever possible, but keep in mind that they constitute an opportunity to hack into the library's network. In a sense, you want to confine laptop users, giving them access to only what they need and denying them access to network drops. Ideally, it's a good idea to have a physical or virtual network just for patron laptops and/or public library computers. It's also important to use the Security Configuration Wizard, a tool that allows network administrators to more easily make changes in security settings. You can find information on how to use this tool on the Microsoft Web site.

Separating Public and Staff Computers

In planning your network and setting up your accounts, imagine an impregnable moat dividing staff computers from public computers. This is one of the best ways to keep hackers from discovering the patron information stored on staff computers. A separate server for the public would accomplish this goal; but also consider purchasing a router that can support two sub-networks. That way you can have a subnet for the public and another for staff use. In addition, a virtual local area network (VLAN) would accomplish the same job without a major investment in equipment. VLANs provide an effective and inexpensive way to separate public and staff functions. If you're inter-ested in more information on VLANs, you might check out an article entitled "What is a VLAN?" on the Tech FAQ Web site (www.tech-faq.com).

Microsoft Shared Computer Toolkit (SCT)

It is fortunate that Microsoft has designed a toolkit that makes it eas-ier to set up and manage shared computers. The company defines shared computers as those "used by many different people who gener-ally don't know or trust each other." Whether you're in a school, aca-demic, or public library, this definition perfectly describes any library's public computers. The toolkit is freely available on the Web (http://www.microsoft.com/windowsxp/sharedaccess/default.mspx). it allows computer owners like schools and libraries to defend their equipment from unauthorized changes to hard disks. It also enables them to restrict users from accessing system settings and other protected data.

Poisoning the Address Resolution Protocol (ARP) Cache

In every life, some rain must fall, and in every librarian's work life, some computer jargon must be mastered. In this case, it is important to know that address resolution protocol (ARP) is a method of finding a host computer's IP address. Naturally, you do not want hackers to discover an address because they can then disguise packets to look as if they're being sent from within the library's network. Poisoning the ARP is a method of disabling communication between two PCs or groups of PCs. It involves placing commands in a batch file to be run by the PC at startup. Some systems analysts say that this technique ends up causing more trouble than it's worth, so work with the library's technical staff to consider the advantages and disadvantages carefully.

"Group Policies"

"Group Policies" is a function of the Windows operating system. It allows administrators to configure and control user environment settings. It makes it easier to copy configuration settings to a large number of PCs. As the library network grows, it becomes increasingly difficult to assure that each and every computer has the same settings. Taking full advantage of Windows Group Policies function allows you to make a change just once and have it apply to a whole group of computers. It is always the weak link in the chain that causes problems, and this is an excellent way to help assure there are no weak links.

Autoruns Software from Sysinternals

Autoruns is a free computer utility that reveals all the software that starts automatically on your computers. It lets you discover spyware or malware hiding on your system and allows you to disable it. Go to www.sysinternals.com, download the Autoruns program, and check to see what executable programs start automatically on your computer. As we mentioned earlier, it's a good policy to have multiple layers of protection because different security programs address different problems. While you're downloading this program, you would do well to download TCP View, which is also available at the Sysinternals Web site. This program is also freely available and allows you to see what ports are open on your system.

Learn to Ping

Ping is a basic Internet program that lets you verify that an IP address actually exists and can accept requests. Ping works by sending echo request packets to a host computer and listening for the "echo response." If you "ping" between a staff and a public PC, you should not be able to get a reply back. Your staff and public computers should be totally separate and segregated from one another. You'll find simple, illustrated instructions for pinging on the IHug Web site at http://www.ihug.co.nz/help/general/guide/ping.html.

Limited Access to Folders

It is also possible to limit the users who have access to any folder stored on your network. Right click on the folder icon in Windows Explorer, choose Properties, then choose the Sharing tab and decide whether you want to Make this a private folder. You can also hide the folder or make it Read only. However, we have a tendency to mix folders containing confidential information with others that require no security whatsoever. Make sure that staff folders are private. Any files and folders containing sensitive information should be stored separately.

The System Log

Every computer maintains a sort of event diary that is called the system log. It contains errors and warnings that require attention. Many people, even trained technicians tend to look at the system log event viewer only after a major problem occurs. Had they noticed warning signs along the way, they might have avoided disaster. It is possible to use the filtering option in the event log viewer to search for suspicious events, but technicians must then make time to look at the results. Like so many other security precautions, this task will not be performed unless it becomes a regular part of someone's daily schedule.

The SANSFIRE Web site

The Internet Storm Center (http://isc.sans.org) provides a free analysis and warning service to Internet users and organizations. It works with Internet Service Providers (ISPs) to guard against the most malicious attackers. The Web site brings together knowledgeable security professionals who discuss a wide variety of issues. This is another example of in-depth protection. Discussions can alert library technicians of security problems before they have been resolved by security software providers. It's a good idea for technicians to make a visit to this Web site a weekly duty.

SAFE WIRELESS NETWORKING

A few years ago, libraries were discouraged from installing wireless networks because of the multiple security problems involved. However, recent technical innovations have made it possible to maintain a wireless network that is almost as secure as the library's wired network. Installing such a network, however, requires considerable attention to security issues. It also requires a somewhat different attitude about security on the part of library staff members. They generally find it a lot easier to keep an eye out for suspicious activity by desktop computer users than by wireless users. Intruders with their own laptops appear just like other computer users. Everything they need is already available to them so they need not install software programs or alter library computer settings. The following are some basic recommendations for maintaining a safe and efficient wireless network.

Changing the Administrative Password

Just as technicians setting up a wired network tend to leave default router passwords unchanged, they may also forget to change the administrative password for the wireless network. Librarians who supervise technical staff may feel uncomfortable bringing up the subject, but hackers know that even the most skilled technicians sometimes forget to make changes. Substitute a strong password for the manufacturer's default password immediately. If you fail to change the wireless network's administrative password, you are allowing hackers to reconfigure the network and defeat any other security measures you put in place.

Suppressing the Network SSID

The SSID (Service Set ID) is the string of characters used to identify your network. The SSID is usually broadcast by an access point, and it is what users see on their laptop screen when they search for wireless networks. If you do not allow the SSID to be broadcast (suppress it), then users must get instructions from library staff and enter the SSID manually. This is a useful way to limit network use to library customers. Although there are other ways to obtain the SSID, it becomes more difficult for unauthorized users to gain access to the library's network.

Enabling WEP or WPA

These security protocols (or rules) encode data being sent across the network through the use of a security encryption key. Wired equivalent privacy (WEP) is an older scheme to secure wireless communications and tends to be vulnerable to evesdropping, because messages are broadcast on a radio frequency. Wi-Fi Protected Access (WPA) is a more recent protocol that involves a system of constantly changing keys. For this reason, it offers much stronger security than WEP. The network administrator must provide a passphrase or key to network users.

Coordinating Wired and Wireless, Public and Staff Computers

Consider where the wireless LAN fits within your organization's overall network design. Make sure that part of the network (one access point, for instance), isn't giving away information that has been suppressed on all the others. Rogue access points sometimes result when careless IT staff or independent technical contractors fail to finish the installation job they started. Remember that a public wireless network may be the most vulnerable part of your library's computer system. In some ways, it should be quarantined to prevent infections from spreading. We'll discuss how that is done shortly.

Don't allow one network station to eavesdrop on its neighbor. It is quite possible for eavesdroppers to open and read the packets of data

unless strong security measures are in effect. Library users are entitled to privacy when they use the library's network, and library
records must be secure as well. Hackers use what is called promiscuous mode to open not only the packets addressed to their computer
but to all the other computers on the network. Network sniffers capture network traffic, sort it by workstation, and make it readable to
the eavesdropper. Although it may seem a little paranoid, it is necessary to operate your network with the assumption that network traffic
is being monitored by unfriendly intruders.

Be sure to protect your network from unseen intruders beyond what
you imagine to be the limits of the library network. Hackers may use
high-gain directional antennas that are able to access wireless networks
well beyond the range that you intended. Isolate your public wireless
network from the rest of the library's computers. This requires both
separation and segregation. You may choose to make the wireless network physically separate. In other words, the wireless LAN has its own
Internet connection and its own hubs and routers. Another good solu-
tion is to separate the public wireless network virtually, but not physically. Even if your library network and wireless users share some
equipment, a VLAN should use separate switch ports, so the packets
traveling over the wired network are invisible to wireless users.

Managing a Wireless Network

Make it easy to manage the wireless network. As networks grow
larger, it becomes impractical to oversee all the computers and access
points, and so security breaches become more frequent. Simple Networking Management Protocol (SNMP) is a good investment for networks of more than fifty computers. Although it increases the cost of
network components, it makes it easier for technical staff to identify
and resolve problems. You can also centralize the management of a
large number of access points with a wireless local area network
(WLAN) switch. Among it's other talents, the WLAN switch can
detect and block rogue access points.

Encryption

If your library uses wireless connectivity for anything besides public
laptops, it's would be smart to encrypt data before they're introduced
to the network. In fact, you may also wish to discuss the possibility

of encrypting data from public laptops with your IT staff. It is much more important to encode information moving across a wireless network than the library's traditional Ethernet network because intruders can access the network completely unobserved.

Firewalls

We often think of a single firewall protecting our entire network from the outside world. However, it's both possible and desirable to have more than one firewall that act to separate a network into zones. Place the public network on the outside of a firewall, or within an untrusted security zone. The term DMZ (demilitarized zone) is sometimes used for parts of the network that cannot be considered as trusted, so wireless access points and public computers are sometimes placed in such a virtual zone.

Multiple firewalls provide multiple layers of protection. The strongest firewall should be placed between the library and the outside world, but additional firewalls can separate public and library functions. It is possible to set up different zones each with different levels of trustworthiness. Again, the library needs to think not only of its own sensitive information, but of the privacy needs of its users as well.

Don't set up a wireless network outside the firewall and adopt a let the public beware attitude. Wi-Fi hotspots like those in coffee shops can be very dangerous places for wireless users. Hacking into computers on such an unprotected wireless network can yield a treasure trove of passwords, credit card numbers, and other confidential information. Because part of the library's mission is to protect the dissemination of information, it must provide safe access to its users. Protect the privacy and safety of wireless users as you would protect the library.

Virtual Private Networks (VPN)

This is a system for setting up a secure channel that allows communications to travel safely through insecure networks. This can be achieved with encryption software installed on both ends of the tunnel, the server and the user's computer. This is a technique that further separates library computers from the public. However, it is not usually very practical to secure public communications since it requires authentication of each laptop computer with a username and password.

Constant Vigilance

Although there are many technical issues involved in computer security, the most important factor in achieving a safe computer environment is really the human factor. Decisions must be made, implemented and become part of the library's routine. Staff must be assigned and reassigned; tasks must be scheduled and verified. Procedures must be written down, disseminated, and performed daily without fail. Technical solutions alone cannot protect the library's computers. It is rather the library staff who must accept the responsibility.

SUMMING IT UP

In this chapter, we've looked at a variety of things that the library staff can do to protect the privacy of its patrons. We've considered policies, procedures and technical functions that can all contribute to a safe computer experience. However, there's no way that you can do it alone. In the next chapter, we discuss ways in which you can make library computer users aware of the dangers they face and suggest simple ways to avoid them. Even when both the library and its users are focused on protecting privacy, there are some threats over which we have little or no power. It then becomes necessary for the librarian to become the library user's advocate. In this role, librarians have a responsibility to support comprehensive legislation that limits intrusions on privacy from both the business sector and from the government itself.

CHAPTER 10
Education and Advocacy

In the last chapter, you learned how to fine-tune your services and employee technology solutions to protect the privacy of your users. Once you secure your computers from attack and purge your systems of unnecessary personal information, have you finished the job? Can you sit back and bask in the warm glow of a job well done? Unfortunately no. Despite your efforts, your users repeatedly put themselves in danger. They do so because they are largely unaware of the risks they face. Although they may occasionally read about extreme situations like identity theft, they generally trust the library to protect them.

THE CHALLENGE OF PROTECTING LIBRARY USERS FROM THEMSELVES

You want to be worthy of their trust, but how can you protect your users from their own thoughtless actions? Since you value their privacy, you do not look over their shoulders. You have struggled to offer them opportunities to view any and all information available on the Internet, free from the restrictions imposed by filtering. You may, therefore, feel uncomfortable discussing their surfing habits with them or telling them what they should or should not do while they are online. You may also find it uncomfortable to confess that your computers are not as safe as home computers, or that your users should not assume that they can use all the same features and services enjoyed by computer owners. In addition, you cringe at the thought of libraries of the past that imposed a plethora of rules on their patrons, and you don't wish to impose further edicts. So, what can you do?

Dangerous Activities

When vacationing tourists sign up for library computers and promptly access their bank accounts, they don't tell you what they're doing. It's easy to conclude that this is really none of your business. Yet you know that this may be one of the most dangerous online activities for public computer users. Even if a keylogger or other type of spyware has not been installed on the computer, there is always the possibility that someone will walk past the computer just as the tourist types his or her user name and password. We must let our users know that this is a very real possibility and alert them of potential dangers in a way that they will find acceptable and is in accord with our own professional ethics.

Taking Responsibility

When librarians identify a problem, they are often inclined to post signs on every available surface. There is one place, however, where a virtual sign can be can be more effective. As users sit down at a library computer, they find themselves staring at a screen that is usually called desktop wallpaper. Your library may have chosen one of the designs that are included with Windows, a photograph of your library, or a screen that describes library resources. Desktop wallpaper, however, provides you with an excellent opportunity to begin educating users about the privacy risks they face. A simple statement alerting users to the risk of identity theft, and asking them not to type or display personal information may be just enough to make that tourist hesitate.

Using desktop wallpaper to communicate is just one of many ways that your library can alert its computer users to potential risks. In this chapter, we will list the information we would like our users to understand before they sit down at a public access computer. After we identify the risks they face and the actions that can reduce risk, we will pare our list down to essentials and divide it into doses that they can reasonably be expected to absorb at a single sitting. Once we have made those choices, the rest is relatively easy. The next step is to structure their library computer experience in such a way that users learn what they need to know *before* they are exposed to danger. Such an Internet education program should not interfere with our users' enjoyment, and it should not take up more time than they are willing to spend. Educators tell us that repetition is essential to learning, so basic information should be repeated in different ways that maintain the user's interest.

Keeping Users Safe

What is it that users need to know to use our computers safely? Since we spent some time getting to know them in Chapter 1, we now have an idea of their skill levels and their interests. We know that we cannot throw a lot of technical information at them because they are probably less technically sophisticated than computer owners. We also know that many of our users are children and teens. Adults may have limited financial resources that reduce their access to information readily available to more affluent groups. The following is a list of precautions to get you started, but you can probably think of additional risky activities that you've noticed in your own library.

Understand That All Public Computers Pose Privacy Risks

Many library users have access to other public computers, like those in school and university computer labs, after school programs, and copy centers like FedEx Kinkos. Your users may be high school students who move naturally from school library to public library to recreation center, carrying their personal flash drives on their keychains. University students may occasionally use at least half a dozen different on-campus facilities and then head for an Internet café at the end of the day. Seniors may take an enrichment computer class at the local community college one day, visit the public library the next, and have lunch at the senior center where they check their e-mail in yet another computer lab. Although they are not public in the usual sense of the word, your users should even consider their own office computers as public when it comes to entering confidential information. Such computers are not really intended for personal use and few safeguards are in place to protect personal privacy. Logins are often shared with other staff members and technicians may not take privacy issues seriously.

Emphasizing that all public computers are at risk makes it clear that this isn't just a library issue. Users will be less likely to assume the library is doing something wrong and will more willingly accept their share of responsibility.

Never Access Financial Information on Public Computers

Despite the convenience of checking bank balances and paying bills online, public computers should never be used for such purposes. Once cyber-thieves have a password (which, as we've seen, can be obtained in a variety of ways), they can change contact information and transfer funds to other accounts.

As we mentioned earlier, completing the federal government's online student loan application online should be done only on a very secure personal computer, but thousands of students annually submit their applications from public computers. The application form requests very complete information on students' own finances and those of their parents. There is easily enough information on such an application to steal the identities of several family members.

Never Purchase Merchandise on Public Computers

It can be difficult to convince your users that they should forego the attractions of online shopping. After all, this is what many computer owners spend most of their online time doing. Nevertheless, shopping involves typing credit card numbers, so it is never safe. Of course, online shopping isn't entirely safe on home computers, but the risk is much greater on public computers.

Everyone Has the Right to Remain Anonymous on Public Computers

Directness and honesty are qualities that our society values highly. We expect people to be who they say they are and tell us the truth about themselves. Before the advent of computers, anyone who used an assumed name was thought to be hiding something disreputable. Inexperienced computer users may continue to feel this way about online contacts. Because so many of the cues that we use to evaluate people are missing in cyberspace, computer users need to understand that virtual meeting places are different from face-to-face contacts. Until we have good reason to know and trust the people behind the instant message pop-up or the chat room screen, it's best to remain anonymous and it is not dishonest to do so.

Users might think of their Internet persona as an alter ego. They can be as honest as they like in communicating with others. Their alter ego can be almost identical to their real selves with only their personally identifiable information removed. Since it is important to keep their personal identity under wraps when surfing the Net, public computer users can create assumed names when applying for *free* online services. Web sites like Yahoo!, Google, and MSN provide many services that they can enjoy and most are free. However, it is usually necessary to complete application forms that request personal information. Many newspapers are also available to Internet users, but they too may require membership. Although service providers don't receive money directly for these services, the marketing data they collect is valuable to their advertisers. Our users need to know that somebody pays for free services. However, there is no law that requires Internet users to provide accurate personal information to marketers, and no one should ever assume that because a Web site asks a question, one has an obligation to answer it. Our users need to understand that it is a computer at the other end, not a human being who might be offended.

Create One E-mail Account for Friends and One for Everyone Else

Library computer users should have one essential e-mail account that they use almost exclusively for trusted friends, relatives, and business contacts. The other e-mail account should be used for online acquaintances, free Web services and other recreational or "throw away" communication. Naturally, this second, non-essential account should be completely anonymous. Anytime users begin receiving unwanted mail, they should be able to close the account without revealing their identity or losing touch with important people.

Avoid Premium or Fee-Based Services

Free services often lack some bells and whistles that can only be obtained by paying a monthly fee for the premium version. Users are enticed into signing up for the free service, and then bombarded with ads for premium features. For example, a Web mail site may offer a certain number of gigabytes of hard disk storage space at no cost, but if users need more storage space, they must pay for it. Such paid services require users to submit credit card numbers and other personal information. Internet service providers (ISPs) often attract members by offering free services.

Ignore E-mail from Strangers

Users need to know that the only people who have a right to know their e-mail addresses are the friends and family members they notified. Their banks will not contact them at their e-mail address (unless they specifically told them to) so when they receive such messages, they must assume that someone is trying to trick them.

If users have given out their e-mail address when signing up for Web services, they may receive messages from the service providers. However, they will never ask for passwords, Social Security numbers, or other sensitive information.

Use Strong Passwords

Since library patrons do not use computers as often as computer owners, they tend to forget their usernames and passwords. They are, therefore, inclined to use the same password for every Web service to which they subscribe. They also tend to choose short easy passwords that can be easily cracked by cyber-thieves. It's possible, however, to create passwords that are easy to remember but hard to crack. The longer the password the better, so simply repeating a word two or three times with no spaces makes it more difficult to crack. Even better, computer users might simply create a short sentence with the words run together.

If Applications Require Accurate Personal Information, Do Not Submit Them Online

In Chapter 1, we met a student using a public computer to complete a student loan application. Little did he suspect that what he was doing was dangerous. The Social Security Administration (SSA) also encourages claimants to use its online forms. In fact, many government agencies, large employers, and financial institutions have all found it convenient to accept online applications, because a computer program can screen applications and quickly identify red flags. Applicants submitting materials by post may be at a considerable disadvantage, but they should understand that they are taking a much greater risk with an online submission. If your library allows patrons to use the library's fax machine, this might be suggested as a good alternative. Financial information is not the only sensitive information that should not be entered into public computers, but it is the one category for which there can be no exceptions.

Never Save Logins

Each time computer users log into a service, they are asked if they want the computer to remember their password. Library computer users may not understand what this means. Saving their login information means depositing a cookie on the library's computer. It is not the Web site that remembers them but the library computer. Programs like instant messengers may save logins automatically unless the function is disabled. This can be done from the "Preferences" or "Options" menu.

Always Log Out

Your users may not understand that they remain logged into a site until they deliberately logout or until their session times out. This means that the Web site being accessed logs them out automatically after a given period of time, but this may not occur for a half-hour or more. Just clicking to a new Web page is not sufficient, since it may be technically possible for hackers to access your Web site as if they were your library users. Whatever personal information users have shared with the Web site then becomes available to the intruders.

Don't Leave the Computer Unattended

Imagine a computer user logged into her e-mail Web site. While reading her mail or composing a message, she walks away from the computer to get a drink of water or visit the rest room. Another user on the lookout for such an opportunity quickly moves in, clicks on her account information, and accesses her personal data. It takes experienced cyber-criminals just a minute or two to obtain the information and return calmly to their own computer workstations. This is, of course, more dangerous when a fee-based service is involved since names, addresses, phone numbers, and even credit card numbers are available. However, even free services store some personal information.

Be Aware of the People Around You

Library users often become focused on their computer screens and engrossed in whatever it is they are doing. They may not be aware of someone walking or lingering behind them. Library computers are often placed so close to one another that the computer user sitting at the next work station has a clear view of his or her neighbor's screen. Library staff members should also be on the alert for such behavior, but they cannot watch each and every user.

PREPARING LIBRARY COMPUTER USERS
FOR SPECIFIC THREATS

Novice computer users generally need a clear list of do's and don'ts while they are becoming familiar with the Internet. As they learn more about the online environment, it is helpful to make them aware of specific types of criminal behavior. If they understand how and why criminals devise scams, they are better able to take precautionary measures. The following is a list of the most common types of criminal activity on the Internet.

Phishing

Phishing can be defined as the practice of sending e-mails that fraudulently purport to come from a respected business. Scammers attempt to trick customers of that company into disclosing personal information. Computer users can be taught to distinguish between a phishing attack and a legitimate e-mail message. Here are some of the most common signs that a message is part of a phishing scam:

- The e-mail appears to be from a bank or other trusted institution.
- The e-mail is upsetting or frightening, encouraging recipients to act quickly without thought. For example, recipients may be notified that their bank accounts will be closed unless they divulge confidential information.
- The e-mail notifies recipients that they have won a prize. Of course it doesn't make clear exactly which contest they entered. Many people enter many contests, and they are sometimes unaware that they are even entered in a contest (as for example, the millionth customer). Of course, they want to believe the prize is genuine, but our computer users must accept the fact that this is highly unlikely.
- The e-mail claims it is necessary to update or verify customer account information.
- The e-mail urges recipients to click on a hot link in the message. Such a link often connects to a fake Web site.
- The sender's e-mail address isn't the same as the trusted business organization's Web address. It may look almost the same but even a difference of one letter or number will send one to a different site. For example, the return e-mail may purport to be from Ebay but the e-mail address is spelled "Eebay."

- When recipients look closely, they discover the message originated with a free Web mail address like Hotmail or Yahoo!.
- The message claims that something bad will happen if recipients don't act immediately.

Fortunately, there are simple precautions that will stop most phishers in their tracks. Even a printed library bookmark can provide enough information to thwart many attacks. The following cautions can be contained in a bookmark, brochure, flyer, desktop wallpaper, or a library program:

- Be suspicious of all e-mail from strangers.
- Remember that banks and other trusted businesses will not contact you online.
- Reputable businesses will never ask for your user name, password, or account number.
- The e-mail address you see is not necessarily the real one; it's easy to create a false identity in an e-mail message.
- Phishers will not use your full name because they do not know it. They may begin the message with "Dear Customer" or "Dear Valued Customer."
- Look for odd spellings or capital letters, This is sometimes done deliberately to evade spam filters.
- Look for grammar and spelling errors that a real business professional would not make. Many scams originate in foreign countries where English is not the primary language. Scammers may have poor English skills.

Precautions

Of course, computer users should delete e-mail they suspect of being fraudulent. However, if you have an opportunity to discuss scams more fully, you may wish to encourage users to take these additional precautions:

- Don't click on a link to a Web site unless you really know where it's going. It is easy to right click on the link, select Properties, and see the real destination of the link. In general, it's a good idea to retype any URL instead of clicking on the link. That way, you can be sure that there is no hidden address beneath the apparently innocent one.
- Enable the anti-spam filter that is supplied by most Web mail providers. Although computer owners have more options for reducing

spam, public computer users can still adjust spam settings on their Web mail accounts. They can do this themselves and they'll find instructions on their Web mail provider's Web site.

- If you're in doubt and worried that the e-mail might be legitimate, contact the bank or other organization by telephone.

Hoaxes

Since the birth of the Internet, some people have entertained themselves by inventing untruths and spreading them around the Net. Sometimes these hoaxes are merely annoying and do no more harm than waste people's time and take up bandwidth. Some, however, are intended to distribute viruses that piggyback on the message. Library computer users can recognize hoaxes if they know what to expect. The following are some common examples:

Fake Viruses and Pyramid Schemes

One frequently encountered hoax takes the form of an e-mail message that describes an imaginary virus sweeping the Internet and erasing entire hard disks. After describing this menace, the message tells recipients what they should do to protect their computer and asks them to forward the message to everyone they know. Sometimes one is asked to delete an important file, an action that could open a virtual "back door" for hackers.

Another hoax asks recipients to forward a virtual chain letter. If they break the chain, something terrible will happen to them. Occasionally an e-mail is part of an old-fashioned pyramid scheme. Recipients send money to the top name on a list and then add their own names at the bottom of the list. Then they forward the message to ten or more people. Library users should know that pyramid schemes are illegal whether they exist in the real world or in cyberspace.

Pleas for Help

A particularly ugly hoax is the type that tells the recipient about someone in trouble. It may describe a dying child or elderly person who desperately needs money to purchase medicine. E-mail recipients are asked to send money to a post office box and forward the message to all their friends. Of course, there is no dying child or poverty-stricken senior. The money goes into the pockets of the scammer.

Some hoaxes make ridiculous promises and it's difficult to understand why anyone would go to the trouble of inventing these hoaxes. For example, e-mail recipients are asked to send old lipsticks or toothpaste tubes back to the manufacturer to receive cash. The hoaxer doesn't seem to get anything out of it except a big laugh at the expense of the company that has to deal with all the irate customers. Though these hoaxes may seem downright silly, library computer users nevertheless need to be warned about them. Seemingly innocuous hoaxes may have hidden agendas and it is never a good idea for inexperienced computer users to become involved with questionable online activities.

Fraudulent Web Sites

Internet users may encounter fake or fraudulent Web sites by clicking on a phishing e-mail or they may encounter them through a search engine. Many fake Web site scammers know that Internet surfers often mistype addresses. They purchase domain names that are almost exactly like those of large Internet e-commerce sites like Amazon. com and Ebay.

Some scammers load the real Web site (the actual site maintained by the trusted business) in their main browser window and then create their own pop-up window on top of it. The Web surfer may be unaware that there are actually two windows loaded and sees only the address bar of the real Web site.

If library computer users have been taught to protect confidential information, such sites offer little danger. For the unwary, however, they offer yet another opportunity to fall into a trap, unwittingly share personal information, or download viruses and spyware.

PRECAUTIONS FOR LAPTOP USERS

More and more libraries now provide wireless Internet access for their users who own laptop computers. So many people are attracted by the availability of high speed Internet access that it has become an extremely popular service. Because these patrons are using their own equipment rather than the library's, librarians may feel less responsible.

Overall, laptop computer owners are more experienced and understand more about the dangers of cyberspace than users of the library's desktop computers. Laptop owners, however, may not be aware of the additional dangers they face when they are away from home. Be sure to include your laptop users in your library's Internet education program, but remember their needs are somewhat different. Theft is, of course, a concern but since they are using their own computers, they need not fear that others will leave spyware on them. There are, however, other ways to tamper with computers that are connected to a wireless network. Here is some very basic advice that should be shared with your laptop users:

Use a Firewall

A firewall is a piece of software that serves as a barrier or boundary. The library should have firewalls in place between the library and the outside world, and between library staff computers and public or laptop computers. However, each laptop computer also has its own firewall. Windows XP includes a firewall that it is usually turned on by default. Antivirus software programs also include firewalls. However, users may not know if their firewall has been disabled. Since malicious code can turn off firewalls and they can be accidentally disabled by other programs, check them from time to time by clicking on the Windows or Mac Security Center.

Typing Confidential Information While Using a Public Network

Since wireless networks are not usually as secure as wired networks, most of the cautions for using library computers are appropriate. Other wireless users can, under certain circumstances, read the information that's being transmitted. If laptop users must type sensitive information, they should first make sure that the Web site displays a locked padlock in the lower right corner of the screen.

Encrypting Data

Most operating systems allow users to encode their files so they cannot be read by lurkers on the network or out in cyberspace. In the case of Windows, it's not difficult to encrypt files, but the procedure is a little roundabout. Instructions are available at http://www.microsoft.com/windowsxp/using/security/learnmore/encryptdata.mspx. The library can also encrypt data as it passes through its servers, but it's a good idea for users to encrypt their own data as well. Since young people may take advantage of wireless connections at libraries, computer labs, and coffee shops, they are vulnerable to eavesdropping by other wireless users. Encryption greatly reduces this danger.

PRECAUTIONS FOR CHILDREN AND TEENAGERS

If adults have a hard time comprehending the dangers that lie in wait in cyberspace, it only stands to reason that children have even more difficulty. Although children often grow up using computers and may be more technically proficient than adults, they don't understand the adult world. They generally lack an accurate mental picture of the people who are reading their messages. In fact, they may have no comprehension of the number of people who are online or the number who might be lurking unnoticed in a chat room.

One of the reasons that many librarians do not support the use of Internet filters is that such remedies do nothing to help children understand the online world. Instead, forbidden sites may simply become forbidden fruit that children are tempted to visit, and filtering software may offer an attractive focus for their hacking skills. Libraries have a unique opportunity to educate both children and their parents. Children who use library computers often come from families that have little experience with technology. Parents may fail to understand the dangers that confront their children on the Internet, or, on the other hand, they may have acquired baseless fears from the more sensational media.

Short, entertaining workshops are a great way to communicate basic Internet safety information. Some libraries have been very successful at bringing parents and children together to discuss both Internet dangers and opportunities. Since most of the safety precautions are even more important to children who may be using their family's home computer while their parents are at work or otherwise occupied, it is also a good idea to include other parents and children who do not use the library's public computers. Whether your audience consists of children, their parents, or both, there are some basic points that should always be included.

Advice for Parents

Parents need to understand that the best way to protect their children from online dangers is to spend time with them, whether children are using their home computer or a public computer at the library. It's important for parents to see the sites their children visit and discuss them together. Children should become accustomed to consulting their parents when they encounter anything online that bothers them or that they don't understand. Online predators obtain information by pressuring children, and making them feel guilty for not trusting them. Routinely consulting their parents makes it easier to "just say no" with clear consciences.

Some parents find that written contracts with their children help to spell out details of what is and is not acceptable. Sometimes penalties are included in the contract, but too much emphasis on rules and punishments can interfere with honest communication. Bringing parents and children together to discuss the Internet opens up channels of communication so it will be easier and more natural to discuss issues in the future. It's impossible for librarians to foresee all the different experiences children will have online. Children need someone who is ready to answer their questions as they arise, and their best source of information should be their parents.

Advice for Children

No matter how much fun or how likeable their online friends may be, children should never reveal any personal information about themselves or their families without parental approval. This is an extremely difficult concept to convey to young children. They have been brought up to be honest and open. Misrepresenting themselves seems like a violation of the ethical values they have been taught.

Even very young children use computers. They may begin with children's software programs featuring Barney or Arthur. Soon they graduate to children's Web sites. One librarian friend believes that this is an excellent time to imbue caution and teach online safety. In planning a program for first and second graders, she decided to appeal to their imaginations. She first enlisted an accomplice, an unseen staff member who sent an instant message to a computer in the children's library. My friend gathered a group of children around the computer and asked them who sent the message. Of course, they did not know, but they had lots of guesses. The librarian asked if it might be a monster. That idea, of course, completely captured their attention and they began to describe the monster.

Then the accomplice sent another message asking the children to be his friend. The children's discussion continued about whether this was a good or bad monster. Finally, the offstage accomplice sent a message asking where the children lived so he could visit them. If, of course, this was a bad monster, it would be very dangerous to give out their address. Children wisely decided not to take any chances. This provided an opportunity for my friend to explain that there was really no way to know who you were talking to online, and that it's dangerous to give out information. At the end of the program, children were asked if they wanted to meet the monster, and the staff member who had typed the messages revealed himself.

A school librarian suggests that children should pretend to be an imaginary friend when they're online. She tells me that they find this much more ethically acceptable than lying. These are examples of different ways to acquaint children with the dangers of the Internet using concepts that they understand. As children get older, they can absorb more factual information about the Internet, but it's important to balance the information they receive. Rational precautions are far more effective than irrational fears. In particular, children should be cautioned against

- Using their full names
- Providing their home address or telephone number
- Revealing where they go to school
- Sending photographs
- Revealing their parents' names or other information about their parents

Passwords and Screen Names

Children quickly learn about passwords when they begin using the Internet. They also have remarkable memories and may remember passwords belonging to family and friends, which they have seen only once. Passwords are top secret. Children need to know that even though the secret password should not be revealed to even their best friends, they must always be shared with their parents. This is another of those ideas that can be difficult to convey, since children treasure their privacy. Most passwords are also created to enter specific Web sites and children need to know that the only time they should ever type it into the computer is when they wish to enter that particular site.

Usernames or screen names can inadvertently give away personal information. Encourage children to make up names that are unlike their real names and avoid using first names.

Marketing Ploys

Children need not be victimized by marketers, especially those collecting survey information. Marketers may not collect information from children under thirteen without parental approval. Children of all ages need to understand that there are many people on the Internet who want to collect information about them for the purpose of making money. They need to know that these people have no right to this information.

Most of us have been taken in by the promises of advertisers. We sent away for a variety of supposedly wonderful treasures that turned out to be worthless. However, cyberspace is the world's largest marketplace, and children are literally besieged by commercial offers. They need to know that such offers are rarely what they appear to be, and if something seems too good to be true, it probably is.

Age-Restricted Sites

Although children should feel free to invent assumed names and other personal information, they need to know that they must not lie about their age to online service providers. This comes up most often when children want to have e-mail accounts. Larger Web mail service providers like Yahoo! and MSN do not permit underage children to have their own accounts, so it is not uncommon for children to prevaricate. If it's okay with parents for children to use e-mail, it's usually best for parents to set up accounts themselves. That way, they'll be able to get into the account if they are uncomfortable about their children's correspondence.

Parents, however, have an obligation to respect their children's privacy as they get older and develop separate lives of their own. If children believe they are being spied upon, they will take steps to banish parents from their world by creating secret online accounts. They will be less willing to ask questions or confide their concerns about unsavory correspondents.

Chat Rooms

Chat rooms are among the favorite online gathering places of children and teenagers. They are also one of the most frequently cited hangouts of pedophiles and other cyber-criminals. Young people using chatrooms need to take the following precautions:

- Find chat rooms that are monitored by adults. Check service providers like Yahoo! and MSN for lists of these child-friendly sites.
- Don't list personal information in profiles. Information for profiles is often taken from the service's sign-up form. Avoid answering questions whenever possible and make up answers when necessary.
- Use a screen name totally unrelated to your real name
- Assume that other chatters may be totally different from what they appear to be. Someone who introduces herself as a twelve-year-old girl may really be a forty-year-old man.
- Don't trust your instincts about a cyber-correspondent's truthfulness. Most of the cues you depend on in your real-world, face-to-face life (like facial expression, voice, and body language) are missing. That means you just don't have enough information.

Social Networking Sites

In Chapter 4, we discussed social networking sites like MySpace and FaceBook at length. Some are open to high school students and some have a specific age requirement for membership. To participate safely in these sites, teenagers need to be experienced Internet users who understand the dangers they may encounter. This poses a problem for libraries who often do not know how old or how Internet savvy their users are. As mentioned before, teens are often the users who need our handouts and our workshops most, but they are also the ones least inclined to take advantage of them or ask questions. Some libraries do not permit users to access social networking sites for this reason, while others hesitate to become censors. If your library decides that it will allow access to social networking sites, you must accept some responsibility for alerting teens to their dangers. This usually means some kind of required program, workshop, or tutorial. Such a requirement can also help to eliminate underage users.

Threatening and Demeaning Messages

Concerns about online predators may tend to focus parental concerns on adults. We should not forget that other children can be cruel and even threatening to one another. Older bullies sometimes deliberately frighten or intimidate younger children. They may also rob them of private information to play tricks or get them into trouble. Much of their behavior is identical to what occurs in the schoolyard, but the Internet offers some unique opportunities for cruelty. Children need to understand that they should immediately cease communicating with anyone who makes them feel uncomfortable. They needn't worry about hurt feelings. Cyberspace is different from face-to-face conversation, and they can and should disappear. Most chat rooms and messaging programs allow users to be visible to trusted friends while invisible to others. Children, like adults, should make frequent use of this feature.

Suggestive Messages

Children may not know how to interpret suggestive messages. They may not understand what the writer is getting at or think they just misunderstood. Children may not understand that they are entitled to privacy and need not answer the questions of adults. They must learn that no one should ever ask them about their bodies. The e-mails and instant messages that Congressman Mark Foley sent to underage Congressional pages shocked the nation. It is important to note that Foley frequently asked the pages to describe themselves, what they were wearing, and what they were doing. Early in the exchanges, these inquiries could be interpreted as just friendly interest. Gradually, however, they became more sexually targeted. Children and teenagers should understand that such questions, innocent though they may seem, are hallmarks of online predators, and should always be shared with parents, teachers, librarians, or other trusted adults.

Meeting Face-to-Face

Face-to-face meetings are, of course, the most potentially dangerous aspect of the online experience. Children must understand that people who suggest meetings are either bad people or ignorant people, who don't understand that they shouldn't be making such suggestions. Even young children should understand that bad people lurk in cyberspace waiting to entrap children. However, such information needs to be presented in a matter of fact way that does not cause children to see stalkers behind every tree and every computer screen.

DEVELOPING AN INTERNET EDUCATION PROGRAM

We now have a pretty good list of the information that our users should know if they are to use public computers safely. But how can we communicate this information to them? How will we make sure that they understand the risks they take and how they can safeguard their privacy?

If you have spent much time helping library computer users, you have undoubtedly discovered one of their biggest difficulties. They don't know what they don't know. When they ask for assistance, it is almost always to cope with hurdles they just encountered. Experienced computer users, in contrast, have a wider knowledge of computer technology. Even though they are not experts, they have a general understanding of their own limits. This is not the case with novices. They are always surprised when they encounter a new feature or function. Corporate managers have told me that this is how they identify job applicants with poor computer skills. When asked a question, experienced computer users describe specific computer programs and skills, while novices are likely to respond that their computer skills are "okay" or "pretty good." This is because they have no idea what lies ahead. Their knowledge of the computer world is so limited that they can't pinpoint their position.

Because they don't know what they don't know, beginners may be reluctant to spend time learning more than basic skills like online navigation. Libraries often find that the users who know almost nothing about computers are the ones least likely to attend workshops, or otherwise participate in the library's Internet education program. Too often, the people who read our brochures and attend our programs are already aware of at least some online privacy issues. This means that if we are to reach inexperienced computer users, some part of our program must be compulsory. It is usually necessary to require that new computer users go through some kind of preparatory experience before they are permitted to use the Internet. Later when they have some experience under their belts, they will be more likely to become voluntary participants.

School and academic librarians may assume that all young people know about computers, but this is far from the truth. Children teach other children to play computer games and it often happens that this is all they know. They're focused entirely on the game, and the wider online world and its dangers are of little interest to them. Children and young people who grew up without computers in their homes know even less.

What are our options when it comes to presenting basic information to people who have little personal experience with the Internet, and who may be more interested in surfing than paying attention to our cautionary advice?

Written Materials

Of course, we can produce pamphlets, flyers, newsletters, signs, and bookmarks cautioning users about dangerous online practices. Again, the problem is that new users are mentally focused on getting online and they may never get around to reading our carefully designed materials. However, interactive written materials are usually more effective than traditional passive ones. New users might be asked to complete a worksheet that consists of a brief chunk of explanatory text followed by a question, followed by more text and another question, etc. Written materials also work well when they are very brief (like bookmarks) and already available at public computer work stations.

Workshops and Library Instruction Sessions

Many public libraries offer a series of brief workshops that cover basic computer and Internet skills, while school and academic libraries may include computer skills in their library instruction programs. Many have been very successful while some others have floundered from lack of interest or participation. Successful programs have the following characteristics in common:

- They are short and don't try to cover too much information.
- They are fun in that they use the entertainment value of the Web to enhance the sessions.
- They include hands on practice. This means that attendees should have computer access during the workshop.
- They are conducted in a separate area of the library free from distractions. If a computer lab is not available, workshops may be held before the library opens or after it closes.
- Incentives are offered to encourage participation. It often works well to offer a half hour workshop with an additional half hour to practice surfing skills.

Internet education programs can be mandatory or voluntary. When library instruction includes computer privacy issues and is incorporated into school and undergraduate curricula, librarians can at least be assured that all students have been alerted to privacy dangers. In public libraries, seniors often get the most benefit from workshops. They have the available time, enjoy the social interaction, and appreciate the relaxed environment in which they feel free to ask for help. School age children are usually registered for public library activities and transported by parents. This means that the library may have a captive audience but workshops will be successful only if they can communicate the subject matter in an entertaining way. My completely unscientific survey indicates that public libraries have had the least luck offering workshops for teens. By this age, they usually have reasonably good technical skills and little interest in privacy concerns. After-school pizza can be an effective bribe for this age group.

Online Tutorials

In general, libraries have found that the most effective way to communicate information to less than enthusiastic computer users is to present it in the online environment. An online tutorial is usually a series of Web pages or a separate software program that presents information to users in small increments and in an organized manner. To progress to the next screen, patrons usually must respond to questions. Many academic libraries have developed tutorials to communicate basic library skills, especially to entering freshmen. Educators tell us that tutorials are a form of active learning and can be more effective in communicating information than more passive printed materials. It is possible to link the tutorial to the computer management software the library uses to authorize and time users. The software can be configured to limit Web access to new users until they have completed the tutorial.

COMPONENTS OF AN INTERNET EDUCATION PROGRAM

Workshops, library instruction sessions, tutorials, and printed materials all have a place in an Internet education program, but they are not interchangeable. The library's goal is to devise a sequence of experiences that gradually prepare inexperienced users to cope with the privacy risks to which they will be exposed. Some Libraries may wish to expand such a program to include basic computer skills, but the focus of the program should be protecting library users from harm.

It is also a good idea to make the program available to the general public. Library computer users are not the only people who endanger their privacy in the online environment. Many computer owners, though they may have more advanced computer skills, continue to engage in activities that threaten their privacy. Make your online tutorials readily available on the library's Web site so they can be used outside the library. Be sure that publicity about workshops is sent to your local radio stations and newspapers so as to attract local residents who are not regular library users. Many people have no idea of the depth and breadth of the library's services so a workshop is a good opportunity to get the word out.

PROGRAM OUTLINES

Now let's look at some ideas for possible workshops, instruction sessions, tutorials and printed materials. Some of the topics can be developed in any of these formats. In other words, they may be expanded into a workshop or shrunk down into a few basic recommendations printed on a bookmark. It is impossible, however, to know precisely how your library computers are configured, so suggestions must be adapted to your particular environment. Can your computer users view the cookies they have deposited? Can they delete temporary Internet files? Each library protects its computers (or fails to protect them) in a different way. As librarians we may install programs and hardware devices to protect our computers, but we are largely unaware of how they affect our users online experience. What can they see? What functions and features are invisible to them? Before developing any educational program, it is important to actually sit down at a public computer and use it as is if you were a library customer.

Once you have determined which recommendations are most relevant to library computer users, it's a good idea to decide how much information you want to include just for computer owners. For example, library users usually cannot alter computer settings to increase or decrease their privacy. Computer owners should know how to make the small changes that can make a big difference when it comes to protecting their privacy.

Topic #1: Keep It a Secret: What Web Sites Shouldn't Know about You

Note: This outline can be used as a brief introductory workshop, instruction session, or tutorial. It can be condensed into thirty minutes although a full hour is preferable. It is intended as a short introduction to privacy issues. If a longer workshop or series of workshops is appropriate, more information about hoaxes and scams can be included. It is equally useful for students, public library computer users, and the general public.

Objective: To alert computer patrons to misuses of personal information on the Web and suggest precautions.

Points to cover:

What Web sites Know about You

- Web sites store information indefinitely
- Web sites sell information to marketers and data brokers (Google, Yahoo! and AOL examples)
- Registration and application forms
- Survey questionnaires and free drawings
- Web sites keep track of their visitors
  o The facts about cookies: what they are and what they do
  o Sensitive cookie content (login and password information)
  o Third-party cookies

Protecting your privacy online

- Guarding personal information
- Keeping information out of Web site personal profiles
- Guarding privacy at social networking and match-making sites
- Creating an anonymous e-mail account
- Beware phishing expeditions and hoaxes
- Deleting history (list of sites visited)
- Clearing browser cache

Tips for computer owners

  o Deleting temporary Internet files
  o Blocking only third-party cookies
  o Setting your personal privacy level
  o Turning off the "Auto-Complete" feature that automatically fills in passwords and blanks on Web forms

Sample Workshop #2

Parents' Internet Workshop: Setting Ground Rules for Children

Note: This material is best presented as a series of workshops to allow time for discussion. If you think you can hold onto your participants for three sessions (possibly one a week for three weeks), there will be plenty of time available to discuss parents' concerns and experiences. You can limit each presentation to about thirty minutes, followed by somewhat lengthy discussion and refreshments. Since this may not be possible, it can be done in two sessions with somewhat longer presentations. This topic works better as a live workshop than as a tutorial or brochure.

Objective: Provide parents with a realistic understanding of the dangers of the Internet and offer commonsense ground rules for online safety.

Points to Cover

- Importance of talking to children about the Internet
- Setting boundaries together
- Internet risks
  - Giving out personal information
  - Exposure to violent or sexually explicit images
  - Solicitation by sexual predators or online harassment
  - Spyware
  - Viruses
  - High-pressure advertising
  - For older children and teenagers
    - Social networking sites
    - Chatrooms and instant messaging
- Important steps
  - Understand the risks
  - Decide what activities are unsafe
  - Reach a family agreement
  - Communicate what children can and cannot do online
  - Make sure children understand the reasons for the rules
  - Encourage children to take responsibility for their own actions and develop good judgement
  - Consider signing a computer use contract
  - Decide how Internet use will be monitored
- Things to consider
  - Children's age
  - Children's technical ability
  - Availability of age appropriate sites

- Suggested ground rules
  - Limit times when children can use computer
  - Specify the types of sites that are okay and the types that aren't
  - Agree that children will talk to their parents about anything that makes them feel uncomfortable or threatened
  - Agree that children will not give out personal information without parents' permission. This includes:
    - Addresses
    - Phone numbers
    - Passwords
    - School details
    - E-mail addresses (Parents may want to create "junk" e-mail accounts for their children that can be used for parent-approved Web site registrations.)
    - Pictures of themselves, their family, or their friends
  - Agree that children will not make purchases online
  - Agree that children may not arrange to meet online acquaintances without parents' permission
  - Distinguish between moderated and unmoderated chatrooms. Decide whether unmonitored chatrooms are okay
  - Discuss and agree upon file sharing programs
  - Require parents' permission to download software, music, and other files
  - Take precautions against viruses and spyware. Children should let parents know if they get an alert from their antivirus or anti-spyware program.
  - Place computers in open areas, not in bedrooms

Points to get across to children

  - Positive aspects of the Internet
  - People aren't necessarily who they say they are
  - Most people online are good people but there are some rotten apples pretending to be nice
  - Problems with online advertising
  - Polite online behavior (netiquette).

Suggestions for working with younger children

  - Sit beside children while they're online
  - Make rules simple and easy to understand
  - Click on real Web site examples
  - Ask young children to share user names and passwords with parents

ADVOCACY

Although librarians can secure computers and educate their users about privacy threats, they are often thwarted by totally inadequate and outdated privacy legislation. Until the laws protecting the privacy of all Americans are more in tune with modern technology, your library users will continue to be at risk. Your commitment to protect them should not be bound by the walls of the library. Working with them every day, you develop a unique understanding of privacy issues, seeing them through the eyes of some of the people who are most at risk.

Share your insights with your legislators and encourage them to act responsibly. What is it that we want them to do? To answer this question, it may be useful to look at some of the issues that Congress has been considering: problems that need solutions, legislation proposed by privacy advocates, and misguided bills that could actually remove some of the few protections now in place. The following are some of the most important.

Social Security Numbers

Although there have been some attempts by Congress to limit the use of Social Security numbers for purposes unrelated to the administration of the Social Security System, they have failed to check their widespread use. If for some reason, you wanted to learn the Social Security number of almost anyone, you can pay one of the many data brokers a small fee to obtain it. It should be illegal to give out any individual's Social Security number without their knowledge. Of course, some exceptions would be necessary, but exceptions should be strictly regulated. It should also be illegal for non-governmental entities to request Social Security numbers for any purpose unrelated to the collection of the Social Security tax. Congressman Joe Barton (R-TX) has been a leader in attempts to limit the use of Social Security numbers. "Whether Social Security numbers should be sold by Internet data brokers to anyone willing to pay, indistinguishable from sports scores or stock quotes ... to me, that's a no-brainer ... Such a practice should not be allowed. Period. End of debate" (McCullagh 2006).

At this writing Patrick Leahy (D-VT), Chairman of the Senate Judiciary Committee, and Bernie Sanders (I-VT) have introduced the Personal Data Privacy and Security Act Of 2007 in the Senate. Its aim is to limit the use of "sensitive personally identifiable information."

Such information includes connecting anyone's name with their Social Security number, passport number, driver's license number, mother's maiden name, birthdate, biometric ID, bank account number, or credit card number. Anyone who holds such information must take specific steps to protect it. Although the bill constitutes a good start in protecting Social Security numbers and other confidential information, it has a number of flaws and offers so many protections to the business community that it's actual effectiveness may be compromised. It is essential that we follow such pending legislation, making ourselves aware of strengths and weaknesses. Let your representatives in Congress know your feelings about individual bills and emphasize the importance of such legislation.

Data Mining

One of the most dangerous developments of recent years has been the creation of vast commercial and governmental databases that contain personal information about millions of people. As has been discussed in earlier chapters, these databases are so huge that practically every moment of an individual's day, every purchase, every personal relationship, every financial transaction, even every mile of highway travel can be tracked. Such information is extremely dangerous in the wrong hands, and there is little evidence that information obtained in this way is actually useful for legitimate purposes, such as combating terrorism. However, armed with such a mountain of data, both unscrupulous government agents and criminals can destroy the lives of innocent people.

Tight restrictions must be placed on the collection of data. Whether it consists of airline data, telephone and e-mail conversations, bank or medical records, legislation must be enacted to limit the sharing of such information. Additionally, the government employees and others who have access to personal information must be strictly limited. Data mining is a topic that is not widely understood. Government data mining is cloaked in secrecy, and all data mining is highly technical in nature. At this writing, an amendment to a Senate bill (S. 4) introduced by Senator John Sununu (R-NH) would require federal agencies to report to Congress on their use and development of data mining technologies. The bill has been approved by the Senate Homeland Security and Governmental Affairs Committee and will be making its way through the legislative process. This is an excellent first step. It may pave the way for additional legislation once Congress is made aware of the extent of the government's projects. Nevertheless, this is not a topic that has gained much attention in the press and interest could easily die out without pressure from librarians. Again, your representatives in Congress need to be made aware of the dangers that citizens face.

Public Records

Transparency in government is the chief reason why records created by government agencies are available to the public. Our founding fathers believed that citizens have a right to know what their government is doing. Since government agencies deal with individuals and their personal needs, many of their records contain personally identifiable information. Birth, marriage, divorce, motor vehicle, and court records are all available to public scrutiny. The problem is that until the Internet, it was not possible to obtain such information without personally visiting or corresponding with the appropriate government office. Data brokers have now collected all these records and brought them together in a single database.

Our founding fathers certainly never intended that any nosy parker could click a button and obtain the complete, and in some cases embarrassing, personal history of his neighbor, girlfriend, or co-worker. They never imagined that easy access to government records would become a favorite tool of identity thieves. Legislation, on local, state, and federal levels, is needed to balance the individual's need for privacy with the society's need for government transparency. There are situations in which access to public records is essential, but certainly the role of data brokers in our society must be sharply limited.

Internet Usage Data

The exploitation of children by Internet predators has become an excuse to collect massive amounts of information about personal Internet usage. As discussed earlier, ISPs store practically every keystroke, every search, and every piece of personal information submitted by their members. This means that vast storehouses of data are available to both business and government. Most of it can be associated with specific individuals, even when their names and account numbers are stripped from the data. As we have learned, the Bush administration has actually attempted to require Internet providers to retain information without considering privacy implications. Laws must be enacted to limit the amount of personally identifiable information that can be stored by Internet service providers and the length of time it can be retained.

The Bush administration has supported legislation that would force Internet companies to design their services in a way that would facilitate wiretapping. It is the view of many Constitutional scholars, that the government has already violated the rights of citizens with its existing wiretap program and further intervention in the design of the Internet could be opening the way for unprecedented invasions of personal privacy by government agencies.

Deleting Online Predators Act (DOPA)

At this writing, the Deleting Online Predators Act has been approved by the House of Representatives but has not yet reached the floor of the Senate. Privacy advocates anticipate that some form of the bill will eventually be approved by both houses of Congress. Librarians have more experience with the way young people use the Internet than almost any other group. They have become accustomed to balancing the demands of both safety and privacy. Few other groups can speak to the issues raised by DOPA legislation with such authority as librarians can.

For this reason, we must raise our voices to restore a sense of balance. As the Act currently reads, children and teenagers who use library computers would lose access to many Web resources that are exceedingly important to them. Libraries that fail to comply would lose e-rate funding. While we understand that social networking Web sites and chat rooms pose dangers, such sites have become extremely important to many teenagers' happiness, social lives, and sense of self-worth. The Act as it currently reads would deny access even to many educational sites because they are considered "interactive." These resources are important sources of information that young people depend on to make decisions.

It is natural that legislators react in fear and anger when they learn of young people who were molested or even murdered as a result of an online relationship. Nevertheless, the rights of young adults must be considered as well. Neither should young people from low-income families, who must depend on library computers, enjoy fewer rights than more affluent citizens. Adults would not accept a law that needlessly denied them many of the activities they most enjoyed.

Privacy Bill of Rights

At this writing, Hillary Rodham Clinton (D-NY) plans to introduce a privacy bill of rights that would give consumers the right to sue businesses when their privacy rights have been violated, freeze credit in the event of identity theft, and deal, at least in part, with the government's obligation to police itself when dealing with their personal information. The "PROTECT Act, the Privacy Rights and Oversight for Electronic and Commercial Transactions Act of 2006" would also require businesses to better understand what data they have in their computers, who has access to that data, and how it's used. Specifically, the Act would:

- Give consumers the right to opt-out or opt-in to the collection of most personal information about how we spend money.
- Give consumers the right to sue and seek damages. The bill creates a tiered system of damages for information breaches and misuse.
- Make consumers' phone records private and make the buying and selling of such records illegal.
- Allow consumers to freeze their credit, where currently credit reporting agencies need only place an alert on their records.
- Give consumers the right to know immediately when their private information is compromised.
- Give consumers the right to know when information about them leaves the United States and provide the opportunity to opt-out.
- Give consumers the right to a free credit report each year.
- Create a "privacy czar" in the federal Office of Management and Budget who would enforce privacy law and insure that "best practices" in dealing with personal information are being followed.
- Protect personal medical records by strengthening the Health Insurance Portability and Accountability Act (HIPAA). Companies would be monitored for compliance with the law and violators would be held accountable.

Whether this particular bill will meet the needs of American consumers is, of course, not yet clear, but the idea of a privacy bill of rights is an important one and should be pursued.

Identity Theft Notification

Corporate lobbies are attempting to reduce their liability for identity theft. This means that personal information including Social Security and credit card numbers may be in the hands of criminals, but the company responsible for the theft has no obligation to let the victims know that they are in danger. In 2006, Congressman Steve LaTourette (R-OH) sponsored a bill that some have called the "worst data bill ever." (Financial Data Protection Act of 2005 (H.R. 3997)) His bill has been criticized for favoring industry interests at the expense of consumers, blocking state laws that enable "identity freezes." Currently twenty-three states have laws that allow consumers to put a freeze on their credit reports and LaTourette's bill would invalidate these provisions. Legislation is needed to increase protection from identity theft, not decrease it. Potential victims of identity theft have a right to be notified immediately so they can take preventive action.

SUMMING IT UP

Because of our long involvement with privacy issues, librarians of all political persuasions possess insights that are not shared by politicians, marketing firms or, in many cases, the general public. Any political party can lose sight of the dangers inadvertently created when its members fight the war on terror. Any business can become so focused on selling its product that it fails to perceive the ethical ramifications of its actions. It is natural that both government and commercial sectors are impressed by new technologies and want to take advantage of them to sell their products or to catch criminals. Technology developed for this purpose, however, has a voracious appetite for personally identifiable information. Heedlessly pursuing these goals might be seen as akin to nurturing tiger kittens with no thought to how the public will be protected from the fully grown tigers. Without safeguards in place, like the privacy bill of rights described above, our library patrons and many other people are in great danger. Although members of other professions have privacy concerns, our perspective is unique and especially valuable. Our legislators on both the left and the right need the benefit of our objectivity and our experience.

REFERENCES

McCullagh, Declan. 2006. Perspective: Congressional confusion on Internet privacy. *CNet News,* July 5. http://news.com.com/Congressional+confusion+ on+Internet+privacy/2010-1028_3-6090314.html?tag=item.

Glossary

ADVISE: Analysis, Dissemination, Visualization, Insight, and Semantic Enhancement. ADVISE is a project within the Department of Homeland Security (DHS). Specific information on the project is sketchy, but an audit report by the Justice Department Inspector General indicates that it is a massive data mining operation that has the ability to store and analyze unprecedented quantities of data. Even though it is not operational at this time, it appears that it has already violated privacy laws.

ARPANET: The Advanced Research Projects Agency Network developed by the U.S. Department of Defense (DOD). ARPANET ultimately gave birth to the Internet.

Biometric data: Biometric information like the examples above can be translated into numerical algorithms (long strings of numbers) and stored in computers.

Biometric ID: These unique numerical algorithms can be used to identify individuals in much the way a driver's license serves as positive identification. Some schools have replaced library cards with biometric IDs.

Biometrics: The development of methods for uniquely recognizing human beings based on unique physical or behavioral traits. Fingerprints, eye retinas, and facial measurements are examples.

CIPA: Children's Internet Protection Act. The Act was upheld by the Supreme Court despite the attempt by the American Library Association (ALA) to have it declared unconstitutional. It requires libraries to install a "technology protection measure" (filtering software) to receive federal funding.

Cookie: Sometimes called HTTP cookie or Web cookie. A cookie is a small file sent by a server to a Web browser. Each time the browser communicates with the server, the cookie is sent back. Cookies are used for authenticating and tracking users, thus posing potential privacy problems.

COPPA: Children's Online Privacy Protection Act. The Act limits the online collection of personal information from children under 13 years of age.

DARPA: The Defense Advanced Research Projects Agency. Part of the Department of Defense, this agency has been responsible for developing many of the large data-mining projects like the TIA (Total Information Awareness) project described below. DARPA earned the scorn of Congress when it misspent large sums of money developing a futures market for terrorists.

Data Mining: Sometimes called "knowledge discovery," data mining is the process of automatically searching huge quantities of computer data seeking patterns. It was originally developed for use in the business world but has been adapted for use by intelligence agencies seeking terrorists.

DEA: Drug Enforcement Administration. An agency of the U.S. Department of Justice (DOJ).

DHS: Department of Homeland Security. The Department has been collecting vast amounts of personal data, much of which is intended for use in its data mining projects, especially Project ADVISE.

DOPA: Deleting Online Predators Act. The Act would force libraries to bar children and teenagers from accessing email, instant messaging, and social networking websites. At this writing, it has not been passed into law but it appears that Congress is in favor of passage.

Encryption: The process of obscuring or encoding information to make it unreadable without a special key. It is sometimes called scrambling.

EPIC: Electronic Privacy Information Center. It is a public interest research center focused on civil liberties and First Amendment issues. EPIC is located in Washington, DC and can be accessed online at http://epic.org.

Firewall: an information technology (IT) security device (either hardware or software) configured to permit or deny data connections. Firewalls control traffic between computer networks by establishing different zones of trust.

FISA: The Foreign Intelligence Surveillance Act of 1978. The act specifies the procedures for collecting "foreign intelligence information" through physical and electronic surveillance. Parts of FISA were amended by the Patriot Act of 2001 to include groups that are not specifically associated with a foreign government.

Fraud alert: Patrons who believe they may have been the victims of identity theft can request major credit bureaus to attach a fraud alert to their credit report. If anyone then tries to open a credit account (for example, by getting a new credit card or car loan), the lender should contact them to verify that they really want to open a new account.

GAO: Government Accountability Office. GAO is the non-partisan audit, evaluation, and investigative Congressional agency headed by the Comptroller General of the United States. It was established by the Budget and Accounting Act of 1921.

ID Theft affidavit: A tool created by the Federal Trade Commission (FTC) to assist victims of identity theft. Its importance is that it provides one form that can be sent to many companies. Victims need not fill out a separate form for each fraudulent account or transaction. The form can be found online at www.consumer.gov/idtheft/affidavit.htm.

Keylogging: Also called "keystroke logging." This is a diagnostic software program that captures the computer user's keystrokes. Such programs are very useful in software development but they are frequently misused by identity thieves to capture confidential information like credit card numbers.

LAN: Local Area Network. This is the term used for a group of computers linked together to communicate with one another in a network that covers a small geographic area.

Link analysis: In computer science, the term applies to the exploration and analysis of associations between objects. In other words, computers can establish relationships between different kinds of data like telephone numbers or bank transactions. In data mining, these functions are performed automatically using templates pin-pointing the kinds of transactions that might indicate terrorist activity. Law enforcement officials can also follow links that connect individuals with their activities and with other individuals, either with or without the assistance of computers.

Malware: A shortening of the term "malicious software." Malicious software is intended to infiltrate and often damage a computer system without the owner's knowledge or consent.

Money mule: A person who transfers money and/or reships valuable, fraudulently-obtained goods. The money mule is often an innocent person who is misled into acting as a go-between in a scam. The instigator of the scam is usually a criminal who operates with impunity from another country.

NSA: National Security Agency/Central Security Service. NSA is an agency of the Department of Defense (DOD). Although its existence is shrouded in secrecy, it has been said that NSA is the world's largest intelligence agency. It gathers intelligence through eavesdropping, especially cryptography. In

2006, it was revealed that NSA routinely monitored millions of telephone calls and e-mail messages within the United States.

NSL: National Security Letter. A form of administrative subpoena used by the FBI. National Security Letters may be issued by the FBI itself without "probable cause" and without judicial oversight. The number of NSLs that have been issued since the U.S. Patriot Act was passed in 2001 appears to be much larger than the FBI reported to Congress.

Packet sniffer: Sometimes called a network analyzer. Sniffers (either software programs or hardware devices) intercept and log traffic that passes over a digital network. While data packets are traveling back and forth over the network, they are vulnerable to capture. Although they are very useful to network administrators, hackers use sniffers to capture and decode sensitive information that is included in the packets.

Passphrase: A sequence of words or text that controls access to a computer system or computer program. A passphrase is very much like a password but is usually longer for additional security.

Phishing: The act of fraudulently acquiring sensitive information like passwords and credit card numbers by pretending to be a trustworthy business or other organization. A typical phisher might send an e-mail that purports to be from the victim's bank.

Ping: A computer network tool that works like an echo. The term comes from the game of Ping Pong and allows network administrators to discover whether the public side of a library network can "see" the staff side.

Promiscuous mode: Refers to settings on network cards. Promiscuous mode allows all network traffic to pass through the card to computers on the network. It can be used by hackers to sniff out sensitive information like passwords.

RFP: Request for proposal. This is an invitation to vendors or suppliers to submit a bid or proposal to provide a product or service. Libraries usually prepare an RFP when they select a library automation system or contract for services.

RO: Read only. In this book, the term is used in relation to radio frequency identification (RFID) chips that have unique numbers preprogrammed into them. This information cannot be deleted and no new information can be added.

RW: Read write. Again in the context of this book, the term refers to radio frequency identification (RFID) chips that function something like a computer disk. Data can be added, changed and deleted.

Semantic Web: Originally, the idea of World Wide Web pioneer, Tim Berners-Lee who envisioned computers capable of analyzing the semantic content of

Web sites. The term has been comandeered by intelligence-gathering projects, especially data mining, to describe techniques for analyzing the verbal content of websites like MySpace pages to generate useful information.

SNMP: Simple Network Management Protocol. Used to monitor network devices, SNMP is a computer management tool that helps systems administrators manage network performance and solve network problems.

Spam: Unsolicited and unwanted bulk e-mail. The practice of sending massive numbers of duplicate e-mail messages arose because there was no additional cost to the sender/advertiser. The nature of the Internet makes it possible for senders to disguise their identity (see "Spoof" below) so spam has also become the primary way that victims are lured into phishing and other scams.

Spoof: E-mail spoofing involves the altering of the sender's address and other parts of the email header to make it appear that the e-mail originated from a different source. Web site spoofing is similar but relates to Web site addresses. The term is also used for caller ID spoofing.

Spyware: Also known as malware. Malicious software that collects personal information about users without their informed consent.

System log: Computers keep track of and record their every action. This logging function or recordkeeping is extremely important to systems administrators. It is in this way that they can learn of illicit attempts to break into their network and take appropriate precautions.

Thin client: A computer (client) in a network that depends mainly on the central server for processing activities. Thin clients lack the computing capacity to function independently.

TIA: Total Information Awareness, later Terror Information Awareness. This was a vast data-mining project devised by the Defense Advanced Research Projects Agency (DARPA) and run out of the Information Awareness Office. In 2003, Congress cut off funding for the project but it appears that it was split into multiple projects run out of various agencies. Project ADVISE appears to be an outgrowth of TIA.

Trojan Horse virus: A software program that at first appears to be harmless. However, when it gets into the computer of an unsuspecting user and becomes activated, it reveals itself as a malicious virus. The term is taken from the Trojan Horse of Greek mythology.

Victim statement: An effective tool for dealing with identity theft. When library patrons and others believe that confidential information may be in the hands of identity thieves, they can complete a statement to be added to their credit file that describes what happened and requests creditors to contact them before opening new accounts.

VLAN: Virtual Local Area Network. A method of creating independent a separate computer network within a physical network. In libraries, VLANs can separate the staff side of the library's network from the public side. Several VLANs can co-exist within such a network.

WEP: Wired Equivalency Privacy. WEP is part of the IEEE 802.11 wireless networking standard (also known as Wi-Fi). It is not considered very secure and is readily susceptible to eavesdropping.

WLAN: Wireless LAN or Wireless Local Area Network. Wireless networks use radio waves to communicate between devices over a limited area. Users are able to move around and still remain connected to the network.

WORM: Write Once, Read Many. Like "RO" and "RW" above, WORM is a term used in connection with computer drives and radio frequency identification (RFID) chips. WORM chips used in libraries could store a variety of information about users checking out books embedded with RFID chips.

WPA: Wi-Fi Protected Access. A more secure type of wireless network than WEP described above WPA data is encrypted and a passphrase is required for network access.

Index

About the Author

Jeanette Woodward is a librarian and principal of the Wind River Library and Nonprofit Consulting Group. After a career in academic libraries, most recently serving as Assistant Director of the David Adamany Library at Wayne State University, she began a second career in public libraries as Director of the Vista Grande Public Library in New Mexico and the Fremont County Library System in the foothills of the Wind River Mountains of Wyoming.

Woodward is the author of several books including *Creating the Customer Driven Library: Building on the Bookstore Model* (2005). Another book for librarians, *Countdown to a New Library: Managing the Building Project* (2000) was intended "to bring librarians who will be participants in new construction or renovation projects up to the mark so they can competently play their part in this process from beginning to end" (*Journal of Academic Librarianship*).

In her most recent book *Nonprofit Essentials: Managing Technology* (2006), she has used her experience as a library administrator to better understand problems facing other nonprofit organizations.

Woodward is also the author of *Writing Research Papers: Investigating Resources in Cyberspace* (1999) and "Cataloging and Classifying the Internet" in the *Annual Review of Information Science and Technology* (1996). She holds a masters degree in library and information science from Rutgers University with further study at the University of Texas at Austin.